My Home Is Your Hon.

It took Mary Russell five years to get a visa to travel to Syria in order to write a book but once granted she's off, on her bike, on local buses and on foot, travelling across the desert to places such as Abu Kamal, Deir ez Zour, Tadmor and Sheizar. Her street Arabic, picked up in Sudan, Palestine and, more formally, at the College of Further Education in Oxford, gets her into a few scrapes but gets her out of them as well. Travelling solo and on a shoe-string, as she always does, she is regularly invited into their homes by friendly Syrians where, inquisitive as always, she notes their living, sleeping and eating arrangements. Hazards along the way include being ambushed by semi-feral dogs, dealing with a request for sex by a Schools Inspector and being stalked by the Mukhabarat.

Returning home after one visit (she made many over the course of ten years) she found a letter on her kitchen table in Dublin inviting her to visit Baghdad. One week after the Twin Towers were demolished, she's off again, taking a taxi from Damascus to Baghdad to explore the marvellous city of Haroun al Rashid.

Reviews

"The intrepid traveller Mary Russell takes her reader on a journey through Syria, throwing herself into modern Syrian society with a contagious enthusiasm. The reader's sympathies immediately go out to the Syrian people she meets along the way, who are now engaged in a desperate struggle for political freedoms from their autocratic government that would have been unthinkable at the time of Russell's visit."

Dr Eugene Rogan St Anthony's College, University of Oxford

Also by Mary Russell...

Survival South Atlantic. Ed. Grafton Books.1986

The Blessings of a Good Thick Skirt. Collins (now Harper Collins). 1988

Please Don't Call it Soviet Georgia. Serpent's Tail. 1991

Amazonians. Penguin Book of Women's New Travel Writing. 1998

Journeys of a Lifetime. TownHouse/Simon and Schuster. 2002

Travelling Light. Gill and Macmillan collection of travel writing. 2004

My Home is Your Home

A Journey Round Syria

by

Mary Russell

Bullstake Press

First published in 2011 by Bullstake Press
A CIP catalogue record for this book is available from the British Library.
ISBN 978-0-9570840-0-1

Designed & typeset by *Moyhill* Publishing.
Printed in UK.
Photographs by Mary Russell
Back cover photo of author courtesy of Freya Rodger

Some names have been changed in this book
to protect the privacy of the individuals involved.

Permissions:

Thanks to united agents (www.unitedagents.com) for permission to quote from *Wilder Shores of Love* by Lesley Blanch, published by John Murray 1954, ISBN 2207255891

Permission sought to quote from the following:

Poems of Wine and Revelry – The Khamriyyat of Abu Nawas.
Trans: Jim Colville. Kegan Paul 2005

The Desert and the Sown
by Gertrude Bell. Heinemann 1907,Virago 1985

Memoirs of Lady Hester Stanhope by C.L. Meryon London 1845

Islam, a Way of Life (on al Ma'arri)
by Philip K Hitti University of Minnesota Press

Kitab al l'tibar
by Usama Munqidth Trans: Philip K Hitti
Colombia University NY 1929

Bullstake Press
5 Duke Street, Oxford OX2 0HX, UK

Dedication

For Eta, Isabella, Charlie and Elizabeth

My Home is Your Home

البيت بيتك

Acknowledgements

I'd like to thank Professor Abdul Nabi Staif for introducing me to Syria and for his hospitality in Damascus, Dr. Ota Haidar for her invaluable advice and friendship, Carol and Roger Fox and Kathy Biddulph who read the MSS and made their individual and helpful comments, everyone at Right Click for their support which went far beyond the line of duty, Mary Eldin, the staff at the Bodleian Library, Eugene Rogan, Tariq and everyone at al Rabie Hotel in Souk Saruja, friends in Salamiyah, Nadia Khost, everyone at Mar Mousa, Phylis and Hassan Mahfoud for their hospitality in Kilkenny, Mohan and Bimla Pandey for their hospitality in Baghdad, Faitti Darwish for bringing me to Jane Digby's former home in Damascus, Moyhill Publishing for doing more than simply printing the book.

I would especially like to acknowledge my debt to both Robert Fisk and Bob Friedman whose first-hand accounts of events in Hama in 1982 were immeasurably useful.

Thanks also to the many people in Syria who opened their doors to me.

Finally, I would like to thank Freya Rodger whose immense patience, hands-on support and professional expertise in the field of publishing has been a major factor in the production of this book.

Syria is a country rich in history but mindful that not everyone likes it as much as I do, I have segregated the high moments in Syrian history to the section called *A little bit of history* on page 296

Mindful too that history is happening, right now, on Syrian streets, I have included a Postscript which refers to events over the summer of 2011.

Contents

Images and Maps

Preface

I first visited Syria the year Bashar Assad was appointed president. The visa office in London displayed a notice telling visitors it would be closed the following week for the election of President Bashar Assad. "You usually wait for the ballots to be counted," I told friends, "before announcing the winner." It made amusing dinner-table chat. Syria, and indeed Arab countries generally, didn't do western democracy. That's how they were. And we accepted it. At least I did: I wanted to go there, after all.

So, with the visa in my pocket, I loaded my bike on to a Syrian Air plane and flew to Damascus where I began a love affair with a country I knew so little about but which took me to its heart. A few things niggled, of course: a creative approach to bus timetables, the absence of road maps and the infuriating fact that so many Syrians spoke English far better than I spoke Arabic, despite what I felt were my serious attempts to learn the language. But these things were easily outweighed by the cheery manner in which people helped me on my way, applauded me when I spoke Arabic (albeit like a two-year-old), tried to accommodate me when they learned I was vegetarian and accepted the fact, as best they could, that I had no particular religious beliefs.

In Syria the question I was asked most often was how old I was. Once home, however, the question everyone asked was: "Is it safe to travel there?" And yes, for a woman travelling on her own and often by bike, to out of the way places, it was incredibly safe. My age, of course, may have afforded me some protection, but Syria was not like some Arab countries where men pestered women in totally unacceptable ways due, a Libyan friend told me recently, to the fact that "Arab men are woman hungry."

Then I visited Tadmor and Hama and learned of the terrible events that had left their mark especially on Hama, noting the crater-like holes, the gaps between buildings still filled with debris, the abandoned houses, the guarded way people spoke about what had happened in 1982. In my diary, I wrote: "...all I can do is reflect on the fact that visitors to Syria, finding it an exceptionally safe country, owe their safety to an autocracy which tolerates no opposition..."

I didn't really want to write that sentence since it shone a light on a very dark moment in Syria's history. Now that moment has returned. The people of Hama have again been shelled, bombed, killed. Some choose not to walk the streets for fear of a sniper's bullet to the back of the head, while others keep their heads down both metaphorically and literally.

Nevertheless, many citizens have continued to walk the streets, in Hama, Deir ez Zour, Damascus, Aleppo, Abu Kamal, Ma'arrat al Numan, Zabdani – all places you will read about in this book. It is in this simple act of walking along the streets that hope for Syria lies.

This book, however, is not about the terrible events that have taken place in Syria since March 2011. That is a book that must be written by Syrians themselves though I have appended a short chapter on the current situation. Instead, My Home is Your Home is a celebration of the country and its people and yes, including its lumpy mattresses, its bureaucracy and its over-zealous bus agents. Engage with the country and its peoples and you will be rewarded.

I have chosen to use Before Common Era (BCE) and Common Era (CE) as it seems inappropriate to date major Muslim events from the birth of Christ. CE is used up to the beginning of the first millennium.

I have been guided by distinguished Syrian friends on the correct spelling of Arabic words. However, I have, in places, used spellings that may be more familiar to non-Arab readers – for example, Mecca instead of Meccah.

I have capitalised all Gods be they of Islam, Christianity, Judaism or indeed paganism hoping, by so doing, to avoid offending anyone.

The Syrian unit of currency is the Syrian pound (SYP). Since my first visit to Syria, rates of exchange have fluctuated enormously. When amounts are given I have put them in context. My bike, for instance, cost £300 which, at the time, worked out at about 18,000 SYP – a lot of money for me and even more for someone in Syria. The room in my one-star hotel in Damascus averaged £8 a night. Hotel prices were very occasionally quoted in US$.

SYP	EURO	STERLING
100	1.50	1.29
200	3.00	2.58
400	6.00	5.00
1,600	24.00	20.00
8,000	120.00	100.00
24,000	360.00	300.00
64,000	960.00	800.00

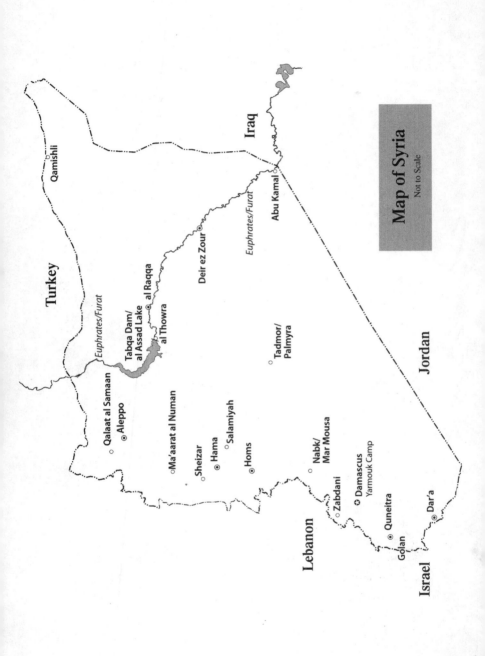

Map of Syria
Not to Scale

Chapter 1

"Bayti baytak – My home is your home"

A hmad comes into the shaded courtyard, carrying a small silver tray on which is set a mug, paper napkin and a teapot containing an infusion of flowers. He approaches briskly, tray held aloft on the palm of one hand, mug and teapot placed on the table with a flourish, the whole action brought to a conclusion with the suspicion of a bow. I sit back and, just for a moment, imagine I'm taking tea in the Ritz instead of in al Ward, a no-star hotel in downtown Damascus.

Ahmad is a student, doing a course in hotel management and I thank him as I start to pour the tea: "Shukran. I'm looking forward to this. I've been thirsty all day."

His smile changes to a look of sad reproach: "You can't say that."

"No?"

Has my Arabic been even worse than usual? Or have I broken, yet again, some unwritten social code.

"No," he replies. "No one is ever thirsty here. In Damascus, there is always water."

So, it *was* a code. But one comprised of conflicting desert ethics: the duty of hospitality versus the right to survival. Not something the average European city-dweller is likely to know about.

Arabs prize water above all else as the source of life, a gift to be given freely – and freely taken. In the old days, however, drink uninvited from the well of another tribe and you might have ended up with a bullet in your head. Not now, of course. Now, they put their hand on their heart and say: Bayti baytak: my home is your home. If I were thirsty, I should have helped myself to a drink of water, as if I were in my own home. But I'm reticent, and, if I'm truly honest, squeamish about using the kitchen which is really only a curtained alcove, with a tap and a sink that often has dirty dishes lying in it as well as bits of leftover food floating in the scummy water.

Still, it's true, what Ahmad says. The crowded streets of Damascus are graced with water fountains whose metal cups, chained in place, are in regular use. Outside the imposing Hejaz Railway Station, monument to the Ottomans' 400 years of tenure, there is a majestic, ornamental fountain to which people come – soldiers, taxi drivers, day trippers, passers-by – to fill their cupped hands or plastic jerry cans. In the old days, it was pack camels or horses pulling carriages that got their water here, as well as pilgrims on the Haj, drinking their fill before setting out for Mecca.

Springs, streams, rivers and fountains are the white gold of hot, desert lands and in Syria there are 76 place names beginning with Ain – which means well. Mecca grew up around such a spring and as a result became an important stopping point on the caravan route between Yemen and Syria. Damascus itself started life as an oasis, watered by six branches of the Barada River – the cool river – which rises in Jabal Lubnan Ashsharqiyah (the Anti-Lebanon Mountains) high up on the plain of Zabdani. From there, augmented by melting snow from the mountains and by springs that bubble up into it as it runs its course, the Barada seeps through limestone rock, passing through hill villages, woodlands and tunnels of greenery until, bursting forth into Ain Fijeh, it opens out into a pool that forms a reservoir which serves the people of Damascus. From there, it descends into the city and divides, going underground occasionally, to resurface in unexpected places. Later, it passes out into the ghuta – the fertile area of orchards and market gardens of the oasis which provide Damascenes with mish-mish, the soft juicy apricots for which the city is famous.

This afternoon, however, the Barada hadn't looked good. Reduced in places to a narrow strip of grey, oozing mud, in others its surface covered by a sludge of algae lying on it like a bloom of green death, pockmarked here and there with discarded plastic bags and drink cans, it was a sorry sight, unpleasant to both eye and nose. A man staring over the railings at this unmoving growth dropped a coin into it. The sludge gawped open, swallowed the coin in a greedy gulp, then closed over again leaving behind an unnerving stillness.

It wasn't always like this. I've seen an 18th century engraving showing pilgrims, massing for the Haj, filling their water bottles from a wide Barada and with camels and donkeys drinking their fill at its banks. Still, it's October now and, after the hot summer, the water level has dropped even lower and will stay like that until the rains start to fall. People talk constantly about this longed-for rain, looking up at the clear blue sky in the hope of seeing dark clouds. The talk is of drought, of Syrians starving next year if the farmers can't get their seeds to germinate this season. A national disaster lies ahead, they say. Thousands will die. They shake their heads mournfully: Allah!

It is indeed a terrible prospect. Yet, when I make enquiries, do a bit of research, read the books, I find there is rarely any serious rain before the end of November. Nevertheless, since the drama has to be maintained, the absence of rain foretells an impending tragedy that must be awaited with shivering anticipation which is why, most days; I join everyone else in looking heavenwards hoping for a watery miracle though knowing, because I am from Ireland and without faith, that there will be no rain for another two months.

And yet, because I am from Ireland and therefore superstitious – you never know. Even now, drinking my tea, I look up and wonder. The courtyard is open to the evening sky. What will happen when the rain does eventually fall? Will we be issued with umbrellas, made to move into the tiny cramped hallway which doubles as a reception and TV viewing room? Or will we be invited to take our tea on the liwan, the covered, raised area at the southern end of the courtyard? Only time will tell.

After serving tea to a few other guests, Ahmad retires to do some studying and his place is taken by Saleh whose facial features – sharp and dark – look as if they have been drawn in charcoal. His shining eyes are coal black as are his long eyelashes. Most days, he wears a stone-coloured baseball cap but when he doesn't you can see his black hair, cut close to his head and plastered across his forehead in a fringe of evenly spaced kiss curls. He is junior to Ahmad and his work involves serving breakfast in the courtyard, washing the dishes and mopping the floor. Though not cleaning the rooms. That is the job of an old man who comes in each morning, strips to his vest and long johns and, in the tiny tiled courtyard just outside my room – where brooms, bikes and spare blankets are stored and where unknown people sometimes spend the night on the battered sofa – he changes into a blue nylon work coat and another pair of trousers before padding off with his brush and bucket.

This is also where I keep my precious bike which is my preferred means of transport both at home and away. My first long distance bike ride was down through France from Le Havre to Marseille where I embarked for Algiers. There, I left it in a hotel when I flew down to Tindouf, in the desert, to do some research into the Saharawi. Coming back, I put the bike on the overnight train to Paris doing the journey in 12 hours which, coming down, had taken one month.

The bike survived all this but a few weeks after returning to Dublin, I chained it to a tree when I went swimming. When I came out of the swimming pool, the bike was gone. "Surprised they left the tree," a friend said.

The insurance paid up and I replaced the bike. The following summer, in Oxford, I left a friend's house one evening to find the saddle had been stolen. The bike shop sold me a smart little chain especially for securing saddles to bikes but the next thing that went was a wheel. Finally, outside Oxford City Library where I had left the bike chained to an immoveable object, I returned to find the whole thing gone.

I hadn't done much research about cycling in Syria but knowing how dull airport roads are, I asked Tariq at the hotel to send a taxi to meet me at the airport and to transport myself and the bike into Damascus. Now it sits outside my room like a dog at a door, asking to be taken out. But right now, I prefer walking. Next week, when I've got the lie of the land, I'll cycle.

Saleh has been pestering me. He wants to travel to Ireland and stay with me while I find him a job and no amount of explanations will divest him of this dream.

"I am poor boy," he says in a hoarse voice, bordering on a whine. "Not much money."

"How much do you get here," I ask, always curious.

"2,000 SYP a month and I work from six last morning until two this morning."

2,000 SYP (Syrian pounds) which is about £20. It certainly seems a long working day for not much money but, I tell myself briskly, there's no point in raising his hopes.

"Well, you can't stay with me because I live with other people and they have no extra rooms in their house," I lie. In any case, I can't see the authorities giving Saleh a work visa though there is no doubt he would work hard and would probably be prepared to live in a cupboard if necessary.

Ahmad lives in a sort of cupboard – the space under the stairs where the worn wooden steps take a sharp turn to the left. A curtain hangs in place of a door and I had my suspicions that it was someone's home when, one night, I saw that the curtain was propped open by two blue flip-flops. Next day, I noticed that Ahmad was wearing them. Despite the ad hoc sleeping quarters, however, he is always impeccably dressed. The students at the Institute of Tourism, where he studies, have a uniform: well-pressed grey slacks, white shirt, navy tie and navy blazer. The female students look especially sexy in this outfit, like a classful of very beautiful, trainee airline pilots.

I don't know what Saleh's sleeping arrangements are but I've discovered that he comes from Qamishli, a border town way over on the Syrian/Iraqi border and that he is a Kurd.

"I am not Arab," he tells me, many times. "I am Kurd."

Kurds make up the Middle East's fourth largest ethnic group with many of them living across five countries: Iran, Iraq, Turkey, Saudi Arabia and Syria. Though twice promised a place of their own, once in 1920 and again following the Iran/Iraq war, they are still stateless even though they number 40 million. Many crossed the Turkish/Syrian border as horse and sheep traders and there are now about one million of them living here in Syria with rights and residential status far from secure.

There is a statue to Damascus's most famous Kurd just outside the citadel and as soon as I arrived here I went to have a look at it. It's an imposing, declamatory statue of a man seated on what I can only call a horse rampant, the rider's arm raised in triumph. Behind him, slumped dejectedly on the ground, are two knights in chain mail. The horseman is Salahadin – the name means honouring the faith – and he's the man who knocked Richard Coeur de Lion off his crusading perch. Richard was the product of the tempestuous marriage between Henry II of England and his French wife Eleanor of Aquitaine. In 1157 Eleanor gave birth to Richard, the couple's second son. The birth took place in Oxford where the king had a palace – a stone still marks the spot. The cost of the midwife and linen for the royal birth was 20 shillings.

Salahadin, the infant's future conqueror, was 20 by then. Born in the Tikrit area (in present day Iraq and birthplace also of Saddam Hussein) his Kurdish family was forced to flee to escape reprisals when his uncle carried out a killing – ostensibly to avenge a woman's honour. They settled in Syria and by the time he was 36, Salahadin had distinguished himself both on and off the battlefield. He was an accomplished polo player, enjoyed hawking and regularly hunted lions in the desert. More importantly, he had taken control of Egypt, on Sultan Nureddin's behalf, and was therefore in good favour. When Nureddin died, his son became Sultan and when this son also died – unexpectedly, at the age of 19 – Salahadin found there was no one prepared to dispute his claim to the Sultanate, least of all Nureddin's widow for he had already taken the precaution of marrying her. It wasn't for another 14 years, however, that the Sultan Salahadin, now ruling from Damascus, would drive away the Christian invaders led by Richard the Lionheart.

Salahadin, first and foremost a soldier, was happiest when in the saddle from where, it was said, he ran his council. He spoke Kurdish at home and probably learned Turkish once he joined the army but he had a special love of Arabic which he learned in the mosque.

It was this mix of bluff militarist, expert horseman, lover of the spoken word and man of the people that made him something of a romantic to his crusading enemies who found it hard to believe that he was what they considered a lowly Kurd. The English thought he must have the redeeming feature of an English mother. The French thought it more likely he had a French grandmother. In the Divine Comedy, Dante refers to him as the "great Saladin, aloof, alone," so that altogether he was everybody's favourite infidel. But despite the French and the English seeking to foist a European lineage on him, Salahadin's background *was* Kurdish, a fact which made him suspect to the Turks who saw in him a warring outsider who had usurped the Sultanate and who displayed his generosity by sharing out his spoils among his own people. The First Crusade, begun in 1096, resulted in the Christians capturing Jerusalem and using it as a base for military excursions into the surrounding areas.

Nearly 100 years later, in July 1187, Salahadin's men surrounded the city of Jerusalem and within six days the yellow banners of the Sultan of Damascus were flying from the ramparts.

It was a time of great celebrations. The al Aqsa mosque was cleansed with rose water and the cross removed from its dome. A layer of marble which had covered the sacred Rock to protect it from zealous Christian pilgrims, who liked to take home chips of it, was removed. By Friday 2 October 1187, with everything in place, the Qadi of Damascus, heralded by black banners, entered the mosque and led the thanksgiving prayers with such eloquence that "the stars left their places not to shoot upon the wicked but to rejoice together". Salahadin had freed Jerusalem from 88 years of Christian occupation. By way of celebration, he sent gifts to the Eastern Christians in the Byzantine capital of Constantinople including an elephant, arrows, horses – and a jar of poisoned wine to be given to any crusader guests who happened to be staying there. The fall of Jerusalem caused consternation back in England and the following year, Richard the Lionheart levied a tax – the Salahadin Tithe – in order to finance the Third Crusade though this ended in an ignominious treaty which left Jerusalem still in the hands of what the Europeans called the Saracens. For Salahadin, after four years of fighting, it was time to head home to his beloved Damascus. Worn out by constant battles, he was content to spend his time living quietly, riding out occasionally to welcome back pilgrims from Mecca and playing with his existing children while continuing to sire more. He had 17 sons in all. Whether he had any daughters is not recorded – a common enough omission by historians. He died, aged 55, on 4 March 1193, only five months after returning home from Jerusalem. The statue outside the citadel in Damascus is of a larger-than-life hero. When I get close to it, I look up at the face: an astrologer had forecast that if Salahadin entered Jerusalem, he would lose the sight in one eye but the crafty Kurd confounded them by not only retaking Jerusalem but holding on to both his eyes.

The Kurds have frequently held a lowly position in whatever country they live in but, in the pecking order of the al Ward hotel, Saleh occupies this base position with a certain degree of pride as if even this is recognition of his solitary, non-Arab status. The other workers – all Arabs – seem to be related to one another while none, of course, are related to Saleh. There are no women around al Ward except, sometimes, Tariq's beautiful Moroccan wife, Zulaykhan.

Tariq's father, who owns al Ward, holds court in the evenings. Apart from Ahmad, there is also Marwan who is a cousin of Tariq, Tariq's brother who is a doctor and who comes in sometimes to help out. Then there is a distant cousin, Ghissin, who has seven children and a false leg. In the liwan, one evening, I was sitting having tea when I noticed Ghissin pulling up the leg of his trousers to reveal a pink prosthetic leg with holes drilled in it. I looked away not certain if it were acceptable to stare at someone's plastic limb. The last time I'd seen such a thing had been when I was writing a money feature for The Guardian on the cost of spare parts. The subject, a 70-year-old man, having shown me his leg, then tried to embrace me so that I had to keep the kitchen table between the two of us as I continued my research. The people in al Ward are a friendly lot and some evenings I sit and chat with whoever is on reception duty. Once, when I reminded Saleh that he had forgotten to bring me a pot of tea which I had asked for, Marwan grabbed him in an arm lock and beat him good-naturedly about the head with a spoon. The sound of the metal against bone was painful and seeing my initial consternation, Saleh howled and begged for me to save him: "Help me, I am poor boy. See what he does."

Now, whenever I come into the lobby, this pantomime is reenacted entirely for my entertainment, with Marwan beaming at me as he thumps Saleh who cries out in mock pain. I'm getting a bit fed-up with the nightly performance. They, unfortunately, show no signs of tiring.

Chapter 2

I have loved two things in the world – women and pleasant scents but I have found refreshment of my heart only in prayer

Prophet Muhammad

"Mankind recognises that the Arab/Syrians invented the first alphabet," says the notice in the National Museum in Damascus. It was scribes at Ugarit, in western Syria, who are credited with the invention, some 3,000 years ago, of a cuneiform alphabet which is based on a symbol that looks like a golf tee and which, when arranged in different ways, combines to make up 30 letters. Now here in the glass case right before me are images of these very golf tees, imprinted on a pillow of clay no longer than a finger and weighing only a teaspoonful of sugar but giving us the price of wine, of olives, of a bale of cloth: an ancient microchip in which is embedded an everyday shopping list. In the next case, from around the same time, are two sling bullets of the sort that David might have used to topple Goliath. Beside them, a replica of a chubby Herme's (the greengrocer's apostrophe having travelled all the way from England to Damascus) and, beside him, a statue of Helios the sun God, the halo of light which radiates out of his head making him look like a devout medieval saint.

In the next room is a seated figure no more than five inches high, which the guide says is Baal, a major sun deity in the pantheon. The museum notes say it's the God El and since my research tells me they're one and the same I've decided to plump for the more familiar Baal. Minute and perfect, wearing prettily pointed shoes, with his hand held up as if to stop the traffic, the tiny God is covered almost entirely in gold leaf and what isn't gold is brilliant, incandescent green.

The museum is a mish-mash of dates and divinities, of Gods and griffins, an exuberant outpouring of ancient history updated by the graffiti of foreigners (Souvenez, Jacques. 1993, it says on the side of one glass case) and brought back into this modern world by the chatter of small schoolchildren in fawn tunics and revolutionary red neck-scarves, the crocodile moved past the exhibits by their teachers at the speed of a conveyor belt. One child, however, breaks away and makes for a statue of a Greek hero, whose family jewels nestle plumply between his legs. The small boy stares up at the Greek, then lifts a hand and thoughtfully strokes the marble balls. The older children giggle knowingly and hurry on.

In the map room, I locate all the places I've read about – al Raqqa, Deir ez Zour, Hama, Homs, Aleppo, Tadmor – and see them stretching out ahead of me like jewels in the sand.

Around 70% of Syria is desert and despite the concrete blocks of hotel towers, the sprawling housing developments, the smooth highway that curves westwards towards Beirut, the streets full of computer shops selling cut-price CDs, the satellite dishes competing with minarets for skyline space, despite all these, Damascus is still an oasis city, sand seeping into it from all directions.

Seen from the air, the countryside around it glows dusty red in the setting sun, the houses flat-roofed, the stony, biblical landscape falling away over the tilting horizon. And though the caravans no longer come and go, bringing silk from China, indigo from India and musk from Tibet, there's still a feeling of movement, of impermanence. People set off to work in Saudi Arabia for five or six years at a time, the road signs read Baghdad and pilgrims from Daghastan, on their way to Mecca, still stop here, selling their carpets at the kerbside to fund the last leg of the Haj. Damascus is a point both of meeting and of leaving.

Outside the museum, art students are making drawings of the fallen pillars, stone troughs and other classical remains that have been collected from all over Syria and brought here to rest among the plane trees of the garden. I sit in the sun and pass the time trying to guess the nationality of the tourists. The French are instantly recognisable, the women in tailored shirts, hair short and well cut, wearing one piece of expensive jewellery. The men, silvery hair curling over coat collars, wear fine wool scarves – red or navy – slung rakishly over their shoulders. The Germans all look like press photographers in multi-pocketed waistcoats and lots of cameras. The English are sensible as ever, the women in flat shoes, pleated skirts, permed hair. The men tall, bony, with short back and sides, stick with their own sex. The museum gardens are peaceful to sit in, the pleasure marred only by the sight of the ornamental pond, bone dry and empty save for two lovely verdigris herons.

Beyond the gates is one of the man-made channels that carry the waters of the Barada River to the kitchen taps, baths and fountains of the city. Its brown and stagnant length leads eventually to the whirling roundabout of Umawiyeen Square where seven lanes of traffic flow unceasingly in a carousel of cars. At the centre of the square is a chunk of concrete curving into the blue sky, a committee-designed construction that the city fathers seem to be trying to enhance by surrounding with segments of green turf set into the red earth. To one side of it is a large complex which – due to the number of cigarette-smoking soldiers lounging at its entrance – must surely be a military establishment but which turns out to be the national TV station. This then is the modern Damascus.

It seems unthinkable that I should be trying to fill in time in a city as intriguing as this one but that is exactly what I have been doing. By midday, however, I can put it off no longer and head back along the Barada for the Ministry of the Interior where I have to get my visa sorted out. When I eventually locate the building and make my way past petitioners crowding the stairs, the corridors, the doorways, paper fluttering from their hands like confetti, I find that I have come to the wrong floor, the wrong building even and, not only that, I have come too soon. A visa, I'm told politely, can't be renewed until it has almost run out.

Forward planning is not on the agenda and I'm reminded of the time I was with some desert people in the Sahara who were surprised to learn that I had bought a return ticket when, they explained, the day, time and even the actual return was not for me to decide but for Allah.

Because it's approaching the two-hour lunch break, the traffic is more desperate than usual with everyone, palms pressed on horns, trying to get home before the end of the world is declared. Damascus traffic bears in from every side like an invading army intent on imposing unconditional surrender on the pedestrian enemy. There are worthy bicycles with over-laden carriers and patched saddles, ridden only by men. There are lots of cars, most of them battered, taken apart and restructured, some taxis – required by law to be yellow – and a lot of public service micro-buses all hurtling along as if the road belonged only to them, as indeed it does. Pedestrians are an afterthought. I stop at the kerbside to take stock. There are two ways of getting across the four-lane highway that divides me from the souk where I want to buy my vegetables. The suicidal way is to strike out into the path of the oncoming traffic and move at a steady pace until the other side is reached. This requires a lot of nerve for, regardless of the number of people trying to cross, drivers do not vary their speed and nor must the pedestrian otherwise the whole interrelated movement will be thrown into jeopardy. Syrians – experienced in jaywalking – manage the crossing with synchronised elegance and I start off that way too but then freeze as a truck hurtles down on me. I have a split second in which to decide do I jump back on to the pavement or dash forward into the unknown. Propelled first by panic, then pulled back by fear, I plunge forward again but immediately retreat realising, cravenly, that, to the Damascene driver, I am yet one more foreign nuisance.

Throughout all these tactical manouveres, the drivers remain courteous and smiling as they whip past, almost shaving off the tip of my nose. No road rage here, no swearing, no paranoid shaking of fists nor psychotic punch-ups and for that I'm grateful.

Now, however, marooned on the pavement and unable to move, I consider the alternative which is to stand there whimpering and hope that the traffic policeman will sigh, as he usually does, then blow a whistle which almost stops the traffic and gives me as much of a sporting chance as I'm ever likely to get.

Today, however, there is no policeman and, frantic with nerves, I grab the arm of the man standing beside me. Unperturbed, he gives me the signal to wait – fingertips closed together over the palm which is held upwards, the hand pumping up and down a couple of times – until he sees a break in the traffic which allows us to cross. For a moment, I feel as triumphant as though I had just walked through a field of fire. Then the adrenalin seeps away as I realise I have to do it all again to get back to the other side, this time laden with bags of vegetables and fruit. Damascus is surrounded by fertile, arable land and further north, towards Homs and Hama, where the land is irrigated by the Orontes River – known to Syrians as the Atissi – there is even more cultivation. As a result, the souks are a kaleidoscope of fruit and vegetables all arranged with particular attention to scale of size, depth of colour and intricacy of shape. Green olives march diagonally across pyramids of black olives. Heaps of spices – fil-fil, white pepper and turmeric – are shaped into precise mounds, each tip brought to a point of perfection. Red apples tessellate with green apples, lemons with oranges. Grapefruit are sliced open to display their juiciness, pomegranates to show their redness. Huge bunches of coriander dipped in water are used to sprinkle moisture on lettuces to keep them fresh. Scallions, cabbages and onions are laid out in abundance. Here, in the souk, is pattern and symmetry with everything – vegetables and fruit – afforded its rightful place in the order of things. And I am not the first to appreciate all this. John Green, an English traveler who passed through Syria in 1736, remarked on the produce in the souk displayed "…in such an artful manner in which they are arranged tempts people to buy them."

And there are other items on sale here as well – rows of grinning sheeps' heads, twisted knots of white, salty country cheese, cuts of meat, bolts of cloth, shoes, batteries, song birds and flapping chickens. Hanging over some nearby iron railings are rounds of flat, limp bread – khubuz – though they have been handled so much I decide to wait until I can get to my local bakery.

Back at al Ward, I overhear an American backpacker phoning his embassy. "I think I need to see a doctor," he tells them. He has enteritis. Gastroenteritis, he emphasises.

I am so determined not to get a tummy bug that I have decided to ease myself into drinking the local water gradually and to drink only boiled or bottled water to start with. So, still unable to face the kitchen, I devise a cleaning system by slicing through a plastic water bottle, turning it on its side and then filling it with bottled water in which I wash my lettuce, tomatoes and scallions. Together with the warm, freshly baked bread from the bakery at the top of the street, this is a feast – for 15p.

I've had to move house, from room number 12 to room number 13. The former was a double and this one is a single so I get to pay a little less: no single-room supplement here. In my new room, I have an iron bed, an unsteady table, a chair, a ceiling fan and, on the back of the door, a hook to hang things on. There is a window which opens onto the small, inner courtyard over which I drape the meagre curtain so that the cleaning man or the people in the rooms across the courtyard can't look in. The bed groans and whinges when I sit on it, screams when I lie down on it. After the first morning, I checked under the mattress and found that the missing coils had been overlaid with one of those large cardboard boxes that washing machines come in. I've asked Tariq if anything can be done.

"In the morning," I tell him, "I wake with a pain in my back because there's a dip in the middle."

Tariq is solicitous and uses his hands to diagnose the problem: "Does it dip this way?" he stretches his hands wide, "or this way?" holding his hands at right angles to his body.

"Well, sort of over to one side." He's promised to look into it.

Al Ward was once an old traditional Damascene house, owned by a rich Turkish merchant and, like all such houses, its main feature is the tiled courtyard with the fountain in the middle. Some of the tiles are cracked and the whole thing needs a coat of paint but it has an air of decayed graciousness that is pleasing. At one end is the tiled liwan where the family and guests used to sit. By day, the liwan is cool and in the evening it picks up the last glorious, slanting rays of the sun. Strewn with couches and cushions, the floor covered with carpets and beside each chair a circular table with fretwork inlaid with mother-of-pearl on which the brass tea tray could be put, this was where the men met to chat, eat nuts, smoke an arghilah, drink tea and do a bit of business.

Now, the liwan is furnished with white plastic chairs and tables covered with plastic cloths advertising Lipton's Tea – a popular brand in Syria. The walls have recently been renovated and a painter has been restoring the strangely 18th century English scenes set into the alcoves which line the walls of the liwan and which show distant vistas of Lombardy pines, trailing roses, ivy leaves and comely maidens in *fin de siècle* attire reaching up to pick bunches of grapes. Set into two of the alcoves are a couple of red lamps that glow warmly when the night air turns chilly. The octagonal fountain is surrounded by trailing plants many of them set in old olive oil tins and the courtyard itself is a forest of vines which weave to and fro forming a canopy of greenery among which hang blue, red and orange lanterns. The fountain is surrounded by more old olive oil tins filled with earth in which the ever popular basil plants grow: basil was the Prophet's favourite herb. At the very top of the green canopy, visible only from the balcony that overlooks the courtyard, are bunches of dates ripening to yellow. From time to time, small birds flit down from the date palm and peck about on the tiled floor for any crumbs they can get, their ticking beaks chiming with the precise click of the backgammon pieces, signalling a quiet game in progress in the courtyard.

At night, with shadows cast by the glow of the lamps, the courtyard becomes a mysterious place that makes people talk in whispers. Off the courtyard are doors leading to what were the living rooms in the old family house and which now are three- and four-bed dormitories. At each end, two unsteady wooden staircases lead to the second floor balcony with more rooms off it. A further, very narrow staircase leads up to the roof where people can sleep in the open – on payment of a very small amount of money. They doss down, these homeless transients, sleeping on mattresses, the contents of their backpacks spewing out onto the floor: bottles of water, underwear, socks, sanitary pads, passports and dog-eared, recycled paperbacks. A Stephen King novel is popular because it's got lots of pages. They arrive off the bus from Beirut or Istanbul, staggering like drunken beetles under the weight of their backpacks and are gone the next day, bound for Amman or Cairo. Sometimes, they say hello or bonjour and, hoping they'll think I'm Syrian, I reply in Arabic but they stare back, nonplussed: Hi is the preferred international greeting.

From the roof it's possible to see Damascus's beloved mountain, Mount Qassioun, as well as the local al Ward minaret from which, five times a day, the muazzin calls the faithful to prayer. All the minarets have loudspeakers attached to them and some also have loudspeakers fixed to nearby buildings so that, once they all get started, the sound, which starts off as a solo voice, becomes a joyous multitude jostling for attention, everyone calling out though none on the same beat – like an exuberant off key orchestra whose maestro has given up and gone home.

Mount Qassioun, known simply as the jabal, rises 1,150 metres above Damascus and has as many legends attached to it as its surface has stones. Abraham is said to have been born on it and Cain to have finally laid his murdered brother to rest in a cave there, after carrying the corpse around on his shoulders for days on end. The Prophet himself, it is said, has stood on its slopes.

I've been doing a lot of reading in the Alliance Francaise where the librarian has allowed me access to the books there. They're in French which is both challenging and rewarding, especially when I come across a choice bit of history like the story of Eleanor of Aquitaine having an affair with her uncle – on the way to Jerusalem with her first husband, Louis IX of France. When Louis found out, he withdrew into himself, took to wearing a hair shirt and gave away a lot of his money. She, for her part, crossed the English Channel and swapped kings: out went Louis IX and in came Henry II. It reads a bit like a crusader soap.

Today, because I wanted to find out more about Muhammad coming to the jabal, I looked up something about the infighting that took place in 656CE, some 24 years after his death when Uthman, the then leader, was murdered. The finger of suspicion was pointed at his rival, Ali ibn abu Talib, whose followers became known as Shia, the party of Ali. But Ali had two important advantages: he was a cousin of the Prophet and his wife, Fatima, was one of Muhammad's daughters. These two facts were indisputable and, at a ceremony in Madinah, he was duly proclaimed the fourth caliph, his position recognised everywhere except in Syria where the Meccan Governor, Muawiyyah, conducted a five-year military campaign against him, finally gaining supremacy, by means which, to this day, are still disputed and are reflected in the continuing divide between Sunni and Shia. I've always felt a bit sorry for Ali. Corpulent, bald with a thick white beard, he seemed doomed always to be a bit of an outsider, a loyal plodder, faithful to the ideals of Islam, "affable, pious, valiant," as the history books say of him. But, despite his impeccable connections,

Hammam in Saruja

he was no match for the glitzy crowd of businessmen from Mecca who adopted Islam but still held to the old tools of favouritism and preference. Ali was Salieri to Muawiyyah's Mozart.

The other reason I like coming to the Alliance is that it is relatively easy to get to on a bike. I took it out of its safe haven today for a trial run and learned that the form, as with walking across a street, is to keep going regardless. Hand signals are out and, having decided I am too young to die, even in a city as marvellous as Damascus, when I come to a roundabout, I get off and push.

Damascus – or Sham, as I am learning to call it as the locals do – was huge in the struggle between the Umayyads and their later challengers. Muawiyyah founded the Umayyad dynasty and moved his seat of power from Mecca to Damascus. In so doing, he initiated an astonishing cultural flowering that resulted in the building of the city's most famous testament to this period – the enormous Umayyad Mosque with its gleaming marble, its colonnaded courtyard and its glittering mosaics, the place I have so far postponed visiting.

The Umayyad rule lasted only some 90 years before it was replaced by another branch of the Prophet's family, the Abbasids, who were supported by the Shia. The Abbasids, in an effort to remove all trace of the Umayyads, destroyed much of what had been built in Damascus and, in 749CE, moved the Caliphate to the new city of Baghdad. The Umayyads, forced to flee, crossed the desert to North Africa and from there, entered southern Spain where they established al Andaloos, known today as Andalucia. The move to Baghdad was a devastating blow to the prosperity and to the cultural life of Damascus: no longer could the great caravan city be called the Queen of the Desert. But this is a resilient city, built to survive the fall of the Roman Empire, the seismic upheavals of Islam, attack by the crusaders, the onslaught of the Mongol invaders and, more recently, 400 years of the Ottoman rule.

In Saruja, where I am living, the Turkish presence is still everywhere. Each morning, when I step out of the al Ward, I cross the narrow cobbled street to buy some sweets from the old man who sells cigarettes, matches, chewing gum and biscuits from a little shop no bigger than a phone booth. We do our business over the wooden counter – three sweets for 2 SYP – and he fumbles in a rusty cigarette tin for the change. If I'm late, and it's getting close to noon, I have to hurry for once the 'asr goes out – the muazzin's noonday call to prayer – the old man will duck under the counter, pull the shutter down, lock up and walk up the hill to the Mosque of the Flowers with its distinctive minaret built like a series of

Saruja shopkeeper opposite al Ward Hotel

cubes, one on top of the other. Syrian minarets, sometimes called
Mameluke or Middle East minarets, are chunky and ornate while
the Ottoman ones are slim and austere, rising up into the sky like
plumes of prayer. Some minarets here, however, are little more than
wooden pulpits grafted unsteadily onto outside walls, a reminder
that, in the old days, their function was not solely a religious one.
From them, warnings of attack by outsiders or of the outbreak of

a fire in the neighbourhood could be quickly announced as well as news, perhaps, of a birth, a death or that a small child was lost somewhere in the narrow, winding alleyways of the souk.

The streets of Saruja are twisting warrens that divide, turn sharply, and disappear round corners or under low arches. They are lined with houses whose lower parts have been built with stone and a mix of date mulch while the upper floors, beams made from poplar taken from the ghuta, have their walls leaning so close to each other as to be only a handshake away. The old doors, one step below street level, are painted maroon or dark green and often have a brass hand for a knocker. If a door happens to be open, a curtain will hang over the entrance so that you are at once drawn in and at the same time warned against prying. Many of these old houses are now derelict, wind, rain and neglect having worn away at the mulch foundations. In the alleyway that runs along the side of al Ward, there are three such roofless houses, each leaning outwards or slipping sideways so that soon a heavy fall of rain will wash away one more precious piece of history.

In more prosperous times, many of these houses belonged to officers of the Ottoman army. At the top of my street, there's a small triangular space where three cobbled streets meet. Tucked into one angle is the bakery where, door and unglazed windows open to passing trade, the bakers can be seen forming rounds of dough into shape, slapping them onto wooden paddles which they feed into the huge woodfired oven. When they're cooked, the rounds of bread are stacked up on the counter by the open window, like books in a sale. Opposite the bakery is a confectionery shop offering sweet, sticky cakes smothered in honey and nuts.

Across the street is a stall where, each evening, you can buy a roll of flat bread filled with lettuce, tomatoes, gherkins and falafel, all spiked with the sauce of your choice. The seller is a genial man, generous with the spicy sauce, who sometimes removes his cigarette from his mouth when he's serving me. On one side of the falafel store is a greengrocer and on the other a perfume shop.

None of these are full blown shops that the customer actually walks into – simply stalls whose wooden shutters are let down to become counters. There is also a shop where you can buy birthday cards, pencils or single sheets of paper to write a letter on. Next to the bakery is a takeaway fasuliyyah shop selling bean curd sprinkled with filfil and drowning in oil. I bought a polystyrene carton of the stuff and found it so oily I was unable to finish it. Close by, under the old willow tree, is the Saruja drinking fountain. Beside it is one of the neighbourhood entrepreneurs – a man who repairs bicycles as well as doing the odd welding job. He has no shop but simply arrives each morning, sets up his gas cylinder on the pavement, attaches a blow torch to it and gets down to business. Sometimes, a horse with red and black plumes mooches across the cobbles, pulling a wooden cart decorated with intricate, tessellating patterns in white and red, its owner calling out his wares which, in this case, is kerosene sold from a tap. Across from the bakery is a bird shop, packed to the ceiling with birdcages, the individual song of each tiny, pulsating occupant known to the shopkeeper.

"Buy?" he asks when I drop in one bright, sunny morning.

"I can't. I've nowhere to put a bird. I'd just like to look."

"Buy," he pleads, "beautiful," and touches two fingers to his throat so that, for a moment, it seems as if he has given voice to a thousand birds.

I love this secret part of Damascus. It's a place unchanged since the days when peddlers and artisans earned a living without being bothered by bureaucrats checking their trading licences.

At the top of the cobbled street, close to the Sudanese café – which is nothing more than a few stools set out on the pavement where customers, mainly Sudanese immigrants, drink their sweet tea – there's an old man in a grubby gallabiyyah who turns up every day with his own stool and sets it in a quiet corner by the alleyway. Someone – I haven't worked out who – brings him a plate of food which he eats, after which he picks up his stool and shuffles off home again. My hotel is in a narrow street less than 100 metres long but in it you will find three tailors, two shoe shops, three barbers, a dress shop and, right next door to al Ward, a man who mends musical instruments. Most of the shops have a small television and a primus stove so that friends – who are always men – can drop in for tea, a chat or watch a bit of television without interrupting business. Yesterday, I saw a man cycling along on his bike watching the television which he'd balanced in the basket of the bike.

Above the street, a cat's cradle of vines and meandering electricity wires weave a haphazard web of daytime shade through which sunlight filters. By night, lit by old orange lamps fixed to the wall, the street is a place to come home to.

I've located Nadia Khost, an energetic woman in her 50s, wearing sensible shoes and well known for her novels set in Saruja. I'd tracked her down in a writers' café and today she takes me on a tour, showing me the niches in which Damascene history hides itself. She moves fast, pointing to buildings, drawing my attention to arches, windows, the fact that the small, twisting streets are clean, washed down and swept: "It is the custom. Everyone is responsible for the street right outside their door. See, like that woman?" A woman, in a long red gown, hair tied back in a pink scarf, sluices water on the cobbles. Nadia nods, satisfied: "The people here, it is their home so they keep it tidy. Not like where I now live, in a block of apartments, with successful business people, ambassadors, university lecturers and the streets are dirty with rubbish left out to rot." She hurries off ahead of me, disappearing, like the White Rabbit, round a corner and down a few steps to where there is a mosque with a couple of tombs and beside them four slabs of concrete arranged round a concrete fountain in ugly imitation of Islamic symmetry. The fountain is empty of water. Nadia gestures contemptuously at this example of urban art and hurries to one of the tombs: "This is the tomb of the Sitt al Sham, the Lady of Damascus. She was the sister of Salahadin. When Saruja was being demolished and rebuilt, they wanted to pull down her tomb but we managed to save it. But look, here, all these buildings are to do with women. Over there, beyond the tomb of Salahadin's sister is the one of his mother and there is the school set up by Sitt al Sham." The doors are all locked but, in any case, Nadia is off again, back up the steps, leading me to where a large house had once stood and where, it is said, the Mongol Timur the Lame stayed while his troops were sacking the city. Intent on trying to imagine what Saruja was like in 1400, I lose track of Nadia and searching up first one street then down another I eventually hear her calling me to look at a decayed but once elegant house whose small, carved timber balcony overlooks the shady little street: "In that house lived the man who managed the Hejaz Railway. His son later became the first President of Syria." She pauses and looks around her: "You see, Saruja was an important place. People don't know that. Even our planners forget that." Then she's gone, back into the bustle of the street to peer through a window.

"Come, look in here."

I look through a barred window and see a small room lit by a single green bulb. There is no furniture in it, only a tomb draped in green – the colour of Islam. It stands there, a solitary witness to the neighbourhood's forgotten history. This is Saruja's own holy person, whose tomb has been here for so long that no one, not even Nadia, can remember whose it is.

In the 1960s, Saruja – much bigger then than it is now – was bisected by the four-lane highway known as al Thowra Street – Street of the Revolution. Families were cut off from each other. People had to learn to negotiate the hell-bound traffic in order to get to the souk. Developers moved in and pulled down old buildings, replacing them with hotels, faceless office blocks and uniform rows of shops. Now there are plans to pull down more of it – including al Ward. Nadia has tried to take on the developers but fears she is fighting a losing battle.

"These roads the government is building all over Syria. They are anachronistic, part of a planning strategy devised and left behind by the French mandate. They were planned so that the French could move their troops around more easily and designed with no thought for the needs of the people of Damascus. They are simply not part of our Syrian heritage." She has published a full-page spread in the newspaper about the destruction of Saruja though first, she tells me, she had to get permission from the President to do so.

My Saruja walkabout has left me in a different frame of mind. Whenever I return to al Ward, I find my shirt clinging damply to my back. The noisy, midday rush hour lasts from twelve to two when microbuses are packed, taxis plough along streets and around intersections like mechanical toys whose owner has lost the key with which to switch them off. I find myself glaring at car drivers, despising the impecunious, complaining backpackers and developing an allergy to al Ward's squat lavatory. In short, I am just one more bad-tempered city dweller, rendered hot and tired by urban madness. And in Damascus!

Nadia's tour, however, has made me realise that it's not just my sugar levels which are running dangerously low. I feel the need for oxygen but also for a large hit of history, not only Saruja's but the broader picture of Syria itself. It is time, I realise, to move on.

In a sense, I have only myself to blame for this perverse wish to escape from one of the world's oldest cities. When I first arrived in Damascus, I decided that I would postpone getting to know the old city – the madinah qadeema – whose walls are only a ten-minute walk away. They encapsulate so much history that I feel I need to take it in gradually otherwise I may overdose. And, apart from that there is the fear, lurking treacherously at the back of my mind, that the madinah qadeema may turn out not to be all I've dreamed of. A few years ago, a casual acquaintance told me, amazingly, that there was nothing to see in Damascus. It was, he said, another badly-planned modern concrete city.

I wouldn't have been the first to risk disappointment. George William Curtis, an American visiting Damascus in 1852, had the same worries: "As you tread the streets, are you disappointed

by these repulsive waters? Do you tremble lest the dream of
Damascus be dissolved by Damascus itself…?"

What I need to do, I have decided, is to go away – and come
back again.

Now that that decision has been taken, I feel energised and,
needing company, join up with a group of cheery 30-something
Australians staying at al Ward who are looking for somewhere
to eat. They head out into the traffic with little thought for the
consequences and I have no choice but to follow. This means
plunging across to the central reservation, throwing a leg over
the waist-high metal crash barrier and then dashing through the
traffic going the other way. Fearful that I might get left behind,
I make it over the barrier in record time and on to the other
side where James, checking we're all there says, with approval:
"Good, we've got the A Team here." Thrilled to be included in that
category, I hurtle over the next reservation with brio – and land
thump on the pavement, bruising my shoulder. Luckily, James
is no longer checking. The chosen destination, unfortunately for
me, turns out to be a restaurant in the madinah qadeema – which I
am trying to avoid. We take a taxi to Bab Sharaqi, the old eastern
gate set into the city walls. However, with the narrow streets
only dimly lit and keeping my eyes modestly lowered, it's not
too difficult to avoid seeing anything that might have spoiled
my future pleasure.

The taxi driver, uncertain as to where exactly we want to go,
makes valiant efforts to understand the cacophony of Australian
accents shouting directions at him: "Bob Sherky, OK? Sherky,
Sherky, *Sherky*. Right, mate?"

Hopeless to explain that Bab Sharaqi is a district like
Manhattan or Sydney's King's Cross and not an exact location
and that it's no good giving him the name of the restaurant – Old
Town – in English even if that's how it's listed in the guide book.
In the end, the driver wisely drops us by the gate itself, leaving
us to fend for ourselves.

We pile into the restaurant and then stop abruptly. A white electronic grand piano tinkles quietly to itself, playing Imagine as if it were an organ. A group of Syrian diners, all men, wearing suits but without ties, turn to look at us. It's more up-market than we had expected. The head waiter, however, in a dinner jacket, menu in hand, smiles a welcome and beckons.

James responds decisively: "I want to eat so we're staying. OK? I'm starved and I want a large plateful of pawsta, even if it makes me sick." Like the American, he too has had the runs. In the end, we all have pasta as well as a bottle of wine which might just have been alcoholic. The table talk is of how to get a false student card – £8 in Istanbul seems to be the best deal – what the dollar (Australian or US) is against the Syrian pound, how all taxi drivers are out to get you and whether it's safe to travel on to Israel. None of this concerns or interests me and seated next to James's friend, Jazz, I listen as she tells me all about her parents' marriage. They had been married five years when the whole thing fell apart and her mother married the man who'd been best man at the original wedding. Apparently, he was the one she'd fancied all along.

Back at al Ward, I pack a few things into a bag, check the time on my little palmtop computer, then lie down, apologetically, on my creaking bed. The coach for al Raqqa is due to leave at seven in the morning and thinking about it gives me a rush of excitement. We will travel 850 kilometres north east of Damascus to the city where the Caliph of Baghdad, Haroun al Rashid, once had his summer palace.

In the middle of the night, I wake up thinking about Jazz's mother, puzzling over whether it was a love story or not. Depended on which husband you were, I decide, and fall into a deep sleep.

Chapter 3

Peacock of the World,
Lion of the Impassable Forests,
Gardener of the Vale of Islam

It was the fabled Abbasid Caliph, Haroun al Rashid, who, in 796CE, decided to build himself a summer palace in al Raqqa, on the banks of the Furat. It would be cooler than his magnificent dwelling in Baghdad and had the added attraction that it would allow him to indulge in one of his favourite pastimes – horse racing. The choice of al Raqqa had an even more important advantage. From here, Haroun could keep a careful eye on what might be happening in Syria as well as using the town as a military base from which to strike out into Asia Minor. So successful were these military exercises that, during his Caliphate, the Abbasids reached the height of their influence. Al Raqqa became an important staging post on the trade route between Baghdad and Damascus and through the gates of its walled city came camel trains from China and India laden with silk, spices, camphor, ebony – and slaves. Pilgrims stopped here on their way southwards to Mecca, merchants and middle-men came and went while the Caliph kept a watchful eye on their comings and goings, using a network of spies disguised as peddlers, travellers and even pilgrims, all of them charged with the task of reporting back to him. Nowadays, al Raqqa is a thriving, bustling desert town, full of tall, thin desert men sweeping along the broken pavements in swirling, black dust-laden cloaks edged with brown trim, black and white keffiyehs angled on the side of their heads as jauntily as any farmer's cap. The women, babies in their arms and toddlers trailing behind them like dinghies attached to a sail boat, wear long dresses in colours that dazzle: flame red, sunset pink, daffodil yellow, fuscia mauve, sky blue, grass green. Their head scarves are fringed with tiny metal discs that glitter in the sun, their eyes are darkened by kohl and their arms gleam with bangles of gold.

By the time I get round to unloading my bike from the bus that took me on the seven-hour journey across the desert from Damascus, however, it's dark and I have little chance to notice any of this. Looking for the hotel which Tariq had suggested I stay in, I find someone tugging at my bike and turn to find a man beaming at me.

"From where you are?" he asks.

"Ireland," I mumble, as I try to decipher the letters of the hotel sign on the wall. They should say Funduq al Nahr, the River Hotel, but do they? I stare hard at them, taking one letter at a time.

The man persists: "What you want?"

"Funduq al Nahr."

"No, no funduq, no hotel. Come, come to my house. Come."

"Thanks. But I think this is my hotel. It says funduq. Maybe another time."

"Why not come? I am English teacher, this is my wife."

And beyond him in the dark, standing on the pavement, I can see a woman, also smiling. "Come stay in our house. Bayti baytak. My home is your home."

It takes me a split second to assess the situation: Arabs are naturally hospitable. This man is an Arab. He probably wants to improve his language skills. I want to see what a Syrian household is like and his wife is smiling in agreement.

"OK. Thanks. I'd love to. But for tonight only. Tomorrow, I must come back to my hotel."

"OK. Is OK."

We pile into a small yellow truck that passes as a taxi here – the man riding up front, under cover, with the driver while his wife, myself and the bike ride in the open in the back.

My hosts' flat-roofed house stands in one corner of a large, empty yard and consists of three rooms: a kitchen, a living room and a sleeping room. As we enter the house, I am hit by an unpleasant wave of stuffy heat and for a moment wish I had resisted all the efforts to hijack me. Then the moment passes and I wonder how on earth I could have had such negative thoughts in the face of this overwhelming generosity. Once inside, and my boots off, we settle down on the rugs scattered across the floor. Cushions are brought for me to lean my elbow on, a tray of tea is put on the ground in front of me, and everyone sits round expectantly, watching, waiting. Drinking my tea, smiling back at my expectant audience, I try to sort out who's who. There are six sons and one daughter – Lara – who constantly jumps up to get me whatever it is she thinks I might need, busily brushes crumbs off the bare brown bottom of her toddler brother, has quick asides with her mother, then returns again to attend to my needs. She is small, dark, very pretty and though she looks about 13 is actually 19 and embarked on a two-year training course to be a primary school teacher. The oldest son is away studying law at Aleppo University but the rest crowd into the room for the show – Rahim, Khalil, Neshwan, Malik and the bare bottomed Hamid. Shamsa, the mother, wears a long green velvet dress with gold embroidery round the neck and cuffs and when she takes off her scarf to reveal her thick wavy hair I see that she is very beautiful, with soft tired eyes and a languid body that was made for reclining. I, on the other hand, sit bolt upright, or lean my back against the wall. This disturbs Abdullah, the husband. A stiff, uncomfortable guest makes the host uncomfortable too and now, changed into a grey gallabiyyah that had been hanging on a hook on the back of the door, he exhorts me to relax.

"Please sit, like this," and he hitches up his gallabiyyah, stretches out his bare legs, drives his elbow into a plump cushion and leans his cheek on his hand. I try to do the same but my legs remain embarrassingly straight, my feet are too far away to do anything with, my hands hang about uselessly and I don't know where to put my head. Indolence is something I shall have to cultivate.

Abdullah is the local school inspector of English and visits his schools by taxi or local bus. Both he and Shamsa are Bedu and were brought up in tents out in the desert, a way of life he clearly still yearns for. "We had sheep and our wheat was watered only by the rain." This last to remind me that the Bedu are nomads who follow the rain clouds and are not given to the sedentary practice of planting and irrigation,

"It was better in the tent," he continues. "It was a natural life and we didn't have so many things on our minds. Now, we have to think about our possessions, our money, what to buy."

But in fact, his possessions seem to be few. There is little furniture in this room – a television which the smaller children divert to when bored listening to the adults, a huge ceiling fan, a frail plant, a canary in a cage, a hanging shelf with a couple of Qu'ranic verses propped up on it and a cheap, plastic cordless phone which rings incessantly. Clothes are hung up on hooks and shoes are left by the door. There are no books in evidence.

Lara disappears into the kitchen and Shamsa seems to wilt a little. She speaks no English but I have enough Arabic to ask her if she is all right. She smiles sadly and touches her hand to her temple.

"She has headache. And blood pressure," says Abdullah "and," patting her shoulder chidingly, "she forgets to take her tablets."

I root about in my saddlebag and find some Disprin – my minimalist first aid – which seem to work for in half an hour, when we gather round the huge tray of food that Lara has brought to us, Shamsa is smiling and laughing at my attempts to speak Arabic.

"Irish people are good people," says Abdullah and, without pausing for breath, "how old are you?"

It's a question I'm well used to by now and my answers vary according to the mood I'm in.

"Fifty."

He nods. "I would like an Irish wife. This one is always tired."

I smile dutifully but have resolutely decided to side with Shamsa.

"Having seven children would make anyone tired," I point out. He nods again and smiles apologetically: "Maybe. Anyway, the factory is now stopped."

The meal is a feast of eggplant, grapes, yoghurt, butter, olives and rounds of flat bread which are draped over a primus stove to heat them. We scoop up everything with bits of the bread which, when it has been warmed sufficiently, is thrown onto the rugs on which our bare feet plus Hamid's bare bottom have come in contact with. I wonder should I worry about hygiene and then decide not to. It could, after all, have been our shoes that had walked all over the rugs. Hamid's bottom I decide not to think about.

When the adults have eaten, the boys all dive in, ravenously consuming whatever has been left while Lara brings out some maté which Abdullah and I slurp up through narrow, metal pipes.

Maté is something that caught on here, brought back by Syrians who went to live in Argentina. "Very good for the liver," says Abdullah, ladling sugar onto his and clearly enjoying it though I find the thick substance bitter and unpleasant.

Since we're getting on so famously, I bring out a bottle of wine I bought in Damascus and which I've been saving for a sociable occasion such as this. It tastes foul – sweet and sticky, like grape cordial – but Shamsa is persuaded to have a little and that cheers us all up. Like an uncomfortable guest, a mother who is poorly casts gloom on any gathering as well. After a few glasses of wine, I'm surprised to hear someone sing Drink to Me Only and even more surprised to find the singer is myself. It's not one of my party pieces.

"That's by Wordsworth," says Abdullah but it doesn't seem worth correcting him.

Round about 11pm, the children depart to the sleeping room where Lara has already unstacked the six mattresses which had been piled up in one corner. In the main room – which turns out to be the adults' sleeping quarters – I am given a mattress and the best quilt which is so heavy I have difficulty lifting it. Shamsa leaves and when she reappears in a pink nightie I go out into the yard for a pee and to clean my teeth and wash my hands at the hosepipe. When I come back Abdullah is stretched out on the mattress he and Shamsa will sleep on. Still in my shirt and trousers, I am uncertain of the undressing routine but Abdullah helps me along: "Please, take off your clothes, be comfortable," he says, smiling and nodding. I take the plunge and remove my trousers, make a big thing of folding them – something I never do – and then get under the weighty quilt where, foolishly and formally, I remain sitting bolt upright, in pants, tee shirt and bra. Somehow, it seems churlish to disappear under the quilt at this point.

"Please," says the ever-helpful Abdullah, "take off shirt. Do not be ashamed."

Even allowing for the inappropriate English, I don't like this turn of phrase but nod, smile and, taking off my T-shirt, lean nonchalantly on one elbow to look at the TV which has been switched on.

Abdullah gestures towards the screen: "Watch. Look. Very good film."

The reception is fuzzy and I'm not terribly interested but out of politeness, I gaze intently at the jumping images. Shamsa, who has been walking round the room picking things up, goes out and Abdullah leans towards me to ask:

"What about your successful life? Is it difficult – or good?"

"Well it's not all that… I mean, it's a bit of both really. It's difficult being on your own, of course, having to do everything for myself…"

He nods vehemently, sympathetically.

"Two months is a long time," he says, "without sex" and to my horror I realise his concern was for my sexual and not my successful life.

Shamsa comes back and we all turn our eyes to the blurry screen where, to my further horror, I realise a porn video is playing – legs and arms turning and breasts heaving in sweaty athleticism.

"You like?" asks Abdullah.

"Well, it kind of makes me laugh, this sort of thing." Conditioned by my convent education I don't feel I can admit to feeling bored. I am, after all, a guest in his house and do not wish to be impolite. Oh God, why did I not stay in the funduq?

"We watch sometimes."

"Yes?"

As he speaks, I notice that he is in fact whispering and that the sound has been turned down.

"For the children," he whispers, nodding towards the sleeping room. I nod back. "Of course."

Shamsa leaves the room again – can it be by arrangement? – and Abdullah leans towards me again: "Will you let me fuck you?"

"No." I stop short of adding thank you, as a polite guest might do when offered a cup of tea.

He says something about his wife – that she doesn't mind – and I'm not surprised. After years of bearing and raising children I imagine she'd like a break, from whatever direction it might come. Then, on cue, Shamsa returns and husband and wife resume their staring at the TV while I pretend to fall asleep though keeping a weather eye out for any untoward movement in my direction. At least there is the comforting knowledge that next door are six children one of whom is 18 and has already shown signs of standing up to his father. He's the one I'd shout for.

The night passes in a haze of heat. My options are to keep my tempting flesh hidden while roasting under the quilt or throw my arms outside and get bitten by mosquitoes. I alternate between both.

During the night, Abdullah gets up and pads into the kitchen, perhaps for a drink but since I am feigning sleep, I don't look.

Next morning, when Lara comes with a glass of tea for me, he is already up and coughing over his fourth cigarette.

"I didn't sleep well," he says.

"Oh, why?" I ask innocently.

"I was worried."

And so you should be, I want to say. He has broken the Arab code of hospitality and I'm glad to see he looks so wrecked. The children get themselves ready for school – all dressing in smart military-style uniforms – while Lara adds the mortuary make-up so popular here right now: pale brown lipstick outlined in carmine that makes the wearer resemble a walking cadaver. Wisely, Shamsa sleeps on through all this, unmoving beneath her blanket.

I say goodbye to Lara and the boys, thank Abdullah for his hospitality, and pedal off joyfully over the rutted red earth to the main road leading back to the centre of al Raqqa.

The sky is blue, there's a pleasant, energising nip to the early morning air and I'm on my way to explore the town of the legendary Haroun al Rashid, to locate the great Baghdad Gate and, best of all, to get my first sight of the Furat al Nahr, the Furat river – which others call the Euphrates.

Chapter 4

Welcome, welcome. I love you.

B est known for his starring role in Alf Laylah wa Laylah, aka
A Thousand and One Nights, Haroun al Rashid became
Caliph of Baghdad in 786CE. His empire, at that time, reached
well into Asia Minor and his military expeditions out of al Raqqa
were so successful that his greatness drew level with and, some
say, finally surpassed that of the other strongman of the period
– Charlemagne.

In fact, the two leaders developed a relationship of mutual
cordiality. Gifts including an elephant, perfumes, fabrics – and
information – were exchanged when it became clear to both men
that, powerful though they were, each needed the other. Haroun
hoped that Charlemagne would hold back the Ummayyads who,
by now, were rebuilding their powerbase in Spain, their activities
there a warning to him that, at some future date, the al Andaloos
Arabs could well be a challenge to Baghdad. Charlemagne, for
his part, relied on Haroun to hold the line against any threat to
western Christianity that might come from Byzantium.

Thus, while this east-west climate of suspicion kept both men
on the alert, al Raqqa was developing as an important staging
post on the trade route to China and India via Baghdad and to
Europe via Damascus.

By the 9th century, al Raqqa was well established. It had its
own water works. Its roads were pleasantly shaded by trees so
that it was possible to travel all the way from there to Baghdad
in relative comfort. Through the gates set into its defensive walls
came camel trains bringing grain and linen from Egypt, glass and
metals from Damascus, silks and perfumes from Persia, ebony
from China. It was a prosperous time for all three cities until

the unimaginable happened. In 1258, Baghdad was attacked by Hulagu, grandson of Ghenghis Khan. The Caliph was killed and the city razed to the ground.

With the dark shroud of death thrown across the Abbasid dynasty, al Raqqa, deprived of its commercial and cultural support, declined. Haroun's fortified city sank back into the desert sand. Over the years, nomads moved in and set up their tents within its crumbling walls. For centuries the town was forgotten, left to languish in the flat, sandy landscape, its fortunes fluctuating with those of Syria under the Ottomans. Living was basic, predicated on survival. To get across the river, people used floating gourds to which they clung. Later, when a steam boat arrived from downstream, returning pilgrims boarded it but were loathe to use the water pump because it was fitted with valves made from pigskin which they viewed as unclean.

Then, in the 1920s, Raqqa was revived when a postal system was set up between Baghdad and Damascus with al Raqqa a halfway point. Before that, pigeons had been used.

But what really put al Raqqa back on the map was the Korean War of the 1950s which resulted in a huge demand for cotton and this was where the town came into its own. The emerging Syrian Republic introduced tractors and pumps and these, allied to a good rainfall, brought prosperity and the phenomenon of powerful cotton sheikhs though these soon presented a challenge to the emerging Ba'ath Party whose ideal state was one in which peasants and government worked together. Part of the Party's programme was the building, in the 1970s, of the huge al Assad Dam with, beside it, the nearby new town of al Thowra. At some point, I planned to cycle out to it from al Raqqa.

Today, however, my focus is here and as I walk through the narrow streets searching for the ruins of Haroun's once-splendid city I can see how it all once must have been. I have decided to stick close to the perimeter of the old Abbasid town and start, appropriately, at the imposing Baghdad Gate. It is clear, straight away, that Haroun was seriously intent on defending his territory for the clay-brick walls – once of double thickness – are strong and sturdy and marked, at one time, with tall lookout towers positioned at 35 metre intervals. There were over 100 of them in all.

Now, within the remnants of the walls, the grass is silvered with sand and, as I watch, two village men stroll onto it, find a palm tree and sink to the ground with all the ease of men finding an oasis in the middle of a desert. The ruined walls curve, disappear, reappear and curve again bringing me finally to a roundabout where there is a statue not of President Assad (neither father nor son) but of a turbaned man who turns out to be none other than Haroun al Rashid. I take his unexpected appearance as a sign that I should break off my walk and get something to eat. Noon has long since passed and there is a growing nip in the air.

The café I find is empty but as I settle down to my salad and chai zurat, a male customer arrives and the café owner, in deference either to my gender or to the fact that I am a foreigner, pulls a screen across the middle of the café so that I am isolated, veiled, ignominiously cut off from the outside world.

The tea is lukewarm, the cheese frozen, the salad tasteless and for once I find myself dreaming of a hot bath, a bowl of spinach cooked in butter, a glass of red wine, a warm fire – and a newspaper.

Cold and tired, I head back onto the chilly streets. The street sellers are piling pieces of wood on their braziers which send sparks flying into the growing darkness. Some people have rigged up long flexes to their one-bar electric fires which they position in the middle of the pavement and which fill me with dread lest I trip over one and either burn or electrocute myself. And what happens, I wonder, when it rains?

Reluctantly, I turn away from the cheery noise of the souk and the camaraderie of the crackling fires and climb the concrete steps to my cheerless hotel whose layout reminds me of a Victorian prison. The main room has six doors leading off it, each one numbered. Mine is Number 6. This main room is empty but for a solitary oil heater with six white plastic chairs arranged round it and, far off in one distant corner, a small television. In the reception area, which is merely a table out on the landing, a stern notice on the wall reads: "Checking in 12. Checking out 12."

My room is simply furnished with a formica table and chair, a bed whose singular hardness is matched only by that of the pillow. On the table is a plastic goblet, on the wall a window too high for me to see from and under the bed a pair of brown plastic slippers to use when padding across the communal room to the shower and lavatory area. I find it distasteful to slip into shoes which have been previously worn by someone I don't know and use my own shoes to get to the shower room. Here, though the water is hot, the air is far too cold to take any clothes off and so I move back to the main room where a group of men are clustered round the oil heater, watching football on the TV. The match is in Saudi and when a player is sent off for a foul, he kneels, cradles the head of his injured opponent in his cupped hands and then kisses his forehead.

One of the men is in police uniform, come to collect the bits of paper every hotelier is required to fill in detailing residents' particulars. This morning, the boy who doubles as a receptionist had asked for my passport. I offered him a photocopy of it but when he shook his head in fright and drew his hand across his throat I relented and surrendered the precious document. Now I know that the men around the oil heater will have been informed as to my name, nationality, age and place of birth. It's called freedom of information by stealth and there's not a lot I can do about it.

I join the TV group but somehow, sitting on an upright plastic chair, holding my hands out to get some warmth from the oil heater while being stared at by six men is a bit unsettling and so I withdraw to my room.

For some reason, I feel cheated. Al Raqqa has failed to deliver. Dutifully, I have walked around the walls of the old city, stared at the great Baghdad Gate, chatted to a few people but it has all been inconsequential, as if the traces of Haroun have been whipped away by a desert sandstorm, leaving me with nothing but the sterile pages of a history book. I go to sleep with the hopeful thought that perhaps my bike ride to the Assad Dam will cheer me up. And it does. The day is dark when I set out but it's 72 kilometres there and back so I need to get going early. As the day brightens, the small square mud houses alongside the road come into focus. Some have low walls around them. A few even have trees to protect them from the desert wind and from the sun. All of them have the ground around them swept clean. The only other traffic on the road are lorries taking sheep to market or cotton pickers to their work.

Then I hit al Thowra and it is indeed a new town, full of declamatory archways and ornate gates. At the first roundabout, a policeman waves me on, guessing – or does he know – that I am headed for the famous dam though when I stop to ask the way to the centre of the city he beckons a small boy and instructs him to guide me.

But the man is a policeman, looking after this most bureaucratic of states and the centre turns out to be the administrative heart of al Thowra with big doors leading to this department and that committee and it's not what I want.

Eventually, I find what I'm looking for: a café. Back in Damascus, with other people falling before the onslaught of some stomach bug intent on targeting foreigners, I have been fastidious about what I eat, have avoided the hotel kitchen, if there is one, have cycled 40 kilometres on an empty stomach and am now very hungry.

The owner comes bounding over to me, his smile beaming across the cavernous dining room: "Welcome to our city. Welcome to al Thowra. Welcome, welcome. I love you."

I wolf down the hummus, deliciously creamy with olive oil in the middle and a decorative frill of it piped around the edge of the plate. The ful is tasty and of course full of protein, the freshly-baked bread is warm, the water ice-cold.

It is only when I have eaten that I take time to notice I am in a sort of Aladdin's cave decorated with streamers and glitter. Although it's October, there's a tiny Christmas tree, complete with lights, on my table. A few Santa Clauses hang from the ceiling and the multicoloured lights of the house are switched on and off, manually, specially for my benefit. Even the cooler display cabinet has been decked out with red bulbs making a hitherto boring object look mysterious. In the background, a radio pours out a musical medley of soaring violin and weeping cello numbers. It's hard to leave this cheery place and I promise to return, which I know I won't.

The dam, when I reach it, is enormous and, peering over the railings, I can see some of the seven gleaming double turbines. The guide book says that no one had lived here for over 1,000 years – which is what most dam-builders assert – and then goes on to say that the name, Assad, was chosen by the workers and by those who had previously lived here. I suspect they had little choice in the matter.

Like the creation of most dams, controversy has surrounded this one. Environmentalists say that 64,000 people living in the inundated area were displaced by the project while the government line is that "most" people remained in the neighbourhood. Perhaps that's why, originally known as Tabqa Dam, it is now known, more prettily, as a lake – Assad Lake, a good PR effort.

Perhaps the people did stay for al Thowra is big and looks prosperous enough. And why not? The US invested US$100m in the scheme with the understanding that it would be built using US construction workers and US materials but somehow it was the Soviet Union that got the job. In fact, so many Russians came to work on the dam that a sizeable colony of them have now settled in nearby Aleppo.

I stop at the centre of the bridge to gaze out across the waters which disappear into the horizon and as I do so, a small put-put draws level with me, slows down for the driver to have a look at me, swings round to repeat the manoeuvre before put-putting away again: it's the local Mukhabarat keeping an eye on the foreign cyclist.

Everyone assumes that I am followed by the Mukhabarat and perhaps I am, though the only time I could be absolutely sure was when I was sitting chatting to a friend in the café of the British Council in Damascus. There were only two of us there when a man came in – a Syrian in a dark suit and with a briefcase – who sat down on a sofa and remained there for some time. Then he shifted his seat and came to sit at a table next to ours with his chair positioned so that he was sitting directly opposite me. All he seemed to be doing was looking though he could, I suppose, have had a camera trained on us. I'd certainly thought it strange for he had no newspaper to read, no notes to check through, no explainable excuse to be there.

My friend slipped a bit of paper across the table. "Careful what you say," it read, "probably Mukhabarat watching us. Say nothing important." It was sensible advice, similar to that given in a poem by Seamus Heaney, Ireland's Nobel laureate: "Whatever you say, say nothing."

I pushed the note back again and my friend nodded: "Probably wouldn't have understood what we were saying anyway," she said.

Further along the dam there's a place where, I've been told, you can see the remains of a tower rising up from the water. So I cycle on for another few kilometres, along a sandy track where beyond, the electricity poles disappear into infinity and everywhere is silence. The road lollops and humpbacks towards the headland and at this point, I lose heart and decide I've had enough. Do I really want to look at another ruin? Instead, I enjoy the view. Strangely, it's a little like the view you get in Donegal, on the road to Ardara when, coming over the brow of a hill, the Atlantic is suddenly laid out in the distance like a mysterious jewel. I turn back and as I do feel a wave of relief flood my heart. What *is* this anyway? An endurance test, a personal fitness exam? Of course I can turn back if I want to and sod the ruins.

Back at al Thowra, I encounter a village bus covered with silver foil and purple glitter, with red tassles hanging from the ceiling. I've always wanted to travel in one so I board and then ask the driver how much but, without warning, what I thought was a public service vehicle becomes a private taxi: "350 SYP," he says, his face expressionless. It should be about 60 SYP. I start to leave the bus which he takes as a bargaining move and we haggle. I can't work things out so he tears off a bit of paper that is wrapped round his falafel and makes some calculations. He's charging me, he explains, for the bike. We settle on 200 SYP.

Then, at the next crossroads, he stops and picks up eight people and promptly charges them 60 SYP.

Back again at the hotel in al Raqqa – strange how a grubby room can become home – the arrangements are still the same: metal chairs in a circle, occupied by the same group of men engrossed in what is surely the same football match. No one registers my arrival and, with a banana for supper, I eat it and then go out to buy some food for my next journey. Tomorrow is Friday which means few shops will be open in the morning.

The boy working the vegetable stall is embarrassed to serve me only four tomatoes at a cost of 5 SYP – about 8p. He's more used to selling things by the kilo. The fruit man is chatty, however, and wants to know which Ireland I come from and then mimes a bit of boxing and shouts Bang! Bang!

"Bang-bang mafish," I say.

"Bang-bang all gone?" he asks and looks disappointed.

Back in my room, I repack my saddlebag and think about looking for the very rudimentary map the Tourist Office in Damascus gave me. But do I need one? From here to there seems simple enough and so I turn off the light and settle down for the night.

Arabs do not like the dark. Perhaps this is due to fear that strangers may creep up to their tents at night and steal their belongings. Or perhaps because wild animals may attack their domestic animals under cover of darkness. Or maybe because a warm fire under a desert night sky is comforting and keeps the djinns at bay. Whichever it is, there is no doubt that they like their lights at night: the trunks of trees are entwined with strings of green bulbs. Narrow streets are laced with overhead multicoloured lights and most hotel rooms, this one included, have a small red bulb which glows like an evil eye all through the night which is why, gasping under the weight of the heavy bed cover, I sleep intermittently, cowering beneath the tiny, scarlet pinpoint that seems to pulsate as I watch it.

Round about dawn, with the first light starting to drain the eye of its evilness, I drift off into sleep snapping awake suddenly as I remember that today I am to cycle to Deir ez Zour which is some 120 kilometres away along a road I am not yet sure exists.

Chapter 5

Tifaddli, tifaddli

It's a marvellous day: the sky blue, the temperature rising, the breeze at my back light enough to keep me cool. I spin along smoothly – unusual in a country where there are often more potholes than road – and after a couple of hours pull in at a café where a few men are sitting outside taking their ease in the morning sun. They're the sort of men you might see in Donegal or Montenegro – skin brown and leathery, eyes narrowed against the wear and tear of life, the hands spread out on their knees strong and bony, ready for anything.

My request for chai brings puzzlement to their faces and they confer. And then I understand. This is not a café, simply a place selling the usual things – sugar, candles, cigarettes, biscuits – where one or two men meet from time to time to chat and thereby help the owner and themselves get through the day without unnecessary turbulence. Or, put it this way: it's a select social club, membership of which is granted by virtue of local residency. Long term residency. Foreign women on bikes expecting to gain admittance to this exclusive, all-male club should pedal on. Until the conference comes to an end, that is, and one of them asks Lipton's or Nescafé and I'm in.

We talk about Ireland – yes I'm from the south. Except we call it the Republic, I explain, and they nod approvingly. No, I don't know Gerry Adams. Well, not personally. And yes, I know about jihad and also Quneitra, Lubnan, Muhammad and Allah. My street cred established, we move on to other matters. One of the old men shows me his driving license. "It's international," he says though it doesn't look it to me. "Yes, yes," he assures me. "I can drive trucks and international tourists." This is the rogue of the group – you can usually spot them by the flirty look in their eye. He would, he says, like his picture taken. As soon as I get out the camera, however, he turns into a young girl, hands fluttering round his gallabiyyah, tossing his keffiyeh back over his shoulder with his hand as if it were long hair. One of the younger men helps out, buttoning his shirt up to the top, straightening his waistcoat, patting the keffiyeh into place. Then they all pose, smiling, outside their friend's shop and as I cycle away, looking back to wave to them, I realise I have no idea where I've been nor where I'm going for though I'd actually stopped to ask the way, I have completely forgotten to do so.

But it doesn't matter: the day is still mine. Being a Friday, the muazzin's call runs like an insistent thread from village to village so that as one voice fades the next one picks it up. The mosques aren't visible from the road – this is the main road between Aleppo and Deir ez Zour – but the call to prayer echoes all round me, carrying me forward to somewhere along the way where I'll find a turn off to the right that will take me in the direction of a bridge over the Furat. At least, that's what the map said when I last looked at it way back in Damascus over two weeks ago.

I pedal on, acknowledging the toots and hoots I get from passing trucks, the cheery stickers on their windscreens shouting Braveheart! King Cab! Hello! A car stops because the driver for some reason needs to tell me he's from al Raqqa. Ten minutes later he's back, on the other side of the road, having done a U-turn. This time, he wants to give me his phone number so that I can call and visit when I'm next in al Raqqa.

A lorry, perilously overburdened with sacks of cotton, sways past, the women clinging to the sacks ululating encouragingly. I pedal on for another hour or so and when I stop for a rest hear a shout: "Tifaddli, tifaddli."

It's a young girl, calling from the door of her house – "Come in, come in" – and since I have an ill-mannered curiosity about the inside of people's houses I accept her invitation to visit. Half an hour later, I'm sitting on the floor of the main room enjoying a tasty brunch of flat bread, tomatoes and eggs scrambled in oil.

The girl, Zainab, the youngest of three sisters, is pretty and fast-thinking. When the words we have at our disposal fail us, it's her quick mind which reaches out towards some understanding. The middle sister fetches and carries, bringing in the jug of water, the tea, the tray of food. The oldest sister, who is 17, smiles shyly and stays in the background, her wings already clipped by approaching womanhood.

This is a well-appointed household with a tractor and a donkey in the recently-swept yard. The main room has a washbasin and a shower cubicle in one corner, carpets and cushions on the floor and a TV on a table. Cooking is done in a separate room out in the yard. The parents are away – the father gone to the mosque and the mother to visit her parents. Left on their own, however, the three sisters behave as hospitably as any adult. It's only when a gentle-faced boy of 14 or so comes in that I learn there are also seven boys in the family. This one is looking for his socks and appeals, inevitably, to Zainab, who locates them in the sock bag hanging on the back of the door. I could have probably told him that myself. The girls cluster round, wanting to know as much about my family as I want to know about theirs but eventually I make a move to go. The turning I am looking for, it seems, is another two hours cycling away and I have to think about getting to Deir ez Zour before dark. Zainab is horrified when I say I have to go. I must stay for a meal, she says, stay until her parents return. Stay the night. And when I shake my head, she tries a trump card: "It's going to rain."

Right enough, the sky is darkening and I don't have very good wet weather gear. In fact, I have none but nevertheless I have to make headway.

At least the day is still warm and, as I cycle along, I try to work out how far I have to go. The turning off to the right should be coming up soon. After that, Halabiyah and the river crossing is about 20 kilometres further on. Then, from there, it's a rough ride as far as the main road with another 50 kilometres to Deir. What lies in between I have no idea.

The villages peter out and I find myself cycling through an empty and silent landscape. Should I have stayed with the family of girls as I had been invited to, I wonder? A truck overtakes me and turns off to the right and I realise this must be my turning as well. The truck stops to let someone off and when I catch up, I call out to the driver: "Halabiyah. Is it far?"

He spreads his fingers and, palm down, seesaws them back and forth "Shuwayy-shuwayy," he says. Sort of. This means it could be quite far. Or not.

"Follow me. I'm going there," he shouts but as I watch in dismay, he revs up and disappears in a cloud of dust. The road now is no more than a track and I have to slow down to handle the ruts and potholes. There are no houses, only the occasional dilapidated animal shelter lacking a roof. It suddenly strikes me that without a tent, I may have to spend the night in one of these and I shiver at the thought. It will be a cold night.

I pedal on, scanning the horizon for a building of any sort better than a three walled shed open to the elements. If truth be known, I am finally nervous, fearful of all the things that come at you when you lack the security of a roof over your head: wild dogs, wild men, jinn. Rain even.

Foolishly, my heart starts to thump. The landscape appears deserted but suppose someone is watching me from afar, someone I can't see, waiting for me to select a broken down shed where I might get some shelter? They might creep up on me under cover of darkness thinking I had something worth stealing.

I could keep cycling, of course, and only seek somewhere to stop once it's got dark and no one can see me. But, the voice of reason interrupts, if it's dark, how are you going to be able to see the animal shelters, none of which are close to the side of the road?

I think of all the women travellers I have encountered both in real life and through their diaries and realise I am a gibbering wimp, without an ounce of courage in my body. In fact, so desperate am I that I even consider praying – something I haven't done since I used to send messages to Saint Anthony to enlist his help in finding lost tennis balls. Saint Jude is the patron saint of hopeless cases but I don't think I've quite reached my nadir. Not yet. I cycle carefully down a gully and come to a stop in the pool of red mud at the bottom of it. Somewhere, like an audible mirage, I seem to hear voices. The shouting of children perhaps. Getting off, I push the bike up out of the gully and over the brow of the hill. There, in the middle of the track, are a couple of small children dropping stones in a puddle to create a splash. Their clothes are ragged and ill-fitting, their hair unkempt, their faces dirty. They stop and I stop and we all stare at each other in silence. Then along the track comes a man, old, lean and upright, wielding a stick which he uses to chase the children away.

We exchange greetings and I will him to keep talking to me until I've established some sort of rapport. He does and as we talk, a young and very beautiful woman joins us. She is tall and straight-backed with dark shiny hair pulled back and partly concealed by a black scarf, which is wound round her head, Bedouin style. She wears a long black tunic pulled in at the waist by a leather belt with a brass buckle. And as she comes towards us, I see that she has the walk of a queen. Take her to Paris fashion week and she would steal the show.

She has no English and I later discover that she can neither read nor write but we converse with ease and, as we do so, I will her to invite me to have tea. Which she does, guiding me into a sort of walled compound consisting of a one-storey flat-roofed house, a few outhouses and a yard with a lorry parked in it.

The old man – her father-in-law – drifts away now that we have engaged in women's talk and gradually, as in a play, characters start to enter stage left and stage right: a woman here, a young girl there, a man after her, another man.

My bike is taken away and put safely by a shed. The yard fills with more ragged children come to stare and so many of them are there that the old man returns with a raised shovel threatening to hit them. But they've heard his ranting before and merely move out of range.

Then an old woman advances across the yard and the children scatter. She is wizened, bent, faded henna decorations on her face and hands – and clearly the matriarch. We nod and smile at each other and soon the whole family is there, lined up, eight or ten of them. All smiling expectantly. And it is then, il hamdhu lillah, that the old woman invites me to stay the night.

The relief I experience is next only to what I felt once as I walked around the French/Spanish border town of Collioure, looking for somewhere to pitch my tent. After cycling 80 kilometres to stay as arranged, with a friend, I had arrived at midnight to find she had moved out the previous day, leaving a note to that effect stuck up the drainpipe but which I failed to see in the dark. It was only after two hours searching that finally, at 2am, I persuaded a camp site to open its gates and let me in. Only then, sliding into my tiny tent as narrow as a coffin, did I feel safe and protected from the elements. It was as good as arriving home can get. Now, when people ask me if that experience put me off camping I have to say no, on the contrary: it simply shows that things work out in the end as it has just done so here, in an isolated, depopulated corner of Syria.

Once they have heard me accept the offer of hospitality everyone drifts away secure in the knowledge that I will still be here next time they venture into the yard. The old woman calls out for a carpet to be brought out for us both to sit on, then for a kettle of water, a bowl and a towel. The kettle is for the old woman to pour cold water over my hands and then over my feet to wash away the dry red dust of the day. The water is blissfully cool and the whole event a ceremony of welcome gracious as no other.

The evening meal is being prepared which means it's time for me to leap over the next hurdle. "When you're here," a Syrian friend had advised me, "don't tell people you're vegetarian.

They'll just think you're Indian. Instead, let them think that you'll die if you eat meat."

"Die? How do I convey that idea?"

"Just say you can't eat meat, as if you had a medical condition."

And helpfully, she gave me the exact words I should use: "Ma fini akul lahem. Abden, abden abden." Which means: I can't eat meat. Ever, ever, ever.

The three abdens, she warned, were really important as they would ram the message home.

So I trot the phrase out to the beautiful daughter-in-law who I now know is called Aisha and she nods her understanding.

The preparations for the meal start. A fire has to be lit, dough mixed for the flat bread, rice brought to the kitchen. The old woman and I sit companionably in the middle of the yard smiling at each other while every so often she calls out orders and gives directions. And then suddenly there's a commotion behind me. I turn my head to see the children screaming in horror mixed with delight, all of them dancing round a headless chicken which itself is flapping its wings and screeching in its death throes. I am looking, I realise, at my supper.

Had I not spoken clearly enough? Not added the all-powerful abden, abden, abden? Had my Arabic been totally incomprehensible? But it is none of these, I finally work out. Simply that here, as in many cultures, fowl does not rate as meat.

The old woman's large, expansive daughter comes and sits down beside me flashing a mouthful of gold teeth across the linguistic divide. She seems to be the senior daughter, aged about 40 and has a rough-skinned country face that at first looks dirty but is really weathered to a shade of dark blue. Her hands are huge, the fingers red and raw-looking and for 30 minutes she kneads a large piece of dough while telling me how much her back aches from doing this as indeed it must for she is sitting crosslegged and has to lean forward to thump the dough in a big aluminium bowl.

Aisha, meanwhile, comes across the yard, a second chicken dangling by its legs from her hand. A teenage boy is summoned

all
c arm
are two
ght, sings
It's a lonely

and pray and
for a pee while
by now, the donkey
crowing. One of the
les at the old woman
some bird or other. It's
memory of it still makes
and a cigarette lighter, a pack
00 SYP pounds which I give
er will be refused or not. But he
king at it and then thanks me, his
ness and gratitude. The old woman
uching my hand to her forehead and
should be giving her this sign of respect.
overtake a herd of goats and carry away
inging of the lead goat's bell.

to despatch this bird which he does, kneeling on its outspread wings to cut its throat and then flicking the knife, blade-first, into the sand when he's finished. He holds the chicken by its feet to allow the blood to flow downwards into the sand and when everyone has drifted away, a couple of dogs slink across the yard to lick up the spilt blood.

A big fire of brushwood is blazing away in a corner of the yard where the dough, now risen, is waiting to be cooked. Balanced on three very hot stones which themselves rest in the fire is an inverted metal bowl. It's a skilled business, this breadmaking, and I watch Aisha as first she tears off a handful of dough then flings it from hand to hand. Miraculously, the piece of dough spreads wide and wider as it skims through the air so that eventually it is like a huge wingless bird flying between her hands. Then, at the right moment. she flips it down onto the upturned metal bowl where it swiftly cooks.

After a while, the senior daughter takes over and checks to see that I am watching for clearly she considers herself the more experienced breadmaker. And indeed she is. Faster and faster flies the dough from hand to hand. Bigger and bigger, thinner and thinner it gets until it's thrown down onto the metal bowl. As it turns opaque, she lifts the dough, now delicate as spun silk, and turns it over for the other side to brown. The trick is to do all this without allowing a hole to develop, something she manages every time.

The men, while all this is going on, are busy loading up the lorry with sacks of cotton. Each sack weighs 200kg and takes four men to manoeuvre up onto the back of the lorry, one of them stabbing a sickle into the side of the sack and using that to heave it upwards. The men, with the old man incongruously dressed in bright, fashionably baggy shorts, heft and pull, stab and push until eventually the lorry is loaded and tied up ready to be driven to Deir tomorrow morning.

A few hours later, the evening meal – I had to step over the head of the decapitated chicken to get into the two-room house – is laid

out on the floor on a large tray: a steaming mound of ri̶
with chicken stew, the whole lot swimming in chicke̶

The old woman invites me to sit with her and̶
start to eat. I do so with my eyes partly shut and̶
closed down, picking up one piece of chicken ̶
quickly before concentrating on the rice. The̶
in, ripping all the meat off with her teeth bef̶
back onto the tray. Ahmad, Aisha's husba̶
the family, is a gentle smiling man who̶
of the room, shaking his head when I ̶
It is only when I indicate I have had ̶
of the family approach the tray.

The house – I have a chance t̶
the family is eating – consists ̶
is used for eating and sleepin̶
a corner, with rugs lining th̶
the walls. There are the ̶
father) as well as a fade̶
dead husband of the ̶
cups and bowls and ̶
from which hang̶
This arrangeme̶
Ireland where ̶
ceiling beams ̶
is a rough drawing ̶

After the meal is cle̶
neighbours, cousins, sisters ̶
One woman arrives carrying a sl̶
though all I can see of it is one fat lit̶
the blanket.

"A baby?" I ask.

"Yes," says her proud husband. "One behind and one ̶
and then I see that she is also very pregnant.

"You can see," says another man, making his fingers into horns
at each side of his face, "he is very busy."

All evening, a series of small children have been coming to
curl up on the lap of the old woman, their grandmother, looking
for a comforting place to fall asleep. A little boy burrows into her
black-clad breasts. A tiny girl snuggles in under her long skirt.
A curly-headed, bare-bottomed toddler sprawls on the carpet
at her feet. One by one, as they fall asleep, they are picked up
and carried off to their appointed mattresses. When it is time
for everyone to go home, a small boy who has fallen asleep on
the floor behind his father, is shaken awake, pulled to his feet
where he stands miserably before following his parents out the
door into the cold, dark night.

Some hours later, I wake and see the old woman asleep ̶
her clothes including her black head scarf, her old arthri̶
thrown up over her head. Beside her on her mattress̶
small granddaughters. The fluorescent tube, on all n̶
downwards in the chromatic scale: G, Fsharp, F, E̶
sound that stays with me as I go back to sleep.

Around 5am, the old woman gets up to wa̶
a short while later, the children stir, go outsi̶
their grandmother waits for them at the door̶
is braying, dogs are barking and a cock i̶
little girls, coming back in the door, s̶
and gives three little chirps, imitatin̶
the divine sound of childhood and t̶
me smile. When it's time to go, I ̶
of cards, a small Irish flag and ̶
to Ahmad, not certain if my o̶
takes the money without loo̶
soft dark eyes full of kind̶
comes to say goodbye, ̶
lips though it is me tha̶
As I cycle away, ̶
with me the gentle̶

Chapter 6

Deir, you are my light

A lthough cold air slices into the back of my throat, the sky is clear and I pedal along with lightness in my heart, released from the slightly onerous task of being sociable. Now, on the bike, I feel apart, occupying my own world, coming and going in the other but free again to retreat into mine. This is the way I live, comings and goings marking the hours and minutes of my life wherever I am. The only person I encounter on the rocky, rutted track is a shepherd, a tough little baby tied to her back. She jogs along side-saddle on a donkey, a flock of sheep just ahead of her. Behind her is another donkey with three children on it. I guess that she's taking the sheep to their place of grazing and will then leave the children in charge for the day. We chat for a few minutes and then I'm on my own again, heading for the river which, after a few kilometres, comes up on my right, its waters churning through rough land that rises abruptly on either side.

Reverentially, I get off the bike to stop and stare and suddenly the thought strikes me: I could bathe my feet in the Furat – the magnificent and legendary Euphrates – as if it were just an ordinary river. Dropping the bike on the grass verge, I slither down the steep bank. The water is icy and running fast but clear enough for me to see that, at this point, it is very deep. On the far side there's a mountain with a village half way up it and the distant voices of children playing there come to me across the river: water-music of the sweetest.

On the road below the village – the high road back to al Raqqa as opposed to the low road on which I am cycling – a truck crawls along it, tiny as an insect, illustrating how wide the Furat is at this juncture.

After about an hour's very slow cycling, I see, on the far side of the river, the high ruins of the fortress of Halabiya and turning down towards them, bump along a stony track that leads to a pontoon bridge. I'm pleased about this for though my guide book had said it wasn't possible to get to Halabiyah from this side of the river, I'm just about to do it: in this land of contradictions, the bicycle reigns supreme.

The bridge dips and disappears out of sight in the middle and, as I bounce along it, I see that it's made up of railway sleepers patched with bits of tin and strips of rubber. Between the large gaps in the boards the water is coldly green and as I pass over them, they groan and heave as if every push of the pedals causes them grief.

I wheel the bike off the bridge to where the Stygian custodian is making a cup of tea in his crestfallen little shed. He carries a mug and a plastic chair outside for me but I follow him back through the door as I want to see what his living quarters are like. Inside are three iron cots on one of which is a sleeping body. The obligatory picture of President Assad is pinned on the wall together with a couple of flags so dirty I can't make out what they are. The guard tells me he is from Latakia and I imagine this is a grim place to be if you come from Syria's sunny Mediterranean coast.

The towering ruins of Halabiya rise against the cliff face each section keyed into the rock as it progresses upwards. The fortress was built in 266CE when the desert queen Zenobia ruled in Palmyra. On the opposite bank is a similar fortification, Zalabiya, and between them, they guarded the outer reaches of her realm. The Romans took both back from her when she threatened to become too powerful but later had to give way to the Byzantines who used the fortresses to protect themselves from the Persians though the latter nonetheless managed to capture them in 610CE.

When the Arabs arrived shortly afterwards, their sphere of influence already stretching far beyond those of their predecessors, the Furat no longer acted as a barrier, merely as a hurdle to be negotiated on the way to greater things.

The bridge custodian wants to drive me to Deir ez Zour and is puzzled when I turn down his offer but it's getting close to noon, the temperature is hitting 30 degrees, it's another 60 kilometres to Deir ez Zour and I want to do them on my bike.

Along the riverbank, where the cotton grows rich and plentiful, there are large groups of women pickers who hail me with raucous shouts and excited ululating. Their overseer, a young man with a smart little motorbike and an important briefcase, comes to chat to me, in perfect English. The women are picking cotton, he tells me, which will be taken to Deir ez Zour, now the main collection point for cotton in Syria.

I pedal on, through a landscape of poverty and squalor, wishing I'd taken the other road. Dwellings here are dilapidated buildings bordered with tattered tents whose sacking flaps and squawks in the light wind.

Suddenly, a pack of semi-feral dogs comes at me from both sides. They are large, with vicious-looking teeth and I can feel the rush of air from their mouths, hear the deadly clacking sound as their jaws snap close to my ankles. There are about seven on one side and five on the other, all white which, for some reason, seems to make them more terrifying. I pedal fast, shouting at them as I go. When I'm finally clear of them, I stop for a drink of water. My heart is racing and my mouth dry: for the first time on this journey I have been frightened.

I've read about these dogs. The advice given is to ignore them and above all not to show fear. I practiced this once when walking along a lane in County Cork. A farm dog bounded towards me, snarling and baring his teeth and making runs at my left hand that hung loosely at my side. It took all my nerve not to move my hand up and out of harm's way and so left it where it was, a few inches from the dog's teeth. Finally, once I reached the boundary of the farm, the snarling stopped, job done.

For a city-dweller, the countryside is a dangerous place. As a child, it was my job to cross the fields with a can to get the milk – a simple enough task in itself except that the farm gate was guarded by a flock of geese who hissed and flapped their wings menacingly so that I had to stand at the gate and call out for the farmer to come and rescue me. There was also the fear that Paddy, the farm horse, would get bitten by a gadfly and rear up in pain, to tower over me like something in a science fiction comic.

Once past the fearsome dogs, I unpack my saddlebags and belatedly delve deep to find the dog dazer, an auditory device which emits a sound too high for the human ear to hear but which is supposed to stop dogs in their tracks. I place it and a small pile of stones on the bag fixed to the handlebars, watched by a man from one of the shacks. He has a mouthful of teeth, crooked and black, and holds by the hand a small child with such a woefully running nose that I pedal away as fast as I can and with no regrets.

A few kilometres further on is a café which has a sign reading "Welcome You", its wall painted like a Caribbean holiday brochure complete with palm trees and golden sand lapped by azure water. A baby lies on a mattress on the concrete veranda, its whining cries thin and miserable. When it hears my steps on the path, however, it drops off to sleep, comforted perhaps by the knowledge that someone is close by: we all need some company from time to time. I've stumbled into a whole little community: a woman, whose feet both point to the same side as in a child's drawing, drags herself up the steps to the balcony then shuffles sideways through the café door. An old woman comes out with a small, curly-haired boy and sends him off to bring her a purple gauzy scarf which she lays over the sleeping baby to protect him from the flies that are buzzing round us.

A man arrives and offers me his wrist: his hands are grubby from work he has been doing on a nearby building. The drink the old woman brings me – made with watery milk and tasting of a synthetic strawberry flavour – is awful and I feel embarrassed at leaving it behind but I have no choice. In any case, I still have another 56 kilometres to do before Deir ez Zour.

After cycling for an hour or so, I stop at a tiny shop and am given the most delicious lunch I could have wished for: soft, freshly-baked bread, olives, tomatoes, cucumber, oil and a spicy sauce to dip the bread into.

The man who owns the shop is Eid Ali. He's 35, his wife is 20 and they have a five-day-old baby as well as three other children including a pretty little toddler with gold earrings who nonchalantly steals bread straight from the mouth of her three-year-old brother. The little boy barely notices this so busy is he staring at me. His father, however, sees what is going on, and takes something from his own mouth – a nut or a piece of gum, perhaps –and feeds it to the boy.

Eid Ali has a grand little shop selling fly swats, boxes of matches, packets of tea and tinned beef. He tells me that his father, now 70, married twice and produced 12 sons with the youngest one still only 16. Eid Ali has sad eyes and a soft voice that would make you want to do things for him and I'm glad that I have to move on with no time to leave my heart behind me. As I cycle away, he runs out into the road after me with a bit of paper: it's his phone number. I am to ring if I ever need anything. But I never do.

The temperature, displayed on a garage wall, has dropped to 25 degrees and even though the road is smooth the going is still tough. The Furat is now a distant thing way over to my left and with the wide flat plain stretching eastwards, my route is bordered on the other side by sheer mountains, great horseshoe loops of them that look intimidating when I see how far they disappear into the distance. Then I find that the road doesn't follow their looping progress but ploughs on in a straight line so that I can now start to count down the kilometres, as I go: 30, 20. Only ten to Deir. I stop to have a drink of water and to pump up my back tyre which always seems to be flat due, I suspect, to the state of the tracks I've been riding on today.

The range of mountains comes to an end and I cruise along dreamily until suddenly I am again surrounded by yapping dogs. This time, I stop in panic, can't find the dog dazer and resort to throwing stones at them. They close in, snarling, exciting each other with the sudden, snapping runs they make at me. My supply of stones dries up and I fear that if I stoop to pick up another one the dogs will seize the opportunity to attack. Suddenly, the lead dog stops, yawns and turns away and I want to kill him for his disinterest.

Deir ez Zour was once an important oasis town, its origins dating back to 2700BCE when it was part of the Akkadian empire. Later, it was taken over by Hammurabi, the great lawmaker. Zenobia incorporated Deir ez Zour into her Palmyran empire but it finally succumbed to the murderous onslaught of the Mongol invasion following which it was allowed to sink back into the anonymity of the desert. Until, in 1985, oil was discovered close by. Now it has been resurrected and has a five star hotel, a full complement of SUVs and is surrounded by drilling projects whose oil flares light up the night sky.

I take a wrong road into the town and find myself among huge lorries turning into warehouses, all of them heavily laden with outsize bulky sacks of cotton. There are women everywhere: the cotton pickers on their way home after their day's work in the fields. Truly, I have never seen so many women together here in one place and, for the first time, I am seeing more women workers than men.

I ask the way of one of the women. As often happens, she has no idea and, as often happens, this pisses me off. Then I ask a teenage boy and he points in both directions which neatly underlines the sexism in my thinking.

Finally, an irrigation engineer in a jeep tells me to follow him and leads me to the Raghda Hotel whose pillared portico, marbled steps and fine hotel sign speak clearly of charges more than I can afford and so I check out a more downmarket hotel further along the street. This one is up three flights of concrete stairs which lead into a dark and gloomy communal area. An old man in a filthy gallabiyyah and a mouthful of broken teeth heaves himself off an iron cot and I know, just know, that I will be leaving sharpish. He smiles cheerfully which delays my flight then shows me a room that is grubbier even than his clothes. Next to it is a squat lavatory that I can't bring myself to look at and next to this is a chilly room which turns out to be the shower room with a boiler, large and as battered as something you might find in the bowels of a Liberian oil tanker and which he keeps asking me to feel so that I can see that the water is hot. The price, 200 SYP, is right but I flee back to the Raghda, telling myself this is one occasion when I will just have to pay the extra and, yallah, B&B is US$15. Yes, the rate is given in US$ – we're in oil country after all – and is far less than I had expected.

Immediately, I start to enjoy the life of the moneyed classes: a boy takes my bike away for me in the style of a car valet and so thrilled am I with this service that I don't even ask where he's taking it to. If it were to disappear, I'd have had it for it is my home, my caravan, in which all my wordly goods are stored and carried.

On each side, I have a pannier where I pack the few things I've brought with me. These include a sawn off toothbrush, toothpaste, liquid soap which I use to wash clothes, my hair, myself, knife, fork, spoon and mug. I don't weigh myself down with a towel but use a T-shirt instead probably, though not always, one that is due for a wash. Anything that needs to be dried I hang from the panniers. I carry a small first aid box with scissors, a roll of elastoplast, pain killers, a few sachets of Lemsip, a tube of antiseptic cream, a plastic bottle to refill each day with water, some water cleansing tablets that tasted so awful when I first used them that I never used them again – and I'm still here. I also carry, for some reason, a wound dressing. I think this was left over from when I travelled to Bosnia to work as a volunteer election observer and was warned never to leave the straight and narrow as the grass verges were littered with unexploded mines.

Needless to say, on my very first outing to a hilltop election station, the driver lost his way and reversed – onto the grass verge – laughing uproariously at my remonstrations. "We know these places," he said. "And we know if we are among friends or enemies. Here, we are among friends." Local knowledge, you see. Except that the following day, a farmer, crossing his field, was blown up by an unexploded mine. I also carry a guide book, in this case the excellent Neos guide, as well as a map which I get from the marvellous map and travel shop, Stanford's, in London. For clothes, I pack a pair of light trousers, with pockets, that can be washed and dried easily, a cotton skirt, two pairs of knickers based on the wash'n'wear principle, a warm sweater, three T-shirts. For shoes: walking boots and a pair of flip-flops. I take a waterproof jacket, which doubles as a cushion to sit on. For gizmos, I take a small wind-up torch, camera, a palmtop computer and a cell phone. Most importantly, I bring a supply of biros and rely on local stationers for exercise books in which to write though I do bring with me from home two very small notebooks – one for addresses and contact details of people I meet along the way and the other in which to write my diary.

People often ask is travelling solo not a lonely way to travel. For me, no. I talk to my diary and can't wait each evening to write down what I've seen, heard, learned and thought about. Fearful that I might forget anything – and you do, no matter how arresting the moment or the image – I jot down as much as I can at the time though often a single word is enough to jog my memory.

I used to carry a small pot in which to boil water plus a small cooker fired by tiny firelighters but the effort expended was never rewarding enough. I also used to carry spare inner tubes and a spare tyre but gave up on that as well. Basically, I work on the theory that there's always somewhere to get a puncture fixed. Once, in Georgia, with a purple blister bulging from an inner tube, I managed to cycle the last few kilometres by binding the blister with Sellotape.

My bike boy returns with two bottles of iced water. The label on one bottle reads: "Bouksin spring at 5,000 feet. The best to prepare baby's food and conserve his teeth healthy." On the other is written: "The Drekish spring is well known more than any other spring of mineral water. Its water gushes out from Bazelt rocks and pours out pure, fresh and useful." Either is good enough for me.

I lie on the bed whose linen is pale blue, well-washed and possibly ironed though not greatly so but who cares? My room is high-ceilinged and freshly painted in a cream gloss. The shuttered windows are open and through the billowing muslin curtains I can see a rose bush and beyond that one of the canals that run alongside the Furat. And all this for US$15 and includes breakfast.

I shower, gulp down a glass of iced water, order a pot of tea, watch a little TV (a quiz show with the male contestants in flares and fitted shirts), spend a couple of hours writing up my notes then lie on the bed thinking that after al Raqqa and a cycle ride of some 120 kilometres, I am in heaven. In celebration of this happy state, I move into Arabic mode: "Deir", I intone, "you are my light, the jewel in my crown, my precious stone". Syria, I love you, I add – and then fall asleep.

I have to renew my visa again but when I get to the office, it's packed and applications take a long time perhaps because some of them look like complete family documents with every member's photograph in it. Many of the applicants are oil workers from other Arab countries.

I'm told to stand at a particular desk and am there long enough to notice that the officer is left-handed and a chain-smoker. The form is in French – that's how relaxed and pleasingly out of date the system is here – and asks me to state both my father's and my mother's first and last names. As instructed, I carry my completed form to another room where Mr Big, with a military cap on his desk, rubber stamps my form and sends me back to the original room and I am free to go.

But wait, this has all gone far too smoothly and, of course, the catch soon emerges: my official date for leaving Syria has been brought forward by two weeks. "No, no," I explain. "I can't go back that soon. I have work to do," and then remember that mine is a visitor's visa and work is strictly forbidden. Mr. Big ignores this anxious outburst, crosses out the offending date and inserts the correct one. A simple solution in a country where bureaucracy is usually Dickensian. Far from the centre of power, however, things are clearly more relaxed.

The Furat here is wide and crossed by an elegant suspension footbridge built in 1924 during the French Mandate. I walk across it and meet a truck spewing out a cloud of killing fumes intended for mosquitoes: the hotel manager told me this morning that Deir ez Zour has been invaded by a plague of insects from Namibia. I've decided I don't like this manager. He never smiles and throws my room key down on the reception desk instead of handing it to me. A man is fishing from the suspension bridge, dropping a plumb line over the side. The fish he has already caught lies on the ground at his feet, its startled eyes bulging, its gaping mouth searching for life. Down by the water's edge, a woman, surrounded by her family of small children, is washing clothes and as the evening light fades, the riverside darkens and the only spot of colour is her scarlet plastic washing-up bowl which flares up red as a garnet when caught by the setting sun. Beauty is where you find it and today I find it in a plastic washing bowl.

If you step back from Deir, you can see that it is a town at a crossroads connecting Damascus, Baghdad and the Kurdish town of Qamishli which, far over to the east, is only a few kilometres from the Turkish border. Now, with something like 14 oil companies looking for the crude oil that was discovered round here in the 1980s, Deir is undergoing a resurgence. Possibly related to this development, which some call progress, I've found the play-acting of a few of the young boys just on the wrong side of good behaviour. They yell at me, thump my bike and even, on one occasion as I walk across the bridge, a young man cycling past me on his bike hits my shoulder a glancing blow – unusual behaviour in a country which prides itself on its courtesy.

There's something about the Raghda – its orderliness, its calmness – that makes me pause and think about this challenging Arab country. When I first arrived in Syria, it was as if I were looking at a vast canvas too wide for me to take in. I had to wait for the details to emerge, for the language to make sense. The sentences were too long for me to understand and I found myself grabbing at familiar words as if they were life belts.

Last night, we learned from the TV that "a [Palestinian] martyr had ridden to his glorious death" on his bicycle, a bomb strapped to his body. There was a woman onscreen giving sign language for the deaf and I was struck by her hand movements. Watching her energetic, expressive performance, I realised that the signer is conveying not just words but concepts: sadness, regret, death.

As are the Palestinian fighters who are almost masochistic in the way they display their wounds as if these bleeding gashes were accolades bestowed upon them in the field of battle rather than brutal and obscene injuries inflicted on them by their all-powerful enemies. Palestinian men, we learned, are now wearing their shrouds on a daily basis in readiness for the moment when death comes to them. It sounds dramatic, glorious even, but as a strategy, is it effective when the US exports more 'aid' to Israel than it does to the whole of Africa? Palestinians may have to stop dying in order to live to do things differently.

Lying in my cool room with a glass of iced water to hand, I realise how simple I make it all seem. And yet, I remember, when working on the first democratic elections in South Africa, how people there said to me: "We've done it. Now all that's left is Ireland and Palestine."

At the time – 1994 – things were not looking at all good in Palestine. In Ireland, however, the idea of both sides sitting down together as the ANC and National Party did in South Africa was simply laughable. Then the miracle happened: Ian Paisley and Gerry Adams did just that. Granted neither man sat at the head of the table. Instead, each sat at the apex of a diamond-shaped table but sit they did and smiled while doing so. When I repeated this story to a Palestinian friend, he shook his head in a gesture of sorrow that made my own heart ache: "So, now it's just us."

The hotel manager has noticed that my bike has a puncture.

"Leave it with me," he says grandly, "and the boy will take it to be mended."

I am astounded. This is the gruff hotel manager I had taken a dislike to. Once again, my judgement has been hasty.

Without the bike, I have to walk to the bus station which leaves me feeling ordinary again, part of the pavement world. Last week, following the engineer's jeep, I was unaware of my extraordinariness. Head down, peddling fast, I had a task to perform like no other. I was invincible, cocooned within an invisible bubble of magic. Untouchable. Now, without the protection of the bike, I am vulnerable. People shout at me, wave, accost me and I have to stop. This uses up precious time and realising I may miss the first bus I wave for a taxi. Once I'm seated, the driver wants a few things confirmed: "Madam, you are from Ireland?"

"Yes."

"And you are alone?"

Clearly, he has already got this information from the hotel manager who has it from my passport.

"And, madam, how old you are?"

I eye him in the driving mirror.

"How old do you think?" I ask.

"Madam," he protests, "I cannot tell. Maybe fifty, maybe sixty, maybe seventy," and he smiles triumphantly, having given himself a large margin of error.

"Just take me to the bus station, please", I say, perhaps more grimly than is polite.

The bus to Abu Kamal is decorated with red fringes that hang from the ceiling and sway from side to side. With red pleated curtains at the windows blocking out the bright sun I feel I am in a litter on a camel. At night, these buses trundle around town and with their interiors lit with red and green fluorescent tubes they look like cheerful brothels on wheels, packed with happy men and women, me included.

Two hours later, we arrive at Abu Kamal and I wonder why I've come: there is nothing here. Then I reach the souk and am engulfed. The market is noisy, smelly, packed with produce and people. The vegetables are plentiful and varied, ferried from van to stall by young boys using wheelbarrows. When not rushing, they walk sedately behind a customer, wheelbarrows metamorphosed into supermarket trolleys loaded with shopping. A stall holder uses a black plastic bag pierced with holes and filled with water, to sprinkle her peppers, coriander, lettuces and tomatoes. Everything is alive including the squawking hens, which their owner cheerfully holds up by the legs for me to photograph. And what on earth am I doing, now, taking pictures of potatoes? Maybe because they make me feel at home. The stall owner tries to get my attention: "Bella donna, bella donna," he shouts and it works. In a minute, I am seated by his side, a cup of tea in my hand, trying to resist his kind but unmanageable gift of a large bag of spuds, deafened by the threatening roars he lets out when a hapless shopper stops for a moment to stare at me though, as exhibit number one, I'm loving it.

Walking back towards the river, I fall into step with two women, a mother, Um Ahmad, who wears a kind of mask held in place by elastic that goes behind the ears. Her daughter Hala is totally veiled with only her eyes showing but these, I can't help noticing, are dark, enquiring and very beautiful. The shape of her veil on the crown of her head too is interesting – square rather than the more usual round. She wears high heels and a very elegant, ankle-length navy coat with gold buttons down the front.

I have ambivalent feelings about the veil. In my convent boarding school, we wore berets to Mass on weekdays but switched to the more formal white veil on Sundays, held in place with two hair clips. Our heads had to be covered even to make the three minute walk from the dormitory, across the corridor and into the chapel where the nuns, to a woman, wore black veils. St Paul, after all, had said quite clearly that a woman should have her head covered in church. Did he, though? I never questioned this, accepting it along with a lot of other things that sought to limit my freedom.

Now, I often see the veil as something slightly sexy, hinting of mystery, protecting a woman from the lustful gaze of others but aware, of course, that this lays me open to the charge of orientalism. Right now, though, I simply think that Hala looks lovely.

Um Ahmad invites me to her house which is large and airy with curtained windows which probably make the rooms dark and cool in summer. The biggest room is devoid of furniture but its walls are lined with plush cushions and arm rests. A nearby store room is stacked with mattresses for sleeping on.

Um Ahmad has five sons and four daughters. Her husband, Ali, runs a small shop and bakery. We sit in the shady courtyard while she directs family matters. Her oldest son, Ahmad, comes to sit with me and tells me he is a chill engineer, working six days on, six days off. It takes me a moment or two to work out he is a Shell employee. He did a degree at Aleppo University before spending five months learning English with the British Council in Deir, the course funded by Shell.

I'm always intrigued by the role of the British Council, considered by many to be the cultural arm of the Foreign Office and possibly more besides. As a guest of the Council in Georgia, I was asked to visit a group of Georgian army officers who, overweight and getting on in years, were struggling to learn English so that they could more fruitfully be brought into NATO. It was an uphill task for them – and for me.

They had just returned from a military conference in Budapest attended by people from other former Soviet countries.

"And what language did you speak there," I asked.

"Russian," their spokesman said.

Now, here in Syria, the Council is working to facilitate an oil company whose reputation in certain countries, Nigeria among them, is decidedly tarnished. Ahmad, however, has his own criticisms: "The water here is now contaminated and they are trying to sort it out but our Ministry of the Environment is not very good. Still, working for Shell is good money." And that, as usual, is the bottom line. Ahmad's father, the baker, comes to join us. He's a cheerful, rotund man, confident in his success as a baker and happy surrounded by a family which he has well provided for. More and more people come to welcome me and it's hard to know who is who. Though Ahmad is married with three children, there's no sign of his wife. A tired-looking woman of 30 or so, clearly pregnant, tends to a toddler and busies herself at the washtub and in the kitchen. Is she a maid or some sort of servant? But no, she is a daughter-in-law though her husband never appears either. No one introduces her and when later we eat, she is not included in the meal. We smile distantly at each other and I find her presence unsettling.

The youngest son of the house, Abdullah, is a beautiful boy of 13, with dark eyes, dark curls and the air of someone who knows he can do no wrong. His mother, his father and Ahmad all roll their eyes and proudly complain about him: a lot of money has been spent sending him on a special English language course but he simply refuses to speak it. "He is lazy," says Ahmad and I'm sure that is the case. I get him to speak a few words – his name, how old he is – and both father and mother scowl genially at him.

Hala has removed her veil and, horrors, she is not nearly so attractive without it or perhaps my orientalism has raised false expectations. Her mother, on the other hand, looks better without her mask which she has slipped down under her chin. I ask the two women why they wear them. Hala, it seems, does it for modern, political reasons from which I infer it is a statement of her Muslim Arab identity. Um Ahmad, on the other hand, does so because that's how she's always done it. She lived in Saudi for a while where women were forced to wear one, something that would never happen here in Syria. Now, without the mask, I see that she is much younger then I thought – maybe 50 or so. Her hair is pleasingly hennaed and her smile is warm.

I sit back in the warm sun. The courtyard is cool, shaded by date and fig trees and scented by lemon and orange trees. There's a small fountain in the middle, surrounded by pot plants: I could stay here forever. And then the food appears – large trays of fragrant rice, spicy rice, steaming lentils and barley, beans cooked with pistachio nuts. And, for me, a plateful of some green vegetable whose name no one can sort out. But one person is not satisfied – Ali, the baker.

"This is not a proper meal," he says in disgust. "Without meat, it is not a meal. I am going to lie down." I get my Arabic wrong and bid him goodnight which raises a laugh since it is still only 1pm. Ahmad's small daughter appears and rearranges the pot plants, tweaking the leaves like a little housewife and singing absentmindedly as she does so – Allah, Allah.

Ahmad smiles and pulls her close to him: "She hears the call to prayer from the mosque." It is a reminder, here in Syria, of how much a part of everyday life Islam is for many people even in a country that is officially secular.

The quiet moment is shattered when a row breaks out across the courtyard: the excluded daughter-in-law is smacking the bare bottom of her toddler in an attempt to get him to sit on his potty. The smarting sound of her hand on his soft flesh is terrible and so loudly does he howl that the baker comes out from his room and shouts for the noise to stop. It's disturbing his afternoon sleep.

On the bus back to Deir, plumes of murky smoke from the refinery dawdle across the horizon. Not yet 4pm and already it's getting cold. An old woman boards the bus in bare feet, a black shawl over her head. Hungrily, she peels an orange and throws the peel on the floor of the bus. Her old hands are worn, the fingers lean and clawed, the nails black.

The bus trundles through the scrub, passing unkempt villages where poverty lies at the front door. The landscape is littered with pipes, ducts, cement conduits. In the distance, the flares light up a bleak land. Clouds roll up from the horizon and as the sun falls below it the flat desert darkens, throwing everything into silhouette. As a consolation prize, a glorious construction of colour emerges with the dark tells topped by layers of deep red cloud and finally, on top of these, a strip of sunset gold.

Back in al Raqqa and resting on my bed, I recall the guide book's description of Abu Kamal– a dull, border town – and rummage in my bag for my notebook to record my own experience. Not finding it, I search my pockets, look under the pillow, under the bed and, getting more and more agitated, I ask at reception. Finally, I realise I must have dropped it on the bus.

I sympathise with Isaac Newton when his dog, Diamond, knocked over a candle and 20 years of research went up in flames. Never mind that the story is probably anecdotal and that, probably also, he never owned a dog, the pain of loss is still unimaginable. I think all this through as I hurry back to the bus station.

"To where, Madam?" asks the only driver who seems moved by my horror story.

"To Abu Kamal."

"And the driver? What did he look like?"

"He was wearing a keffiyeh," I say and the man shakes his head.

"Madam," he begs and gestures around him. "Please look." I do and of course every single driver is wearing a keffiyeh.

Back at the hotel and resigned to the loss of a week's writing, I set to, noting down everything I can remember, confident that whenever I have accidentally erased something on my computer I have nearly always been able to rewrite it virtually word for word.

But though the lost notes represent the bad news, the good news is that the bike has been returned in better condition that it had been when handed over. The puncture has been repaired, the brakes tightened, the handlebars realigned, the steel rims cleaned so that now they sparkle.

Before going to bed, I finish writing, noting that three kilometres down the road from the souk at Abu Kamal is the Iraqi border, closed since the Syrian and Iraqi Ba'athist parties fell out with each other. Nevertheless, the rusty old sign still said Baghdad. One day – though I don't know when – I will cross that border and head for the city of Alf Laylah wa Laylah. It has been written.

Chapter 7

Red Silk in Aleppo

In Aleppo, I have a choice of two hotels that match my pocket, both in the same side street, in what was clearly the car tyre district. It's easy to go shopping in Syria because those merchants selling similar goods tend to stick together so that just as, in the old part of town, you have the perfume souk, the spice souk and the silk souk so in the newer part you have the car tyre street, the wheelchair street and the pens, drawing pins and notepaper street. If you don't find what you want in one, you can pop in next door and try them. In Damascus, even national airline offices come all in a row: Iran, Gulf, Pakistan, Yemen – and Austria.

Shopping here is a wholly personalised experience when even the most mundane objects are presented for your temptation and delight. In the souk, spices are displayed in vivid pyramids of colour – orange, mustard, murky green, black. Fruit and vegetables are laid out in careful diagonals of green (avocados), yellow (melons) and red (pimentos), the patterns ever expanding and always seducing. Most visually exciting of all though are the car tyres which come giftwrapped in fluorescent pink, blue and purple and decorated with sparkling strips of silver and gold.

The Syrian shopkeeper works craftily – and creatively – to entice you in to his web. To provide for a need you yourself are as yet unaware of. Cardamom in my coffee? Of course. How could I have forgotten? Pomegranate juice? Nothing better. A hen for supper? See how it flaps its wings – it wants to go home with you. Well, no, perhaps not but thanks anyway.

In a wheelchair shop in Damascus they also sell portable lavatories for use by invalids, one of which consists of a lavatory seat placed over an ornamental plastic garden urn. A simple arrangement and better than the more high tech one which has a clear plastic bag suspended from the lavatory seat so that everyone can see what you've actually done.

I've opted for Madam Olga's hotel and now we sit in the upstairs reception area of the hotel, she and I. Shrivelled into her chair, head sunk into her chest, a blanket over her knees, she dozes, her minutes on this earth marked by the ticking of the clock whose hands point to eight even though it is not yet six. A small brass chandelier hangs from the ceiling. French windows with latticed panes lead to the stairs. They have a tiny brass lever which clicks quietly into place as you close them behind you. The floor is tiled and the wall lamps give off a comforting yellow glow on this chilly November afternoon. There is a print of Van Gogh's sun flowers on the wall. Hotel Spring is a small piece of France left behind when the mandate came to an end just 60 years ago.

Madam Olga continues to doze and I continue to wait. I have enquired about tea and it is coming, I am told, though I will have to wait longer for my room: because I have arrived unannounced it is not yet ready. One half of the French windows opens quietly and a Japanese guest comes through to drop off his key. Madam Olga's hooded eyes open slightly, a foot under its blanket stirs briefly before she returns to her slumbers.

The tea, I know, will come in its own good time and since the coach journey from Damascus has been long – four and a half hours – I am happy to sit here for a while before setting out to explore what is, historically, a cosmopolitan city in a way Damascus has never been. In Aleppo, you can slip into French if your Arabic fails you. Or indeed Russian. During the Soviet period, many Syrians were educated in Russian universities including the last president and his brother, the former training as an aircraft pilot and Riaafat, his brother, taking a degree at Moscow's Patrice Lumumba University. So many Russian workers stayed on here after the Tabqa Dam was built that there is now a whole Russian neighbourhood whose shop signs are in the Cyrillic alphabet. In fact, the Syrian tourist industry is targeting Russian holiday-makers who can feel quite at home here. Lots of people speak their language, an Orthodox church is never very far away, there is a Mediterranean coastline and yes, in the new capitalist Russia, the visitors have money to spend.

But this is all a very recent development. Aleppo's history goes back to 2000BCE and indeed before, when it was already functioning as a small but prosperous city-state ruled over by a succession of dynasties for, by then, the huge movement of peoples from the valley of the Euphrates to central Syria had begun. The Persian and Byzantine Empires fought over it until 624CE, when a truce was reached. Finally, 13 years later, the Arab Muslims marched in through the Gate of Antioch and peacefully occupied Aleppo – or so the historians say. I have difficulties with the idea that the advance of Islam was always achieved without bloodshed. What great colonial power ever managed to do that? In more modern times, Aleppo's story comes to life in the great or infamous names connected with it: Abraham, Salahadin, Baldwin, Tamburlaine (known here as Timur) and even the fictitious Othello.

The heart of Aleppo has always been its iconic mound fortified by a moat which powers up from the land like a subterranean explosion of unstoppable strength. The mound has never been properly excavated but the remains of a Hittite temple, decorated with symbols of the moon and sun, dating back to the 9th century BCE have been found there. Topping it is a citadel which rises 378 metres above sea level and towers over the city like a warning. The sides of the citadel, lined with stones and with grass springing up between them in the rainy season, are tilted at an angle of 48 degrees rendering the fortress virtually impregnable.

The capture of Jerusalem by the Turks in 1071 sparked the First Crusade and led to the Muslims strengthening the walls of the Aleppan citadel against expected counterattacks by the invaders. But while the crusaders failed to take the city, other enemies struck, again and again. In 1260, the Mongols tore through Aleppo, burning and destroying everything and though what was demolished was rebuilt, the defences were not enough to repel a second Mongol onslaught, this time led by the fearsome Timur the Lame who arrived with his army in 1401, on his way to Damascus. Despite its fiery history though, Aleppo was, by then, firmly established as a major trading metropolis on that most magical of routes – the Silk Road.

Silk was cherished in China and coveted in Europe with the Syrian Silk Road providing one important conduit whereby this precious fabric reached India before being traded on to the religious and secular courts of Europe.

A good millennium later, it reached the small convent school where I boarded, our Sunday uniform – a cream outfit full of pleats and tucks and with a prim little collar – was made from a fabric that was shiny and stiff. Our tussaw dresses, we called them. Only later did I learn that it was not tussaw but Tussore, a town in India which gave its name to a silk fabric made from the fibre of the wild silkworm.

Export of the silkworm out of China was forbidden for centuries but it was the Chinese themselves, however, who finally freed up the silk trade. Wanting goods from the west, including glass and silver, they liberalised their trading practices and by 300CE the silk worm was being cultivated within the Roman Empire. By 400CE, the Byzantine Empire had its own silk workshops in Constantinople. This interest in the product gave the trade an important impetus and a few centuries later, silk was being valued at three quarters of its own weight in gold.

Many legends have been attached to the elusive thread. One story concerned a couple of crafty monks who finally managed to smuggle some silkworms out of China by the simple expedient of concealing them in a hollowed length of bamboo though that story was also told of the sainted Willibald who, in around 740CE smuggled balsam out of Jerusalem in a specially hollowed-out cane.

By the 4th and 5th centuries, the silk trade was well-established. Craftsmen in Aleppo and Damascus learned how to dye the silk: cinnebar for red, malachite for green, indigo for blue, acorn cups for black and clam shell powder for white. They also learned how to weave silken cloth and by the 5th century Aleppan and Damascene silk – that soft, whispering glistening fabric so desired by the Byzantines – had found its way to Italy and France. And when the great Damascus-based Umayyad dynasty collapsed in 750CE, the survivors, first washing up in North Africa then moving to Spain, brought the silk industry and its many crafts with them.

At the khans – and there were some very big ones in Aleppo – customs were levied, trading permits issued and goods weighed. The mighty camel trains had to be watered and housed and their handlers provided for. Accommodation had to be found for foreign merchants – safe accommodation if good trading relations were to be maintained.

So it was that silk took on an unrivalled primacy among traded goods. Princes of the church paraded in it, judges processed in it, kings held sway in it, women adorned themselves with it, emirs reclined upon it and courtesans draped themselves with it. The walls of Byzantine basilicas were hung with silk. In Rome, the apartments of the Popes were furnished with it and even the papal burial shrouds were made of silk – spun in Islamic Damascus. Curtains of blue and silver silk hung in the courts of Constantinople. Divans were strewn with embroidered silk cushions and drapes. Cardinals were elevated to a position of glorious mystery unattainable by ordinary people. Cloaked in capes of purple silk threaded with gold, they enacted the sacrificial mystery of the Mass, performing in secret behind silk screens.

Still surrounding the Aleppan courtyards today are upstairs balconies with rooms leading off them where foreign merchants could stay and where the trade consul might do his work. Certain favoured countries, among them France, England and the city state of Venice, were even permitted to send ambassadors to Aleppo rather than to the court at Constantinople as was usually demanded.

English merchants were singled out for special treatment. A charter of privileges was granted by the Sultan Murad in June 1580 which stated that "...the peoples of Elizabeth Queen of England, France and Ireland the most honourable Queene of Christendom...may buy and sell without hindrance and observe the customs and orders of her owen countrey." Three years after the granting of this charter, the first English trade consul was appointed.

By 1793, there was a thriving English Factory, or commercial centre, in Aleppo and, in his book dedicated to the "gentlemen of the English Factory", Alex Russell describes a city full of pistachio trees, myrtle and roses though all this was marred for him by the stench from the manufacture of catgut (for musical instruments) and perhaps spoiled too by the fact that ordinary people had to get on with the business of living which involved collecting cattle dung, charcoal and leaves to burn: winters, though short, could be bitterly cold.

I stretch my legs out on to the tiled floor. Light is fading from the sky. Madam Olga's granddaughter has taken her place behind the reception desk. When I enquire again about a pot of tea, she pings a bell on her desk and a man appears from downstairs where the staff all seem to sit watching television. The ping disturbs Madam Olga who starts to transmit, blending Arabic with French. She is angry, very angry. Her eyes, now wide open, glitter beneath her fringe of dyed black hair. The afternoon's siesta has revived her and her voice is low and strong, its peremptory tone energising us all.

"What are you doing?" she asks the man. "Going to get tea for this madam here," he replies, raising his face to point towards me with his chin.

When another man appears, she asks: "And you, where are you going?"

"Up." he says briefly. They all seem used to her imperious ways.

She directs proceedings, pointing out duster and polish, bemoaning the fact that my room is taking so long to prepare. A more senior man appears from downstairs and bravely engages with her. He leans over her chair, answers her questions directly. Shouts when she shouts. Eventually, they both subside. People drift away and soon there is no one left in the room except myself and Madam Olga. She dozes – and the clock ticks. From somewhere outside comes a disembodied click: the microphone is on and the muazzin starts his familiar evening call to prayer. I have been told that Madam Olga used to run a brothel and, if it is true, I imagine it was a pretty efficient organisation.

When I eventually descend the stairs to the street, I am disoriented. There are no familiar landmarks. The sign advertising the hotel has disappeared, the corner is no longer a corner for one of its sides had gone. I pause to get my bearings. A red fog hangs over everything, veiling the city. Car headlamps emerge and recede like huge, disembodied eyes. Footsteps are muffled and voices quietened. I turn right and then think I should have turned left. I walk to the end of the street into a major thoroughfare and find it frighteningly silent, empty of people.

This may be a city of high fashion and smart restaurants, of prosperous businessmen and well-heeled women, a city with an impeccable history of high culture. It is a city proud of its cosmopolitan connections with Paris and Rome and London. But it is also an Arab city whose souks are thronged with women in long gowns, some veiled, the crowds jostling to share the narrow space with overladen donkeys, with village women carrying their shopping on their heads, with men in keffiyehs and fierce moustaches pushing market trolleys piled high with tomatoes, potatoes, courgettes, spinach. It is a city only a breath away from a biblical place of black goatskin tents, a desert of sand and stones and stunted trees where people squat by the roadside waiting for time to pass. A place where a sandstorm can blow in at any time, changing the urban landscape, covering it with a film of fine red dust like a memory that can never be forgotten.

When the red veil lifts, I take a walk up towards the citadel and then decide to walk all around its outside perimeter. I've met a German architect who is working on an eight-year urban renewal programme for Aleppo. The plan is to restore some of the old city and maybe thus persuade people to stay there and not move out to the tower blocks rising up around its edges.

Aleppo is growing at an alarming rate with some 50,000 people arriving every year, and though only 10% of Syrians own cars, the demand for them is growing. The restoration work is long overdue especially in the eastern side of the city from where the desert sandstorms blow and where recently arrived citizens have built whole complexes of illegal dwellings – on land supposedly set aside for agriculture. And the reason the government does nothing to enforce its own laws is that it can't – or won't – meet the demand for housing. There is, of course, no shortage of new privately-built housing which you can see to the west of the city because, as the 62nd English Trade Consul told me, Syria has been closed off from the rest of the world for so long that the money is being spent internally – on houses and cars.

On my way back around the citadel, I have the usual encounter with a young man: "Madam, from where you are?"

"Ireland," I say grudgingly. I hate being accosted like this and try to give away as little as I can without being downright rude. It's me against them.

"Ireland!" he says as if he has just found the Promised Land. "Welcome! Top of the morning."

I am, of course, disarmed and have to smile. He has a brother who owns a supermarket in Dublin. Where, I want to know because, as it happens, my part of Dublin is full of halal shops. He doesn't know and hesitates – though only for a fraction of a second – when I ask his brother's name. He has many brothers, he explains but, and he smiles winningly, would I like to see the old synagogue?

The presence or absence of Jews is always a puzzle in a country which has such fraught relations with its neighbour, Israel, but which numbered in its population many Jews who made a substantial contribution to its culture. Many left, however, in the 1960s, encouraged by the American promise of grants of up to US$600 per family.

The synagogue, what remains of it, is now a mosque – the mosque of the snake – and in the courtyard is a well where, I am told, you can drown your mother-in-law. I digest this bit of unsavoury information – I am, after all, a mother-in-law myself – and then learn that, by an amazing coincidence, the uncle of my new friend has a craft shop only two minutes away from the mosque and would I like to go there for a cup of tea?

The uncle's shop gleams with gold and sparkles with light which bounces off brass lamps, glass dishes, beaten copper trays, glowing gold fabric. Silk hangings sway in the heat from an electric fire. Long black silk coats trimmed with gold braid, velvet waistcoats, embroidered cushions, white chemises, red and black keffiyehs, multicoloured village dresses – all are scattered carelessly about as if they are of little worth.

The uncle brings me some tea and casually, while we chat, sets out his wares: a silver necklace, a topaz brooch, some jade and turquoise earrings. We are engaging in a little foreplay and I don't know where to look.

I admire everything but am careful neither to show undue interest nor to enquire the price. And when he produces a crimson silk scarf I look away because this is what I really want. That and a hanging lantern fashioned in copper, its edges cut into patterns, its sides dotted with red and blue stones.

I explain that, though I like everything he has shown me and that I admire the craftsmanship, I am unable to purchase anything as I have only a rucksack which is already too heavy. As soon as I say that I see the trap: a silk scarf, then, which weighs nothing. See? He lets it float lightly into the palm of my hand – and I am nearly his.

But determined as I am not to buy, it would be foolish not to at least ask about the lamp. In a second, he has it down, bites off the end of the bare wire, gives it a twist and shoves it in to a socket so that it lights up red and comforting. There is no mention of the price.

"No, sorry, lovely but too heavy." The two men confer briefly.

"My uncle, "says his nephew, "would like you to have this lamp and because you are his first customer from Ireland he will sell it to you for only 1,000 SYP."

1,000 SYP? Divide by this, multiply by that and it comes to £17 and would look lovely in my sitting room in Dublin.

"OK," I say, both uncle and nephew far too polite – and astute – to comment on my sudden volte-face. I am weak and have given in but the victors treat me not as one vanquished but as an equal partner in the transaction and thank me as if I have done them a favour by parting with my money. They want me to feel good about it.

"We are both pleased you have bought the lamp," says the nephew. "Last week, he sold one just like that for 2,000 SYP." He touches the silk scarf thoughtfully, stroking its softness and it would be churlish not to buy it. After all, it was made here in Aleppo – and comes three for the price of one. Outside, I walk back up the street towards the citadel. On the corner is a shop I have looked in before and no sooner have I paused at the window, than the owner is out on the doorstep: "Madam, welcome. From where you are?"

"Ireland."

"Ireland? Ahlayn. Welcome. My brother is in Ireland. He has a shop there."

"I know," I say, and refuse to be seduced even by the picture on the wall inside of Oscar Wilde.

Chapter 8

The man who lived upon a pillar

After the sandstorm – the rain. It comes with a vengeance, thudding down by day and by night, splashing into huge puddles in the middle of the road, churning up the piles of refuse and debris at street corners, pouring along the gutters, spewing off rooftops and, when it encounters a break in the kerbstone – where kerbstones exist – flooding the footpaths. Together with the sand, it combines to make a sticky mud that forms a red coating on my shoes so thick it actually weighs them down.

Across the street from the hotel, a group of men and boys shout excitedly, circle something on the ground then lunge, stamping it with their feet: the torrential rain has flushed a rat out of its sewer which is finally battered to death with a piece of wood.

This is not a country of umbrellas and raincoats and I worry that people going out in shirt sleeves, cotton coats or sweaters will get wet and catch cold: a very European way of thinking, of course. What they do is huddle in shop doorways, dash across streets. Stay at home until it's all over.

For once, I take a taxi and tell the driver where I want to go. I am on a mission to track down a man who, it is said, intends to climb up a pillar and stay there in the fashion of San Samaan (Saint Simeon) who did just that some 1,600 years ago. The driver's meter is mafish which means he can't give me an idea of how much the journey will cost. Still, it's a rare event to be in one at all so I sit back and enjoy the ride.

"Cold, isn't it," I say by way of making conversation and the driver nods. When we get to the far side of town, he pulls in – and asks for 40 SYP which is far more than I had expected and in any case we are at the post office not the Catholic Orthodox Church

I had requested. I argue, expostulate, make a show of being annoyed, give him 25 SYP and walk away, his shouts following me down the street. It is only later in the day that I realise my appalling mistake. When I commented on the cold, I had put the wrong emphasis on the word bareed thus inadvertently turning the word for cold into that for post office – which was where he took me to. Thus did I add to the Syrian's possible perception of foreigners as being brusque, ill-mannered – and mean. Not that they would ever say that: they are far too civil.

My journey to the Orthodox Church has been both circuitous and virtual, taking me from Syria to the US via the internet and on to a university near Dublin that had once been a training college for young priests. I had read somewhere that Karim Ephrem, a priest of the Syrian Catholic Orthodox Church, had apparently said that he would emulate Saint Simeon by ascending a pole and staying there. It seemed a challenging project but though I managed to track Karim Ephrem to Maynooth, just outside Dublin, where he had studied, there the trail had gone cold.

When I reach the church, an evening ceremony is in full swing – a sort of high vespers, I guess – with the celebrant dressed in red and gold robes attended by little boys in white smocks adorned with red crusader crosses. The brass chains of their thuribles rattle and the spicy smell of incense fills the air. As usual, however, this kind of thing makes me feel nervous and unsettled, reminding me of a church feeding on the ignorance and superstition of its followers, who are usually women, just as much of the congregation is this evening.

The bishop hurries in, pulling his clerical cloak on over his black, plastic raincoat then bending to get a skullcap from the cupboard where the communion bread rolls are kept until they can be consecrated. He takes his place on the throne by the altar steps. A couple of little boys approach, peck at his hand like magpies investigating his crimson and gold ring before shaking their thuribles at him until he is enveloped in a cloud of incense and has to wave them away with an irritable flick of the wrist.

A priest holds up a large brass disc on a pole attached to which are a thousand tiny discs which tinkle like bells when shaken. Other priests gather round dressed in robes and black caps and looking like a group of medieval judges. At some point, the curtains are drawn in front of the altar and the secret bit begins. All I can see are the feet of various priests as when the curtain on a stage has not been lowered properly and the stagehands can be detected moving the set about. Of course this is exactly what it is – a bit of theatre, a dramatic re-enactment of the crisis points in the life of Christ, ending in the Last Supper and the crucifixion. The betrayal by Judas Iscariot is never included, of course.

Against a background of chanting which, to my ears, sounds shrill and unmusical, there's lots of kissing of hands and bowing and waving of the thurible with everything done in threes – that magical, mystical triangular number beloved of so many religions.

The Catholic Orthodox Church in Syria is unique in that its ceremonies have changed little since its inception and the language used is Aramaic.

This church which I have come to was built in 1926 to serve the needs of the 50,000 or so people in Aleppo who follow the ancient Syriac rite. God, in those far-off days, was a word too sacred to utter but pagans, Christians and Jews found a way round this by using the word Alaha which signifies the concept of divinity. In Hebrew, the word El is often used. Now, however, the modern Syriac word for God is Aloho and when painted up on the walls of the church looks vaguely Arabic in its cursive style and lettering. The walls are decorated with all the other old faithfuls: the twelve apostles, the Virgin Mary and assorted saints. There is a red light by the tabernacle and above the altar the paraclete descends, its radiating panels of gold spreading across a brilliant blue sky. Directly above the altar is the crucified Christ, clad in a crimson robe. Above, is a mosaic of the Forty Martyrs – those 40 Christian soldiers who, in about 316CE, were forced to stand naked on a freezing lake until they too froze.

Around the altar are small arches and in their ledges rest tiny plaster cherubs, giving the feel of a boudoir which the heavy red velvet altar curtains do nothing to dispel. I take time out to make a few notes and a man who has been counting up money at the back of the church taps me on the shoulder and indicates I should uncross my legs. Suddenly, I am 12, sulky, being told the same thing by a nun at my convent boarding school: to cross your legs is unladylike and will certainly make the Virgin's nose bleed.

A six-candle electric candelabra casts a subdued light across the faces of the people – mainly women – who have come together for Vespers. Some wear scarves over their heads and forage for money in their handbags for the collection. All sing in that jagged tone you hear around here which grates on an ear unaccustomed to the sound – a cross between a whine and a complaint. To comfort myself, I stroke the pillar beside me which, made from limestone, is wonderfully smooth to the touch. Suddenly, the woman beside me grabs my hand and shakes it, smiling mournfully. Then we all shake hands. The women bless themselves the same way as is done in the west and I hide my smile recalling the old joke: spectacles, testicles, wallet and watch. In the pew in front of me, a small girl practices to get it right, over and over again, faster and faster until her hands are a flurry of movement and her mother has to tap her head to stop her. At the back, the men are still counting the money – in fact they were doing exactly that last time I was here three years ago.

It was Ephrem, a 4th century holy man, who laid down the rules for this church: prayers should be chanted by both male and female followers. "The monks," the money-counting man tells me, "were supposed to chant seven times a day but then the musselmen came and made it five." Aramaic, he adds, is easy to learn because it has only 26 letters but, looking at them, I think I'll pass on that.

When I enquire about Karim Ephrem the man smiles dreamily. Karim, he tells me, was born way over by the Iraqi/Turkish border in Qamishli, a Kurdish town which boasts a number of

Mar Cyril, Patriarch Vicar of the Eastern United States
aka Ephrem Karim

eastern churches. He apparently had every intention of setting up
a platform to live on until he got called to a higher plane. Now, he
is Mar Cyril, Patriarch Vicar of the Eastern United States. When
we finally meet, I can see that, affable as he is, his corpulence
would make him totally unsuited to spending any time up a pillar.

It's still raining when I come out onto the street with men
gathering up the hems of their gallabiyyah like fastidious young
girls as they negotiate puddles and blocked gutters.

I head for my room at Madam Olga's. The radiator is on, the
bedside lamp – unthinkable in most rooms of this price – casts

a warm glow on the pink and white cotton sheets and though it's only 7.30pm I get into bed with Timothy Mo and his Monkey King.

Next day, I decide to head for Qalaat Samaan, where the original Ephrem started it all. Waiting at the bus station is an American woman with voluminous hair, faux-peasant outfit and a rucksack. I get the impression that she hasn't spoken to anyone for days because when she meets me, she doesn't stop. Her story begins as she travels by bus through Turkey. She's there to suss out local stuff she can sell back home. Ten scarves bought for next to nothing there will sell enough in the States to finance this trip. Sell 20 and she's making a profit. She knows this because she's done it many times before. Her story is that her bus, travelling down through Turkey, stopped for a break. It was only when she was back in her seat again that she realised she was on the wrong bus and that the one she wanted was already disappearing over the horizon, taking her rucksack with it. Lesson Number One: take your rucksack with you everywhere you go. Luckily, the bus waited for her at the next stop but then, just over the Syrian border, she realised one side or the other had failed to stamp her visa. She walked back to have this done at the border control and when she returned, found the bus had gone – with her rucksack. Lesson Number Two: same as Lesson Number one. This time, it waited for her further along the road. When she got to Aleppo she didn't know of any hotels. The first taxi driver she asked didn't know of any either and the second one was "an animal" who found her a hotel but asked for 500 SYP. Lesson Number Three: plan in advance even if it's only jotting down the name and address of a couple of hotels. Lesson Number Four: Don't treat local taxi drivers as if they were guide books and then complain when they charge as if they were. Still, she had enough nous to get herself a forged student card for US$21. I denied myself the pleasure of telling her she could have got one in Turkey for half the price. When our minibus turns up we climb aboard. The standard fare is the equivalent of 25 cents which is not at all bad for a 35 kilometre journey. "Can we negotiate this?" my American companion asks. "Will he give us a deal because there's two of us?"

The landscape north of Aleppo is scattered with white stones. Two donkeys, drawing a plough, leave a turf-brown ribbon of upturned earth across it. All the houses – clear and regular in their shape – are built in the local white stone and shine spectacularly in the sun.

The bus only goes as far as the small village of Deir Ezzeh where the houses are especially pleasing, some faced with dressed stone and others plastered and painted yellow and orange with the kerbs painted black and white. It was a place I wanted to linger in but Qalaat Samaan was still eight kilometres away – or four kilometres, depending on who you asked. Either way, it would be a pleasant walk but as we discussed this a pickup truck stopped and offered myself and the American woman a lift. The passenger, bringing home a pile of flatbread that he'd hung over his arm like a raincoat, climbed into the back to make way for us. The driver took the long way round in order to drop us off at the gates of Qalaat Samaan but when I offered him 30 SYP he shook his head and patted my arm: "We are Kurds," he said simply, by way of explanation. "All Kurds here. Not Arab," he continued, anxious that I understood. In fact, I understood only too well.

The Kurdish population is divided between Iraq, Syria, Turkey and Iran, each group separated one from the other by arbitrary borders drawn up by the former colonial powers of Europe. There are some 40 million Kurds worldwide, making them the fourth largest ethnic group in the Middle East. In Syria, they make up 12% of the population. Although their national history predates Islam, the Kurds have no country of their own though their right to statehood was recognised in the 1920 Treaty of Sèvres.

They have suffered terrible injustices in Syria – and indeed elsewhere – falling foul of registration processes which failed to take account of their nomadic lifestyles. Apart from this pocket close to Turkey, the majority of Kurds live in the north eastern region of Syria, around Qamishli, and though the driver made it clear he and his neighbours were not Arab, the Syrian constitution does not recognise this and defines all its citizens as Arab. By implication, the Kurdish language is not given official recognition despite the fact that, for most Kurds, it is their mother tongue. And so it seems that the Kurds enjoy – if that is the right word – an uneasy status in Syria which is dependent on some very arbitrary conditions relating to where they were on the night of 5 October 1962 when a census was taken. Many Kurds, unaware of the upcoming census, were subsequently labelled "foreign" because they failed to register on the day. Those unable to produce documentation showing they lived in Syria prior to 1945 were stripped of their citizenship. The aim of the registration exercise was to identify Kurds who might, for instance, have crossed the border from Turkey into Syria after the first world war and who therefore could be classified as illegal immigrants – a group of people that few countries want to deal with these days. Thus their status has left them in permanent limbo.

I have to wonder, yet again, how it is that people deprived of their identity and their human rights, still find it in their hearts to share what they have with others even if it's only a seat in a pickup and, in the case of the Kurds, to do it with loud and cheerful good humour.

At Qalaat Samaan, my American companion continues to plague me. "This guy has asked me to pay one whole dollar to use the bathroom," she shouts to me from the shack that contains a squatting lavatory. "Is that right?"

Of course it isn't but the man had seen her coming, raincoat flapping, hair awry, droopy skirt – and an accent that spoke of dollars. When she rejoins me, she is without her raincoat and I wonder why I bother to point this out to her. Further, she has taken so little interest in the countries through which she's been passing that she thinks the Arabic notices she's been looking at are in Cyrillic. But most annoying of all is that, at the gate, she gets in for free with her forged student card while I pay 300 SYP. After that, I hurry to lose her among the stones and pillars of Qalaat Samaan.

Saint Simeon was an eccentric, a holy hermit or a total headcase, depending on your point of view though it is possible, of course, to be all three at the one time. Born the son of a shepherd in Antioch in 390CE, once Simeon became a monk, he engaged in some very strange habits which involved burying himself up to his neck in earth or wearing a belt studded with points so sharp they drew blood. The more blood, the happier he was. It was the sort of thing that people love and in no time at all he had acquired a large following many of whom came not just to stand and stare but to hear his fiery sermons and, by touching him, take away some of his saintliness. To prevent people getting at him, he ascended a pillar three metres in height and, when this failed to deter the would-be touchers, he raised it again and again until finally it was 18 metres high on which was positioned a substantial platform with a railing around it.

However, standing still for hours on end has its limitations and so for some light relief and no doubt also to get to heaven more quickly, he took to lowering his head to his feet, with arms outstretched, meanwhile continuing to pray.

It was an amazing spectacle and one which, understandably, drew even greater crowds some of whom made a tally of the number of times Simeon did his head to toe routine. The record was 1,200.

Simeon had an aversion to being touched especially by women who were forbidden not only to come near either him or his pillar but to even come within his range of vision. This exclusion order applied equally to his own mother and the one woman who ignored this injunction was struck dead where she stood, legend has it. Simeon died in July 459CE after 38 years on his pillar and his Byzantine followers immediately set about building a basilica in his honour. His body was mysteriously spirited away to Constantinople while architects and artists were brought from there to work on the building. Thus the whole area became a place of pilgrimage bringing prosperity to those involved in its administration and maintenance.

A city developed and flourished as people made their way up the winding hill path to the famous site. With the advent of the Arabs and Islam, however, it fell into decay though its walls were strengthened when Byzantium regained temporary control of it in the tenth century. Simeon turned out to be the first of a number of pole-lovers, setting a trend which many stylites were to follow. Some upgraded by building a little roof over their heads or even a small hut. Some added to their glory by standing on one leg and for different lengths of time with the record held by Alypius who stayed up on his pillar for 67 years, the last few spent lying down because, not surprisingly, his feet were sore.

Now, standing among the ruined basilica, I am in my element, literally. The air is fresh and pure and a warm breeze lifts the leaves on the trees. We are about 2,000 metres up and below is the village of Deir Samaan where Simeon had his very first pillar. Looking westwards, I can see the Nur Daglari mountains which are actually over the border in Turkey. Stillness lies across the hillside and the heat – after the sandstorm and the rain of Aleppo – is like an unexpected gift. Peace is here, in this quiet place, and it's hard to imagine what it must have been like when thousands crowded the area to gaze and marvel at the strange man remote on top of his pillar. The space once covered by the basilica is enormous, witness to what organised religion can achieve when ambition and money work hand in hand: the basilica was the largest church complex of its kind in this part of Syria. In fact, it's not one basilica but four, laid out in the shape of a cross with the famous pillar at its centre. At the southern end is the baptistery – an eight-sided building enclosed by a four-sided one. I sketch it in my notebook and find the octagon and the square have acquired four triangles, one at each corner. The halls on either side of the final pillar – now no more than a chunk of stone that has been chipped at over the centuries by relic-hungry pilgrims – serve different purposes. One was used as a hostel for pilgrims, another reserved solely for the monks.

The remaining Corinthian pillars are magnificent, decorated with the ubiquitous palm fronds and supporting arches that are still standing 1,500 years after they were erected. The grandness of Qalaat Samaan is stunning but so too is the knowledge that it has all faded to nothing. The craftsmanship, artistry and fame have shrunk to being a small tourist attraction in a land that has been taken over by another creed.

Even as I have these thoughts, the voice of the muazzin soars up from one of the minarets in Deir Samaan, calling the faithful to prayer. The sandy-white dirt road, lined with poplars, curves away down the hillside and the morning sun lights up the villages that populate the land far beyond Deir Samaan. The muazzin's voice dies away and Qalaat Samaan is returned once again to its peaceful silence. Here, I am happy and at peace. And, to make things even better, there is no sign of the avaricious American woman.

Chapter 9

"The flute speaks only when it is
touched by the lips of a friend."

Al Ma'arri, the philosopher

Temporarily evicted from Madam Olga's – my room had been booked in advance for two days – I move into another hotel close by. This one is more Arabic than French with a central communal area strewn with cushions and with rooms leading off it. We are two flights up so there is no fountain in the middle but there is the next best thing: a miniature ornamental one sitting on a table that lights up and is driven by a noisy little engine that whirrs and whines and which I can hear even when I'm in my room with the door shut. Which is why, when there's no one around, I sneak out and, pulling the switch, am rewarded with blissful silence.

My room is narrow with a small window so high up I have to stand on the bed to look out through it. As usual when I find myself in a strange room where I will have to spend the night, I review my emergency exit options. Standing on tiptoe on the bed I peek out the window and upgrade my options to red-alert. There is a drop of about 40 feet into the yard below. Should I need to get down into it in a hurry I wouldn't be able to because the window aperture is too small, it's blocked off by a square of wire mesh and it's jammed shut anyway.

I check again and no, there's no escape and I wonder what I would do if there were a fire – a recurring worry I have wherever I am, which is why part of my life strategy is always to know how to get out whether I'm in London, in Syria – or in a relationship.

I used to be a nervous flyer and when my children were small would sit them in a row then refuse to let them get up to go to the lavatory in case this upset the balance of the plane. Now I'm more relaxed though I do still check that line of lights on the floor that is supposed to light up and guide you to the nearest exit when the cabin fills with smoke. And should there be a crash, you won't find me among that band of brave heroes who gets everyone else off the plane first. I'll be scrambling over men, women and children secure in the knowledge that it's not my time to die. Theirs possibly but not mine. But now, here in Aleppo, I realise I have broken a cardinal rule: I have taken a room from which there is no exit except, of course, down the stairs though, in my nightmare scenario, this is exactly where the fire will be raging.

Then, at around 9.30 in the evening, the lights fail and darkness descends, imprisoning me in my cell. I feel my way out into the central communal room where I see a faint light flickering on and off as someone, climbing the stairs with a candle, rounds the bend of each landing. The footsteps are light and slow and I wonder if a cobwebbed Miss Haversham will appear but it's the boy-receptionist. He has climbed three flights of stairs to bring me a candle all for myself.

Now I have another worry: a third-floor inferno started by a candle. I could avert that by blowing mine out but what of other people on the third floor some of whom are probably smoking in their rooms at this very moment. Would they take the same safety precautions? On the other hand, I could leave my candle flickering away but what happens if it blows out accidentally? Ah, yes, of course, a torch. I always travel with a small one but naturally, this essential item is in my rucksack which I have left at Madam Olga's since I am only gone from her establishment for two days.

Next on my worry list is the door: should I lock it? If I do and then try to open it in an emergency and, fumbling with the key, manage to drop the candle and thus start a fire it will combine with the one surely raging outside – started by one of the third-floor smokers – and together they will create a conflagration worse than hell itself. The electricity breakdown is due, I suspect, to the storm which has been blowing outside, the brilliant white flashes lighting up the grey flat roofs of surrounding buildings.

The lights come on again at 1.30am and thankfully I extinguish my candle but immediately regret my impetuosity: what if the electricity fails again? I have no way of relighting the candle and so I lie in bed staring at the ceiling for the rest of the weary night. Next morning, as I pass through reception to leave, I see the candle boy is asleep on the floor in front of the door, his clothes piled up beside him. I suspect he too has had a bad night.

At the minibus station, I ask what time the bus to Ma'arrat al Nu'man leaves.

"Whatever time you like," says the ticket seller and I work out from this that there are any number of buses I can choose from. So, employing what, for me, appears to be brilliant logic, I get a ticket for the one at the top of the queue at which point the bus behind pulls out and leaves. The driver of my bus is sitting on the kerb enjoying a smoke and a chat with a few friends but gets up when he sees me boarding his bus. The bus itself is a decrepit but colourful stopping bus with metal seats. Beside me is a woman breastfeeding her baby boy with a small girl on her lap whose head of gold-tipped curls rests against her mother's other breast. A toddler sitting between us leans his forehead on the metal bar of the seat in front and goes to sleep.

My feet are cold and when I look down I see why: they are floating in the puddle of icy water which has gathered in the runnels of the metal floor because the rain is still falling and passengers are dripping all over the bus. We racket along and through the steamed-up windows I can see a group of nomad tents by the side of the road surrounded by a carpet of red sludge in the middle of which a boy shepherd squats amongst his herd of goats. The driver calls out various destinations and I strain to hear Ma'rrat al Numan. It's about an hour's drive south of Aleppo but takes longer because getting out of Aleppo alone has taken us 20 minutes. We turn right off the main Damascus road and into Ma'arrat al Numan and it's like the edge of every other town in Syria with rubbish dumps and car repair shops and tyres, windscreens and exhaust systems stacked up along the muddy edge of the road. There are no pavements, only pools of water streaked green and blue by engine oil. I get off at the top of the town and start assembling my meagre vocabulary in order to get to al Ma'arri's tomb.

Abu 'ala al Ma'arri or, to give him his full and glorious name, Abu 'ala Ahmad ibn abd Allah ibn Suliman al Tanookhy al Ma'arri, was a writer I think I might well have got on with. He had a quirky, iconoclast take on life – a refreshing antidote to the strict, humourless way in which religion in Islamic countries today is sometimes both presented and perceived. He was also a vegetarian and a sceptic – and therefore a very rare bird indeed in these parts.

Al Ma'arri was born in Ma'arrat al Numan, in 973CE and spent the greater part of his 84 years here. An illness left him blind from the age of five and he was forced to develop other compensatory skills, including that of an exceptional memory, which allowed him to study at Antioch, Aleppo and Tripoli – three of the great centres of learning at that time. His literary career was helped by the fact that he had a small private income. In his 30s, he travelled to Baghdad where he established himself as a writer with very individual views and where he was much in demand at literary get-togethers. Those same views, however, worked against him when he decided that rather than sully his art by selling his work he would simply recite it or offer it for discussion. Such high ideals, however, required a patron and unable to find one, and his own private income not being enough to survive on, he ran up against hard times and two years after arriving in Baghdad left it again to return to Ma'rrat al Numan. By then, he was 37 and on the way to adopting a lifestyle that was to characterise him for the rest of his long life. From then on, he withdrew into himself, renouncing the excesses and vagaries of contemporary life. His own was governed by three things: his blindness, his writing and his solitude.

If this had been all I had to go on, I might have written off al Ma'arri as an eccentric recluse. However, his views marked him out as a very rare writer indeed for he spoke loud and clear of possibilities other than the orthodox. The idea that there was only one true religion was one he rejected out of hand and, writing some 70 years before the First Crusade, was remarkably prescient: "Religions have only resulted in bigotry and bloodshed with sect fighting sect and fanatics forcing their beliefs onto people at the point of a sword. All religions are contrary to reason and sanity."

His major work is Resalat Alghufran which is thought by many to have influenced Dante's Divine Comedy and by some to have actually been its inspiration. His scepticism and his humanism shone through in a world of careful conformity and adherence to the accepted norms. No surprise, therefore, that his works often attracted criticism from his more staid Muslim contemporaries. His journey to and from Baghdad, together with his writings, made him famous and the Persian poet and traveller, Nasir ibn Khusraw, on his way to Mecca in 1047, stopped off at Ma'arrat al Numan to visit his blind, 75-year-old contemporary al Ma'arri.

"There was living there," Khosraw wrote, "a certain personage called Abu al-Ala who, though sightless, was the chief man of the city. He possessed great wealth and slaves and numerous attendants and it was as though all the inhabitants of the city were of his people.... There were continually with him some 200 people from all parts of the world to attend his lectures on poetry and diction."

At the gates to the museum in Ma'arrat al Numan, I try to engage passers-by mixing my mangled request for directions with hand signals but, though anxious to understand me, most shake their heads in bewilderment as I speak the wrong words or lose my place in the carefully composed sentence. I resort to making a drawing but my attempt at a tomb looks more like a bed in a brothel than the last resting place of a revered poet. And so I move into charade mode, covering my eyes and feeling about as if in the dark then laying my hand flat and parallel with the ground, all of which, though it seems pretty clear to me – blind man now dead – doesn't work for the last puzzled man I have stopped. If only I had looked up the Arabic word for tomb in my dictionary which, now, of course, is in my rucksack back in Aleppo. Nevertheless, I persist, covering my eyes again to imitate a blind person walking along bumping into things – and hit the jackpot. The man nods vigorously and we engage in a sort of verbal charade.

"Up street," he says, "finish."

"Finish," I repeat and nod to show I understand perfectly for it is indeed simple enough: Go up the street then stop. Next, he sketches in the air a large square. "Big, big," he says, and gives a passable imitation of someone sawing off his left arm. So that's turn left at a big building.

"Coming, coming," he says encouragingly and I nod: I have to keep going. Finally, he turns to his left, widens his eyes and stares hard, mouth open in wonder which means that at that point, if all goes well, I should be there, staring right at the tomb. We smile at each other in delight, having scaled the language barrier and met each other on the far side.

Now all that is left is to perform the civilities. He leans his head to one side and giving a little twist to his wrist asks: "Min wain?"

"Min Irlanda."

"Ahlan."

I thank him for his welcome: "Shukran."

We part and he bids me farewell as he goes off down the street: "Hello," he shouts, over his shoulder.

"Hello," I shout back.

The tomb is located within a small complex called The Education Centre where a couple of teenage boys come forward offering help. They are eager to tell me about al Ma'arri – that he told people to be kind to all God's creatures, including animals. That the three most important things to him were his eyes, his pen and his home, a view he himself expressed in his own writings:

> *The wants of my soul keep house*
> *Close-curtained, like modest wives,*
> *Whilst other men's wants run loose*
> *Like women sent back, divorced.*

The tomb is surprisingly small, clearly made for a very short man and pleasingly modest for one so all-embracing in his ideals:

> *A church, a temple or a Kaba stone,*
> *Koran or bible or a martyr's bone –*
> *All these and more my heart can tolerate*
> *Since my religion now is love alone.*

Yes, a man I would definitely have got on with.

My teenage guides know all about Ireland, they tell me, because they have seen the film Braveheart. I don't spoil their pleasure by telling them that though Braveheart was in fact filmed in Ireland it is actually about Scotland. Ireland has the same problems as Palestine, they continue, and even though they seem just a little bit disappointed to learn that I am not from Belfast they move on cheerfully to music. Boyzone is a clear favourite. What about Sinead O'Connor, I ask. "Is he rock and roll?" one of them asks. So I don't even bother to mention the elderly Bono.

Ma'arrat al Numan is a busy market town set up on a hill, its minarets visible from the main Aleppo-Damascus highway. In the old days, people walked up and down the steep, dusty streets but nowadays the cool way to travel is by 125cc motor bike – that's if you are a man, of course: the women continue to toil on foot, from home to shop to school, carrying their goods and their babies as best they can. These small bikes are as noisy and troublesome as gnats, their riders aiming them diagonally across the intersections if that is the quickest way to get from one side to the other. I count 19 in a short stretch of street, all with engines revving up, none proceeding in an orderly fashion but darting out from one corner or nipping around another one. Occasionally, there is a woman riding side-saddle on the pillion or maybe a father with two small children on the back as he takes them to school. They are not a mode of transport I would care to try.

When I leave the Education Centre, I ask the way back to the museum and the man in charge gives me directions: "Ala tool", he says. Straight on.

Dodging the motorbikes which buzz around me like angry bluebottles, I set off and resist turning to stop when one of them revs up and shouts at me in an effort to attract my attention. It's noon and hot, the time of day when I am short of patience and so I ignore the persistent call of the shrill little engine until the driver positions his motorbike smack in front of me so that I have no choice but to stop. I prepare to do battle but luckily hold fire: it's the man from the Education Centre come to offer me a lift because he was worried I might not find the museum. Which is how I end up riding pillion on one of these odious little machines – and finding it more fun than I had expected.

The Ma'arrat al Numan museum was once a magnificent khan, the Murad Bahsa Khan, and the notice on the gate reads:

This oasis was built for the poor and wayfarers by the protector of the Sultanate copybooks of the divan Murad Galabi and different kinds of damns of the God, angels and people will fall on that rich man who prevents a poor or his animals.

The Murad Bahsa Khan, said to be the biggest in Syria, served many needs for it was a resting place for camels and their handlers, an inn, a storehouse, a bathhouse and a souk. Now, its large, tree-shaded courtyard is lined on each side with arched cells in which are exhibited mosaics whose magnificence indicates the high level of living that existed among the prosperous citizens of Byzantium in the 5th and 6th centuries. Perfect as intricately woven tapestries, the mosaics – which covered the floors of Byzantine villas – depict animals, trees, plants, bulls, lynx and peacocks. Each subtle detail – shadows, strands of hair, folds of cloth – are conveyed in the minute positioning of pieces of coloured mosaic no more than three centimetres long. Thus are stories told and legends kept alive. In one image, a rabbit is shown eating a grape – rabbits tended to live in vineyards – and the coded message is that to eat a grape is to partake of the drink of eternity.

Ma'arrat al Numan suffered terribly at the hands of the crusaders. The winter of 1098 had brought famine and when the crusaders besieged the town, things went from bad to worse: "A terrible famine racked the army in Ma'arrat al Numan and placed it in the cruel necessity of feeding itself upon the bodies of the Saracen [Arabs]," said one report.

So starved were the invaders that they tore flesh from the buttocks of their enemy and roasted this human meal but at times so insufficiently that they, in their turn, suffered: "And so the besiegers were more harmed than the besieged." An even more graphic account tells us that "our troops boiled pagan adults in cooking pots; they impaled children on spits and devoured them grilled."

The feeding frenzy lasted from 11 December to 13 January and when the crusaders were ready to march off on to their next assignment, they set fire to any dwellings they had not already destroyed.

Less than 100 years later, in 1170, Ma'arrat al Numan was again destroyed, this time by a massive earthquake.

Chapter 10

"There is a place beyond right and wrong –
I'll meet you there."

Al Rumi

I've been thinking about cycling the 310 kilometres from Aleppo to Damascus but things are working against me: Ramadan is starting soon and I want to be back for that so I've finally decided to put the bike on the bus and move southwards to Hama and save a little time that way.

The coach station, like all coach stations in Syria, presents a noisy, seemingly chaotic scene with men hugging and patting each other on the back or walking around hand in hand. The women sit quietly with their babies and their bundles. Young boys sell glasses of tea from urns strapped to their backs, students stand slightly aloof from this melee and – noisiest of all – bus agents shout out destinations, with all of them, to a man, homing in on me to grab my arm and frogmarch me to their own individual bus (it's what they're paid to do, after all) though still managing to smile cheerfully when I refuse their offers.

"Ba'din", I say and I mean it. I *will* come back later.

First, however, I have to inspect the buses. Some are decorated outside with multicoloured geometric patterns, finished off with shiny chrome panels, their aisles packed with sacks of potatoes, cabbages, carrots and huge plastic bags of lavatory rolls. On the roof are more bulging sacks which means that at every bend the bus will rock from side to side like a drunk on his way home from the pub and, while the other passengers slumber, oblivious to their imminent deaths, I will sit bolt upright trying to work out where the nearest hospital is and what exactly is the number of my travel insurance policy. In Arabic.

One up from these exotically decrepit buses are the aged coaches, optimistically called bulman, with grubby curtains, torn sun blinds, metal seats and ashtrays full of cigarette butts. Then there are the state-owned Karnak coaches which are quite adequate but which, throughout the journey, usually show dreadful 1970s films: the men in flares and the women in bouffant hair styles can be a dead giveaway. Finally, there are the true Pullman coaches with comfortable upholstery and neat, pleated curtains at the windows. Most of the time, however, I plump for Karnak as they seem to go nearly everywhere and their prices are reasonable.

The other reason I have to pause for breath is that I need to work out my refusal strategy which means rehearsing a way of saying no in a manner that shows I really mean it for, to the local entrepreneur, every foreigner exists for the sole purpose of being sold something to, whether it's a silk scarf, a grubby bundle of paper money, a tour of the city or indeed a bus ticket. The trick, which I have to work on all the time, is not to engage in an exchange of any sort for Arabs like nothing better than a prolonged, friendly conversation – unless it's an argument, in which case they are in their element.

My aim, therefore, is never to reveal where I'm going. The slightest mention of a possible destination and, with one wave of their magic wand, the bus agents will have me on a bus, their bus, of course, where I sit fuming while all the other buses – cleaner than mine, far safer looking than mine and with drivers in uniform – depart one after the other leaving me sitting in a bus not of my own choosing and which shows no sign of ever leaving the bus station. The problem is that this lack of cooperation on my part can lead to more complications. "Madam," the bus agents plead, "*where* are you going. Hama? Damascus? Haleb? Tadmor? Please say." It's a bit like that game in which your opponent tries to trick you into saying yes or no. So, to maintain the upper hand in this battle, I use my trump card and pretend not to understand a word they are saying be it Arabic or English and for this, I go into Irish mode. "Ni thigim bearla," I say smiling apologetically: I don't understand English. They look at each other in mystification and, by repeating the three words, hope to make something of them. Then they try to reach across the linguistic gap: "From where you are? France? Germany? Japan? England? Bulgaria?"

I shake my head, shrug my shoulders helplessly and say again: "Ni thigim bearla." And they frown: "Ni thigim bearla," they say and then ask each other: "Which country is that?" and smile kindly at me and tell me I'm welcome anyway, wherever it is I come from.

When my chosen bus finally reaches Hama, I cycle into the centre of the city and sit near the clock tower for a while to get my bearings. Tariq has given me the name of a hotel and I need to locate it on my disintegrating map.

A man approaches me and nods in greeting. "Where are you from," he asks with a very slight American accent. When I tell him, he smiles and shakes my hand: "Welcome." Then he sits down beside me and I guess he wants to talk.

"Do you know much about Hama?" he asks.

"No, not very much," I say carefully. No one wants to talk about Hama's recent history or, if they do, they are as cautious as I am.

He has come back to oversee the harvesting of his potatoes, he says: "My family have many potato fields south of Hama." Situated as it is in the rich fertile valley of the Orontes, Hama is famous for its potatoes. His conversation is desultory as if he really wants to talk about something other than potatoes and indeed so do I but the initiative must come from him.

He left Hama, he tells me, to live in the United States five years after the terrible event that left so many people dead. I guess he is about 37 so was 19 at the time – a dangerous age. Finally, he takes the plunge. "Many people were killed here," he says.

I nod. 1982 remains a fearful year in Syria's modern history.

"No one here will talk about it," he says, glancing round

him and lowering his voice. "They are too afraid but I'm not. Look around you. You see all these new buildings? They were built afterwards. The dead lie beneath them. Cemented into the foundations. We are walking, every day, on top of their graves. Thirty-five thousand people were killed."

I suspect this is an exaggeration but say nothing. "They were killed or they just disappeared. Boys of fourteen, never seen again. Some people are still in prison, after twenty years. And some had their houses taken from them and given to Palestinians and they had to move in with relatives." He shakes his head. "They have elections here but it's not like in America where you have two people you can vote for. Here, it is only one and if someone opposes them, they are put away." I ponder on all this, uncertain if what he is telling me was true or not, though I have read accounts of the massacre by journalists like Bob Friedman and Robert Fisk and the account more or less tallies.

His remark reminds me that when I originally applied in London for a visa to come to Syria, a notice was displayed on the railings of the passport office: "This office will be closed next Tuesday for the election of the President, Mr. Bashar Assad." At the time, it made an amusing anecdote. "Most countries wait for the votes to be counted," I told a friend, "before announcing the winning candidate."

That had, of course, to be set alongside the democracy debacle of the US presidential election in Florida which brought George Bush to power. Together with Syrian friends, I had watched this on TV in Damascus. "Is this the democracy the west is so proud of?" they commented and I could only nod.

The violent events in Hama, nonetheless, remain a brutal moment in Syria's history and I recalled a totally unrelated conversation I'd had with a government official in the Ministry of Tourism. We were discussing foreign investment and the difficulties of getting tour operators to come to Syria as long as there was political instabililty in the neighbouring countries of Israel and Lebanon.

"We had our own problems here too, with the people in Hama," said the official, "but we soon dealt with them," and he sat back, contentedly drawing on his cigarette.

What he meant was that, in 1982, the government of President Havez Assad moved swiftly to put down an uprising in Hama, in the process of which between 10,000 and 15,000 citizens were killed not all of whom, one has to assume, were insurgents. Many Syrians felt that Assad had no option but to suppress this insurrection as it posed a possible threat to the country's wellbeing. Others felt he had overreacted, to put it mildly. Another view is that the Muslim Brotherhood uprising simply served to make matters worse for those who wanted to move things further. "They made it all take that much longer," I was told.

The man in the bus station shakes his head again as if still in disbelief at what had happened in his city less than 25 years ago. Two members of his family had been among the dead and he had survived because he was visiting relatives in a nearby village at the time. Perhaps he was wise to get out when he did: it was certainly preferable to lying dead beneath a pile of rubble.

Hama's main attraction is its lovely, graceful norias. Designed and constructed in the 4th century, these huge wooden wheels, some with a diameter of 22 metres, had a series of wooden buckets fixed to them, maybe 40 or 50 per wheel, and as the wheel turned, each bucket scooped up water from the Orontes River. When the buckets reached the top of the wheel, they were tipped over and their contents emptied into a stone trough from where the water was conveyed, by aqueducts, to the surrounding farmlands where it was used for both irrigating the fields and for drinking.

Though they are no longer put to agricultural use, those of the norias which have not been braked are still left to turn, driven by the force of the mill stream so that the sound most associated with Hama is a low, ethereal whirring and moaning as if all the spirits of the river have come together to sing its praises. It is a slow sound – the voice of wood and water each working on the other to produce a harmony not of this world.

Now, as I think of the massacre, it seems as if the voices of those who had perished in Hama can still be heard in the groaning of the continuously-turning wheels. This is fanciful thinking, of course. The uprising was bloody and ugly and bore no relation to the norias with their siren songs and their veils of silvery water falling continually from the great revolving wooden wheels. I take a walk across the bridge and over to the other side of town to see for myself what is left of those fatal three weeks in February 1982.

To get some understanding of the whole complex story, it is necessary to go back a further two years to June 1980 when an assassination attempt was made on the life of Havez Assad. Assad had himself come to power in a coup at a time when Syria was riven with internal disagreements and when the security of its borders with Lebanon and Israel required constant vigilance. His rule was strong, powerful and autocratic and though he held Syria together it was his political opponents who paid the price for this stability.

The Assad family belongs to the Alawites, a Muslim community from the mountain villages in the north-west of the country. Not overtly Islamic and distantly related to the Ismailis who in turn are connected to the Shia, the Alawites tend towards modernism, wearing European clothes and not laying great stress on attendance at the mosque: Assad's Syria was to be a secular state.

Because they are not mainstream Islamic, the Alawites have formed a close-knit group within Syrian society and it is this factor to which many attribute their continuing political survival. That and the fact that, during the French Mandate, the Alawites were used by the colonisers as a buffer group, many of them encouraged to join the feared Troupes Speciales du Levant, set up by the French.

So, although the far more conservative and middle class Sunni form 75% of Syria's population of some 18 million, it is the Alawite – who make up only 10% of the population – who run the country.

Not surprisingly, Havez Assad had his enemies, among them the Muslim Brotherhood, many of whom lived in Hama. It was they, consisting of the middle class and the urban poor and forming an alliance, from time to time, with the trade union movement, who started to raise money, to organise an opposition and finally to issue a manifesto calling on the government to honour the Human Rights Charter. When these demands were not met, the Brotherhood declared Hama an autonomous, Islamic emirate and took their struggle onto the streets.

On 27 June 1980, two hand grenades were thrown at Assad while he was in Damascus and the reprisal was swift: less than 24 hours later, the president's brother, Riafaat Assad, masterminded the mass execution of between 600 and 1,000 people who were already being held as political prisoners.

The following year, in November, a car bomb, detonated by the Brotherhood in Damascus, killed 64 people. Within weeks, Riafaat again went into action, placing some 3,000 undercover agents in Hama in preparation for an all-out attack on the city which began on 2 February 1982, a cold wet night when 500 security men, many of them members of the feared Mukhabarat, the Syrian secret service, were sent into the old part of Hama where they gunned down an estimated 50 people whom they suspected of being in the Muslim Brotherhood.

A jihad was announced and a call to arms went out via the microphones on the minarets and although a three-week urban battle raged throughout the small alleyways, underground tunnels and souks of the city, the Brotherhood were no match for the weaponry Riafaat had at his disposal. Helicopters hovered over the city while tanks bombarded it, steam rollers flattened it and cyanide gas, it was reported, was pumped into it. Something like one third of homes were destroyed leaving 50,000 people without shelter. Many of those who died were left where they fell and later cemented in when workmen were sent to rebuild the city in an attempt to eradicate the scorch marks of battle and wipe away the blood of soldiers, policemen, insurgents and citizens. Erasing the memory was a different matter.

The politics of Syria are not those which pass for democracy in Europe. Assad's supporters claim that his Machiavellian aim was to make the country a modern, secular state unhindered by religious strictures, hence its official title: Syrian Arab Republic. His critics point out that his methods, which included torture, were indefensible and that in any case calling the country Arab ignores the presence and rights of its Kurdish citizens.

One way or the other, it was the people who suffered and as I walk around the town, I can see evidence of it everywhere. New office buildings have risen from the rubble. In between, lie great empty spaces where once were homes. New shop fronts border the streets but walk behind them and you see dereliction: a house pockmarked by mortar shells, beside it a half destroyed building, beyond that, a piece of wasteland the huge gaping hole gouged out of its centre filled with nothing other than reminders of what had happened 25 years ago.

I pause outside a butcher's shop where the goods on sale resemble a hands-on lesson in biology. On a tray is a row of skinned sheeps' heads complete with grinning teeth all of which will make a nourishing soup. Beside them are the entrails – livers, kidneys, hearts, stomach linings – and above them, swinging from a metal hook attached to the awning a clutch of silvery-white gizzards gleam moistly in the weak sun.

My walk takes me through the areas that had been at the centre of the battle, where the Cham Palace Hotel now stands. Nothing, apart from the hotel, has been built here and the clay around it lies like a still-sore open wound. There is a terrible newness to everything: the uninterrupted view down towards the city, the shining limestone walls, the smooth road that curves up to the entrance like a driveway. The silence.

I go into the hotel hoping to get a cup of coffee but my feet echo in the marble lobby and the receptionist shakes her head: "No, sorry. We have no coffee here."

I leave the hotel and walk round the citadel – no more than a hill with a makeshift café at its summit – and along the lovely elevated walkway (also new) by the river. Glancing down, I can see that there had once been houses built by the river's edge. An old row boat rots by a decayed dwelling, tall weeds growing right up to the door. To live by the Orontes in Hama must once have seemed like heaven: unlike the Barada in Damascus, it is relatively free of plastic bags.

I head for the Great Mosque and locate it down a quiet side street, the courtyard a safe haven, the stones warm now in the midday sun, the yard peaceful, protected from the noise of traffic by its high walls. This is a much-loved mosque which has, at the centre of the courtyard a small room – the treasury – which is supported by eight pillars, where the well-off citizens stored their wealth. It is similar to the one in the Ummayyad Mosque in Damascus, on which it is modelled, except that the one here is totally devoid of decoration and somehow is all the more pleasing for that.

In the shady cloister, the caretaker sits on a plastic chair, a small boy in a blue school tunic, leaning on his knee. Perhaps he is the caretaker's grandson. There is always, I notice here, an easy, tactile bond between men and small boys.

I feel so relaxed that I too sit down for a while before venturing into the prayer hall and there I find yet another link with history. Like many places in Syria, Hama goes back well before the Greeks, as a friend in Damascus always reminds me, back to the Neolithic era in fact, and as a result has had many names. In biblical times, the Hittites called it Hamath. Under the Romans, it was Epiphania. During the Christian era, when its name was changed again to Emath. The Byzantines built a basilica on this spot which in turn was turned into a mosque now known as the Grand Mosque.

As I walk through the doorway into the prayer hall, I see these stages of history laid out before me for, beneath the plan of the prayer hall, lies the shadow of the basilica whose pillars, leading on either side towards the altar, indicate a cruciform shape over which the southerly orientation towards Mecca had been laid. A man puts aside his Qu'aran to welcome me and to point all this out before returning to his reading.

Outside, the small boy still leans against his grandfather and the sun still shines on the basalt and limestone minaret as it has done for centuries except that here, as in many parts of Hama, the minaret is newly restored. And this is something to celebrate: when the Grand Mosque was seriously damaged, in 1982, because a prescient council had carefully archived them, the architects rebuilding it were able to use the original plans dating back to 1168.

The weather is still unsettled. Dark foreboding clouds climb up from the horizon and the al-Nouri water wheel casts a moving shadow on the old mosque nearby. Tomorrow, I will wash away the sorrow of Hama by going to the hammam. All I can do today is reflect on the fact that visitors to Syria, finding it an exceptionally safe country, owe their safety to an autocracy which tolerates no opposition. Even President Havez's brother was no exception. In 1983, when the President had a heart attack and Riafaat made a bid for power, he was banished from Syria, allowed to return to his native land only for funerals – though not for that of his brother.

Chapter 11

Uncovered at the hammam

Abdullah, who runs the hostel where I am staying, has many jobs including that of travel counsellor. He likes his guests to get out and about. To see everything. At the moment, he is helping a group of backpackers find a minibus that will take them to Qalaat al Hosn, the well-known crusaders' castle sometimes known as Craic des Chevaliers.

The main room – which I have renamed the student union bar although it is beer-free – is buzzing with people swopping information about the cheapest place to stay in Damascus, the quickest way to get to Amman, how to get the most out of a taxi driver, where to have a free read of a guide. The answer to this last is here: Abdullah offers photocopies of the relevant pages from one of the backpackers' English-language bibles. But there are people here also speaking French, American-English, German – and Japanese. The Japanese look out for each other. In the guest book, there is always page upon page, in Japanese, of information about the location the handwriting neat, key words underlined, maps drawn in minute detail, directions colour-coded, tiny cartoons inserted to illustrate a particularly interesting mosque or museum. Some of the pages are laid out so well they could qualify for a prize in graphics.

Others entries are short and to the point: "Don't stay at the Pyramid Hostel. The boy on the desk there tried to get into bed with me…Don't have a shower in the hostel at the back of the market in Amman. There's a hole in the ceiling and the owner looks through it."

Once he has the minibus sorted out, Abdullah turns his attention to a tiny American woman with plaits who looks about 13 but who is actually a divorcee with a three-year marriage under her belt so she must be at least 22. Her visa has expired and she doesn't seem to think getting it renewed is a priority. Abdullah knows differently. "Get it done or they will throw you out." She makes a pretty little moue which must have worked before in other situations but it cuts no ice with Abdullah. "They will put you out," he repeats. "It is that simple."

Abdullah speaks English with a Liverpudlian accent for although he has never visited England many of his guests are from there and the accent is catching.

"So where are you from, anyway," I ask.

"Here. I was born here in Hama," and he pauses, "but I'm not really from here. My parents were driven out of Palestine in 1948."

For a moment, history hangs between us, the huge wrong done to his family palpable but invisible. There is nothing useful to say that won't have been said already and after a polite pause, I ask him about the nearest hammam.

"There is one but it's only for men. The other one, near here, is not a very good one," he says doubtfully.

I set out and, as usual, I get lost and am rescued by a man who gets off his bike to lead me along past one of the norias, under an arch that brings us into a narrow alley bordered by high walls where he knocks on a door and shouts through to the woman on the other side. The door in the wall opens and I am admitted to the Hammam al-Osmaniyeh.

Although some hammams – usually the older and more pleasing – are for men only, most have times set aside for women. In the days when homes did not have their own bathrooms, the weekly visit to one was a vital part of family life.

This one is full of women and my arrival causes a slight stir though one woman encourages me by calling out Bravo! for which I am grateful: it's quite daunting to be stared at when you are fully clothed whereas being stared at when you are stripped down to your knickers gives a fresh and profound meaning to the word vulnerable. I pull in my tummy and then, looking round me, wonder why I bother.

I am taken over by the woman in charge who, like a camp commandant – a kindly one but a camp commandant never-theless – orders me to hand my clothes to her then to follow her to a room where a couple of women, their bodies old and collapsed, are sitting on the ground pouring water over themselves and their many rolls of fat. They look like Buddhas although one has long plaits which hang down her back like sorry rats' tails.

Funny how fixed we are in our cultural outlooks: to me, it seems quite frivolous and certainly undignified for an older woman to have long plaits – unless they are wound round the head in a decorous and matronly fashion. Or the woman is a native American. So I lift that bit of cultural baggage from my shoulders and set it to one side for the time being. The camp commandant asks if I want a douche and apparently I say yes – my Arabic is never totally reliable – because I am brought to yet another room where there is a tap from which warm water flows into a lovely round bowl of worn marble before cascading unceasingly over the delicately curved rim. I am handed a jug and told to pour the water over myself and when I have done this a few times, I too have to sit while the commandant washes my hair, my legs, my arms, my breasts then scrubs my back with something that looks like a blond, matted wig and feels like a pot scrub but is, in fact, a chunk of shredded palm fibre.

When it's all over, I'm given a cotton towel which is nowhere near adequate to cover me and sent to sit on a padded seat alongside the old woman with the plaits. It is then the fun starts. Around us gather the women, a couple of whom have drums which they start playing and, in no time at all, we're singing and clapping. A few begin to dance and it's quite pleasing to watch one fat woman weaving and dipping to the drums while another, older woman essays a bit of shimmying. And so, shake, rattle and drum, we while away the time and I wonder why Abdullah had said it wasn't a very good hammam. I think it's great – until the drum is put in my hand and I have to perform.

When they've tired of the jollity, the women get out their food and share it with me – torn-off strips of flat bread sprinkled with lemon juice which charges the taste buds and has me accepting a second helping.

Outside, after the farewells and my empty promise to return (I'm leaving Hama in a day or so) I walk off down the alley and am overtaken by the old woman whose plaits are now concealed beneath her various veils. Though she has a limp which I hadn't noticed before, she moves along swiftly and sturdily, carrying on her head a white pillow case of clothes she has washed at the hammam. I turn left to walk along the alley and imagine what it must have been like in the old days to hurry between the high walls perhaps to make for the lovely old mosque by the bridge. In the fading light, a man in black robes steps out of a door set in the wall, pads silently across the paving stones and goes down an alley, though, when I draw level with it, all I catch is a glimpse of his robe disappearing round another bend. I walk on, passing the Azem Palace, once the very opulent home of the Ottoman ruler of Hama, Assad Pasha Azem, the ornate paintings of the woodclad ceiling a hint of the dazzling lifestyle the Turkish family enjoyed. In 1742, Assad Pasha moved to Damascus where he became governor and there he built an even more stunning palace.

I'd visited the one here in Hama on a previous visit and was struck by the doll-like models used in the palace-museum. They stood in groups, limbs awkwardly sticking out at painful angles as if their legs and arms had been broken and wrongly reset. The faces of some of them resembled people facing a terrible destiny, mouths open in a silent scream like Munch's refugees. Inappropriately, this particular group represented a wedding party. Syrians, it is safe to say, do not excel at making lifelike models.

الرجاء
ترك الحذاء
خارجا

Please
leave shoes
out

Notice on door of al Nuri mosque, Hama

The alley opens out into an irregular square, if there is such a thing, and I duck my head to enter the low doorway before stepping down into the sunny courtyard of a small mosque.

Imagine, and we're talking 12th century here, a tall, dark-featured man whose bearing indicates he is used to his orders being obeyed while his strong physique tells us he is a sportsman, a skilled horseman and formidable polo player. He prays regularly whether in the mosque, on the battlefield or when he is out hunting in the desert. He doesn't drink alcohol and is considered to be a just man.

And there is something else about him that is striking: the cut and fabric of his clothes tell us he is a wealthy man but a wealthy man with a difference for this is Nureddin, uncle of Salahadin and his great pleasure is to spend his money on building mosques, hospitals and schools. He is the epitome of Kurdish nobility though this is not a description his enemies would choose.

To those Franks who have come to Syria and taken possession of the land, Nureddin is a fearsome soldier and his habit of harrying the foreigners in their mountain fastnesses has been so successful that the Byzantine Emperor himself, Manuel Comnenus, has had to come to stop him in his tracks. Nureddin's prowess both on and off the field was rightly recognised when, in 1174, he was appointed Sultan of a very large area which included Syria and Egypt.

Here, in Hama, his memory is cherished as the builder of this friendly little mosque which nears his name: the al Nuri mosque. The caretaker welcomes me, indicating I should pull my scarf over my head but saying also that it is alright to leave my shoes by the door. In a place as peaceful as this, with few people around, I can't imagine anyone showing an interest in them.

The long, narrow prayer hall is plain, its white-washed walls unadorned. I stand for a few minutes and then another visitor comes in – a tall, slim young woman, elegant in an ankle-length coat, wearing high heels and black gloves. As she moves down the steps, she lifts the veil away from her face in order to see where she is going. It is a movement of extreme grace.

Back out in the square, I notice a long tent has been erected at one corner. It is a funeral tent, open at one end and lined inside with chairs where the mourners will sit. I've seen the same sort of tents in South Africa except there, the tents are filled with people singing, swaying and clapping their hands. Here, there is an air of hush to things. People stand about talking quietly, the women with their heads close together as if gossiping and I wonder if one of them is a bereaved wife or mother. The evening is starting to get chilly and a brazier has been lit round which the men gather. Beside the brazier is a table laden with food though no one is eating anything as if, somehow, that would be an act of self-interest inappropriate to such an occasion.

I leave the wake behind and cross the river by the bridge which is lit by some lovely old lamps that glow warm and yellow in the darkening evening. A taxi comes towards me illuminated inside with green and red lights so that it looks like a Christmas tree on the move. Light and colour is everywhere. A couple of veiled women pass me by, arm-in-arm and laughing. The evening is a good time to get out and about: the day's work has been done, the father is home and everyone is ready to enjoy themselves.

On al Quwatli Street there is a café I know which sells shalawat al-jibna, the sweet cake for which Hama is famous. All the cafés and cake shops display it and it hangs in the windows like sheets of thin, yellow pastry. When you order some, it comes rolled up, filled inside with soft white cheese and drenched with honey syrup.

I pass the shop advertising "seson frute and juice frish" and turn into the pastry shop though what I really want is a cup of tea. And I want it my way, bag out, very weak. No sugar.

"Madam," cries the jovial man at the counter, "you can have the tea exactly as you wish."

And yes, it comes as usual, with the Lipton bag leaking its dark secret into the water, exactly as I don't want it.

"Madam, how is that?" the man asks, beaming.

"Perfect." In the face of such a smile, what else is there to say?

Syrians will dally and dawdle over a coffee, arghilah or game of chess but the tea or ice cream break is over in a flash. While I am still settling myself in, two men sit down, are served with some halawat which they eat silently and quickly and are gone within five minutes. Beside me, a father and his small son order ice cream and halawat and despite the fact that the child plays about with his ice cream and that the father dips into it from time to time, they too are gone before I have even sampled my Lipton's tea.

Back at the hostel, the student union bar is quiet. The American woman has left for the border where she has to get her entry visa renewed. "She is lazy," says Abdullah which surprises me as I rarely hear Syrians criticise anyone. Good manners won't allow it. Since I have him to myself, I ask him a few questions about the president who is being pressured to present himself to the UN commission of enquiry concerning the assassination of Lebanon's former Prime Minister: Hariri.

"He won't go," says Abdullah. "Why should he? Bush wasn't asked to explain why he invaded Iraq or answer any questions about Abu Ghraib Prison." Which is as good a way as any to put it and preferable to the endless examinations, explanations and accusations that politicians and pundits engage in.

"And what about Syria's ex-deputy president?" This man, Abdul Halim Khaddam, now living in exile, has been on television denouncing President Bashar Assad.

"Is it safe to do this?" I ask. "Do you think he might end up dead?"

Abdullah shrugs: "It could happen. But not by us. By some other country but of course Syria will get the blame."

Chapter 12

Sheizar Castle

I check out the road map and calculate it is about 40 kilometres from Hama to Sheizar which I can easily do, there and back, in a day, though opinion is divided on what the road is like.

Abdullah thinks it's too narrow for comfort. His brother Amir, feeding slices of cucumber to the hotel's cockatoo, disagrees: "No, it's good. Very flat."

The cockatoo listens to us, head to one side, its dark beady eyes like raisins set in a tangle of yellow feathers. "He likes cucumber," says Amir. "because he can pick out the seeds. Don't you?" he says to the cockatoo. "Anyway, go. The road to Sheizar is flat, all the way. No problem."

This last clinches it for me and next morning, at 6am, I set out, my fingers white and pinched and so icy stiff in the cold dawn air that I'm unable to move them to shift the gears on the bike.

Being a Friday, the streets are empty and free of cars so that I can not only smell the jasmine but even get a hint of freshness from the rose bushes and lelandii hedges that border the parks. The pavements shine in the early morning sun and it's a double pleasure to know that I will be cycling through all this again on my way back.

I walked the route out of town yesterday to make sure I knew where I had to go. But it was nothing like the map I had so that I walked on and on through stacked rows of high rise housing developments and upmarket apartments with balconies and green slatted sunshades and which eventually gave way to individual houses built to palatial standards with ornamental gateways and paved frontages. Clearly, there is money in Hama.

Amir is right: the route is pleasantly flat with very little traffic and the bike skims along a road bordered on either side by fields of ploughed clay so thick and red I can almost taste it. I make a guess at the distance I'm covering: 16-24 kilometres and only two or three villages along the way but none of them open for a cup of tea and a piece of flatbread.

The sun was rising as I'd cycled out of Hama but now it's thawed my fingers and thrown a long shadow that just manages to keep ahead of me. I negotiate two roundabouts and start the slow ride downhill to the Sheizar turnoff, watching out for a right turn towards the school. Once a city and now little more than a village, Sheizar has a sense of ordered dereliction to it with the usual line-up of disembodied car engines, chrome bumpers, tyres, stacked batteries and men with oily rags in their hands. Then I catch my first sight of the impressive ruins of the once-great castle, high up on a long ridge, home of the famed writer and diplomat, Munqidth, whose name I always have trouble pronouncing.

Sheizar – the name is a corruption of Caesar – is often classified as a crusader castle but it is not. It came to prominence during one of the crusades, it is true, but the site dates right back to the time of Alexander when a regiment of his soldiers were based here. Later, as happened so often in Syria, it passed from Arab to Byzantine and back into Arab hands again. By 1080, Sheizar was virtually an independent city-state, ruled over by the Sultan of Sheizar, Ibn Munqidth of the powerful Munqidth family though it is another member of the family – Usama ibn Munqidth, nephew of the Sultan – who is more readily remembered.

Usama was born in 1095, two years before the first wave of Frankish or European crusaders arrived in Syria. He was not only a man of great wit but also one dedicated to walking a survival path that led through what was then a land strewn with political and diplomatic minefields.

His life – he died two years after Salahadin reclaimed Jerusalem – spanned a period of great upheaval in Syria. It was a time when son killed father and mother killed son, when the dowry a woman brought to a marriage was more important than the woman herself. When betrayal was as common as loyalty and truces lasted only until the next political murder, the next unpaid ransom.

Perhaps because of all this, Usama learned the value of staying alive since as long as there was life there existed the possibility of trade-offs and compromise. He therefore became an experienced and astute diplomat with – and perhaps the two go together – a fine appreciation of the absurdities of life from which he developed the ability to describe the times he lived through in a manner that is both shrewd and witty. His autobiography – Kitab al I'tibar – is one of the best chronicles of that volatile period.

Sheizar is situated on a bend of the mighty Orontes river and, in the old days, the Munqidth family controlled this important crossing point. The castle, what's left of it, is situated on top of a narrow ridge that drops away sharply on both sides and is further surrounded by a moat fifty metres deep, making it more or less impregnable – and pretty hard to get at too with a bike.

The usual crowd of children arrive to pull and poke at the brake and gear levers. From this raggle taggle group I single out one lad who seems quiet and determined: this is the one I appoint guardian of the bike. That still leaves all the others who offer themselves as guides and interpreters and who, since they are local children, feel the need to assert their *droits de seigneur*. So it is that, as one, we move up the shallow steps – worn smooth and bleached white in the sun – across the moat to the narrow, arched entry. Above the covered gateway is a rectangular gap in the stone – the murder hole – from which a defending soldier could neatly despatch into the next world an unwary and unwelcome visitor. A bucket of boiling oil was all it took. Once inside the ruined stronghold, the children leap like goats from rock to rock, jumping across gaping chasms and hurtling towards the edge of the cliff with the sort of noisy abandon I can only envy. Nevertheless, I find their presence irritating and, idly, I wonder if one or other of them were to fall over the cliff whether or not the others, in a show of solidarity, might follow suit.

The castle, once it had been fortified by the Munqidth family, was used by them for forays against the aggrandising Franks and if I close my eyes I can hear the throng of Arab foot soldiers milling about, the sound of horses' hooves clattering across the bridge – this was a well-known area for breeding Arab horses – and the mundane sounds of children playing, of clanging cooking pots, of ordinary family life. For Usama ibn Munqidth was an educated, courtly man who conducted his affairs with style and elegance and, being a Sunni, with genial formality. The diplomatic skills displayed by Usama were not his alone. Following the appalling cannibalistic massacre at nearby Ma'arrat al Numan and fearing the same fate might await Sheizar, his uncle the Sultan chose avoidance rather than confrontation by doing a deal with the Frankish leader, Richard de Gilles, whereby Sheizar's citizens were to be left in peace in return for which de Gilles was granted permission to go shopping in Sheizar market for Arab horses.

It was during this time of intense and protracted diplomacy that Usama got to know the Franks and to wonder at, if not accept their, to him, strange and unintelligible ways. At their lowest level, he regarded them as less than dogs – an opinion shared by many and based on the terrible happenings at al Ma'arrat al Numan, when the Franks were accused of eating their enemy. Cannibalism, however, was not the only aspect of Frankish behaviour he had to deal with. "The Franks," he wrote, "are void of all zeal and jealousy. One of them may be walking along with his wife. He meets another man who takes the wife by the hand and steps aside to converse with her while the husband is standing on one side waiting for his wife to conclude the conversation. If she lingers too long for him, he leaves her alone with the conversant and goes away."

Used to a degree of formality in his dealings with women and men, he found himself both intrigued and amused by the strange behaviour of these Franks. While in Nablus once, he came across the story about one of them who, arriving home one day – one has to assume unexpectedly – found another man in his bed, together with his wife. The Frank remonstrated with the intruder who explained that he had been feeling tired, had found a made-up bed and had simply got into it.

"But my wife was already in the bed," protested the Frank.

"True," replied the cuckolder, "but as it was her bed I could hardly throw her out of it."

However barbaric as he might have regarded the Franks, Usama remained mannerly in his dealings with them. At one time, he became so close to a crusading knight that the knight addressed him as "my brother" and when it was time to return home, the knight proposed taking Usama's teenage son with him where he could be given an education and learn the rules of chivalry.

To Usama, the prospect was appalling: "Thus there fell upon my ears words which would never come out of the head of a sensible man, for even if my son were to be taken captive, his captivity could not bring him a worse misfortune than carrying him into the lands of the Franks."

However, being the gentleman he was, his rejection was couched in language so diplomatic and courteous as to give no offence. "By my life," he told the Frank, "this has exactly been my idea. But the only thing that prevented me from carrying it out was the fact that his grandmother, my mother, is so fond of him and did not this time let him come out with me until she exacted an oath from me to the effect that I would return him to her." The Frank accepted Usama's reply not as a rejection but as a perfectly understandable explanation as to why the plan could not be put into action.

The shouts of the children bring me back to the present day. They stare at my face, peer down into the neglected wells to see what it is I'm looking at, run ahead of me so as to get to wherever I am going before I do myself. They squabble among each other about who should walk beside me. The eldest child, a skinny girl of about 12 who plays the role of mother from time to time by hauling the younger ones back from the cliff edge, clacks along in a tight skirt and high heels and yet never falls, never trips, never loses her step. Eventually, I manage to bribe them with the few biscuits I have in my bag. If they go away, I say, I will not only give them the biscuits, I will graciously accept skinny girl's invitation to tea at her house. They are gone in a flash and I have the place to myself, time to stop and stare over the cliff edge at the river below, to walk along the worn path that winds through the ruins; to think about the glory days of Sheizar Castle which, though it withstood attacks by Franks and Byzantium, was destroyed in the end by the forces of nature.

In 1157, Syria was shaken by a series of earthquakes that affected cities as far apart as Aleppo and Beirut, with the valley of the Orontes suffering badly. At Sheizar Castle, the Sultan was celebrating the circumcision of his youngest child when the ground shook, time paused, the partygoers held their breath and then the great edifice came tumbling down, crushing this gathering of Munqidths: only a sister of the Sultan survived. To Usama, who was in Damascus at the time, came the heartbreaking news that his whole family had been wiped out. Though he himself lived for another 30 years – he died aged 93 – the earthquake brought to an end the period of greatness that Sheizar had enjoyed. Now all that remains are the broken arches, the fallen stones, worn paths and grassy slopes around the ruined castle – and Usama's chronicle of that time.

The guardian of the bike is standing where I left him, faithfully doing his job. I hand him a few coins and in an instant, an older boy has grabbed the money and run off. It happens so swiftly that there is nothing I can do except shout at the retreating robber. A man who has watched the whole thing shrugs his shoulders and I am left with a small sad boy and a circle of begging hands for once the children have seen there is money about they are not going to leave. However, I am mildly annoyed – it's too hot to be very annoyed – and refuse to dispense any more handouts. Instead, I take the small boy by the hand and lead him to the house where I am to have my coffee, leaving him outside to wait until I come out again. Inside, the skinny girl introduces me to her extended family, most of whom are visiting from Aleppo. The house is sparsely furnished, a television the main piece of furniture in the room. The hospitality, however, is grandiose. I am offered olives, cheese, flatbread, boiled eggs and coffee and after these more things are brought to tempt my appetite: hummus, tomatoes, aubergines, biscuits. Eventually, I manage to make it clear that I will have to leave and at the gate of the house I give the small boy another couple of coins and send him running, praying that he reaches home before being robbed a second time.

I cycle back to Hama in time to catch the bus to Damascus and when I cycle up the narrow street to al Ward I get a warm welcome from Tariq's cousin, Hakim. Or perhaps is he a brother? Relationships here are flexible.

"We have missed you," he smiles. "Where have you been?"

"Hama."

"Ah, me too. I was at a funeral there. For my uncle."

"What happened to him?"

"He came to Damascus for an operation on his leg."

"And the operation wasn't any good?"

"No, no. The operation was successful. But my uncle didn't wake up after it."

Chapter 13

*"Betrayal is written on every page
of our history books"*

The poet of Tadmor

There's something about Tadmor that's troubling. Nothing I can put my finger on. The sun shines, the sky is blue. The hotel is empty and the room, though basic, is adequate. Nevertheless I feel disorientated. Nauseous. Hot and feverish, I sleep for two days. The boy knocks on the door, more urgently each time and I ignore him. One evening, I get up, go downstairs and sit in a café and, in the growing darkness, watch people amble about.

A wedding procession wheels into the square – trucks and cars with horns blaring. In the second truck, a lone young man in suit and tie. Is this the bridegroom? A bus full of ululating women brings up the rear. The noise and shouting is at first deafening but fades as the cavalcade hurtles off towards the Roman ruins.

It's peaceful sitting here although I have a myriad of things to do like going to the museum, checking out the ruins, walking around town. Meeting people. Instead, I sit here and watch the man at the next table. What hair he's got is sandy and there's a paunchy thickness to his waist. If I watch him for long enough he'll talk to me and sure enough he does. He's a translator – German into English – and is based in Germany. The postcard he has in his hand is to his mother in Manchester.

"She doesn't know I'm in Syria," he says. "When she finds out, she'll worry. She thinks it's the same as Iraq."

The wedding party returns and does another a circuit of the roundabout accompanied, this time, by two outriders on decrepit 125cc motorbikes. The Englishman says he feels undercurrents of something here, as if the locals are holding back. I think of telling him that I believe in spirits or, more correctly, in a spiritual presence and wonder if our mutual feeling of unease is related to the desert djinn. I've read somewhere that during the building of the Temple here – we're going back some 2,500 years – the builders inadvertantly freed a djinn from its previous prison. But freedom has its price and in return, the djinn, restricted by a leather belt, was required to work to pay for his unexpected liberty. A village woman, however, undid the belt and let him go. Ungratefully malicious, he turned her to stone and now at night, far out into the desert, he can sometimes be heard laughing.

The Englishman has rented a room in another hotel where, for a bit of extra money, he gets a two-bar electric fire to guard against the cold of the desert night and I think longingly of this. Cold is what I'm feeling and so I splash out on a plate of spaghetti which is silly. Why on earth order an Italian dish in a two-bit café in a small town in the middle of the Syrian desert? Though when it comes it's what I want – hot and filling – but swimming in oil and I just make it back to the hotel before I'm sick.

Next day, I lie in bed surveying the room: blank cream walls. Door painted brown. Single bed with striped sheet and pillow-case. A wooden table and purple plastic chair. There's a shower cubicle in an alcove with an electric cable peeping coyly from the wall, looping over itself and then disappearing into the wall again. Through the insect screen on the window, I can just see a leafless tree and beside it a listless, dusty olive tree.

I sleep and dream I have to sort out a mound of papers to do with payments and although it's simple addition, nothing tallies. If I had some paper clips it would be easier. I wake up feeling tired. The boy calls through the door, his voice plaintive: "Babu, why do you not walk out and look? I want to tidy your room but every day you sleep."

I tell him to come back later then I get up to tidy the room myself before scattering papers on the table, spreading a map out on the bed, making it look as if I've been working and not merely sleeping.

When I left the café the other evening, the boy walked beside me, escorting me back to the hotel and as we entered the bare space furnished with a plywood desk and red plastic telephone so that you might just about call it a lobby, the phone rang. I quickened my pace to get away from him as he went to answer it but by the time I'd reached the first landing, he'd sprinted past me and was there ahead of me, holding out a clutch of old postcards of Tadmor. "Very good, only 75 lira," he pleaded. How can I explain to him that I don't like tourist postcards, never send any and that the less I spend on things like that, the more I will be able to give him as a tip?

I leave my room so he can tidy it, and return to find it immaculate. The floor has been washed, the washbasin cleaned. And, yallah, a clean towel folded and refolded so that it resembles some sort of exotic table napkin. My papers have been shuffled into neat piles. My silk scarf is folded into a triangle with the right-hand angle neatly aligned with the edge of the table. My sun-glasses have been placed in the middle of my pair of nail scissors with an earring set at each corner. Form and order in everything. I stand looking at all this and suddenly there is a knock on the door. It's my breathless room servant wanting to know if everything is alright.

There's another wedding procession in the evening which includes a refuse collection truck, an interesting innovation since its flashing hazard lights – red and orange – add to the gaiety of the occasion as does its klaxon which rides up the chromatic scale then down again, many, many times. Eventually, the anxious unease from which I'm suffering lifts slightly, enough for me to get out and explore the comparatively modern town of Tadmor – its ancient ruins, almost a kilometre away, known as Palmyra, the oasis town of palm trees set in the middle of the Syrian desert. The whole settlement, with its sulphur springs, goes back a long way. It was a trading post during the time of Solon, the Athenian lawmaker who died in 559BCE though the earliest record of its existence dates to around 1900BCE. The Bedouin had made a living from working the trade routes and had come into their own with the invention of the saddle, which enabled them to carry huge loads and travel far greater distances than before. It was the Romans, however, who, in the 1st century put the town on the map, renaming it Palmyra. Here, they built the stupendous colonnaded streets, Senate House, baths, theatre, customs house, triumphal arch and magnificent Temple of Bel.

The reason for this development was two-fold. On the one hand, Palmyra had become a customs town of major commercial importance, funnelling huge caravans through on their way from India and China to the Mediterranean and back again. Secondly, the Parthians – Rome's main rivals in that part of the world – were expanding and had to be contained. Palmyra thus became a buffer zone between the two, with Rome trusting that the Palmyrans would not go over to the other side. In fact, Rome would be betrayed – and by a woman.

But walking among the long, regular rows of pillars of this once great city, the desolate stones long since fallen to earth, the broken water pipes and cracked pavements – the very emptiness of it all – makes me turn away and instead cycle among the walled lanes that wind backwards and forwards in this hidden part of town. Here, small channels of water running alongside the sandy paths snake round corners like threads leading into a labyrinth. They are the lifelines of the oasis bringing water to the date palms and vegetable gardens of the local people. It's cool in here and shady, the water glimmering in the sun, the palm leaves green and shiny, the whole place quiet and solitary.

I cycle round a corner and suddenly come face to face with a barefoot man whose mouth is full of blackened teeth. I field the usual questions – from where you are, how old you are – then cycle on. Strange that because a man is barefoot he is slightly unnerving. After all, in my own childhood in Ireland, children went to school barefoot in order to save their shoes for Sunday best – assuming that they had shoes, of course.

My bike ride around Tadmor brings me to the tourist office – a room consisting of a chair, a table and a man sitting at the table drinking tea. I have come, I lie, to find out something about Tadmor. In fact, I have dropped in because I don't feel like cycling any further.

He smiles and says Afwan and waits. We both wait. Tourism in Syria is not, as yet, a developed industry and since it seems officious to ask a series of questions related to exact times of arrival and departure of Tadmor buses, I wait for some information to be given voluntarily but of course this doesn't happen. Which is why I continue to sit, a sycophantic smile on my face: this sort of thing brings out the worst in me.

"If there is anything you need to know," the man asks courteously, leaving the phrase hanging in the air. Perhaps he hopes I will go away and he can return to drinking his tea in peace. But I don't go away. I have nowhere to go.

"Well, what can you tell me?" I ask.

"About what?"

"Anything. What do you want to tell me about Tadmor?" I have thrown down the glove.

He assembles his features into an image of seriousness and says, in a deep voice: "Culture. Tadmor is full of culture." And that seems to be it.

In fact, I probably know more about this ancient settlement than he does. Every day, for months before I came to Syria, I crossed the paved courtyard of the Bodleian Library in Oxford, showed my reader's ticket and climbed the stairs to the Lower Reading Room, searched out a chair that had arms to it and settled down to read as much as I could. The Bodleian is my second home and is the place where I once had to question my own identity. It happened when I applied for a reader's ticket while studing for an MA at the School of Peace Studies at University of Bradford.

"Would you like to tell me who you are?" the admissions officer asked as I sat before him. What? Here, now, in the awe-inspiring Duke Humphreys Library? With everyone listening?

"I'm Mary Russell," I mumbled.

Then I had to swear, though not on my mother's grave, that I would not deface the books, remove them from the library, nor set fire to the library. I handed over my £10 to receive my reader's ticket – the search engine to what I can only describe as a throbbing fount of knowledge.

Tickets, at that time, were handwritten in perfect copperplate and some years later, when issued with a new plastic card that carries an image of me that is truly horrific, the old ticket was torn in two and tossed into a wastepaper basket. Only when I left the library admissions office did I realise what I had done and had to go back to retrieve the two halves. "This is history," I explained to the administrator. Reunited, the two pieces of the ticket now sit as one in a peppermint tin on my desk in Dublin. Sometimes, I take it out and look at it.

My Bodleian research is always erratic and unorganised, turning up details of cotton-growing on the banks of the Euphrates, a list of Bedouin tribes in eastern Syria, a recipe for honey jam, the name for the Kurdish New Year (Nawruz), the story of how crusader ransom money financed the building of a famous hospital in Damascus together with other seemingly unrelated facts.

It was in the Bodleian Library that I read about Zenobia, self-styled Queen of the Syrian desert and the woman who, for a relatively brief period, ruled Palmyra and the surrounding areas with a murderous rod of iron. I'd thought at first to add her to my list of great women in history, filed under queens and tucked in with Boudicca, Eleanor of Aquitaine and Grainne Mhaol, the Irish queen who saw herself as equal to Elizabeth I. But when I delved into Zenobia's background, I wondered if I should revise my view of her.

The bare bones of the story is that she reigned from 267-272CE and was the daughter of a Tadmor chieftain, Zabaai ben Salim. She herself married the local chief, Septimus Odenathus and, on his death, ruled as regent during the childhood of their son, Valballathus. These are the facts.

Palmyra, at that time the most southerly fortified area in the Roman Empire, was a thriving oasis city sustained by waters from the Afga spring. On its eastern edge lay the valley of the Furat and on the western boundaries the fertile lands watered by the Atissi, also known as the Orontes.

At first, its rulers maintained their neutral position in relation to the two powerful empires that bounded it – Rome to the west and Parthia to the east – but gradually, as it developed as a power in its own right, its rulers got a whiff of what could be gained from extending their jurisdiction. With Palmyra nominally part of the Roman Empire, Odenathus cooperated with Rome in collecting taxes and imposed the Palmyrene Tariff, written in stone, literally, in 137CE and now held in the Hermitage Museum in Petersburg.

This tariff codified trading standards and laid down charges for the use of water, with individual taxes levied on the sale of salt, slaves, fish, dry goods, wheat, wine, myrrh, skins – and prostitutes. There was also a tax on olive oil for the area at that time did not produce its own, relying instead on sesame oil. Foodstuffs generally, were not taxed but it is interesting to note that there was a high tax on refined oils which were used as unguents by both men women. The Palmyrene Tariff gives a fascinating insight into the commercial and social life of Palmyrans at that time. The camel trains that passed through the city were enormous, often numbering 2,000 with a further 300 donkeys to carry surplus baggage. The caravans carried oil, spices, grain, straw, salted fish, wax, dyed fleeces, wools, bronze and marble statuary, wine, skins, fresh and smoked meat, slaves, almonds, pottery and much else. The caravans were usually led by an experienced horseman whose job it was to locate water supplies and wells en route, making sure that water skins were adequately filled for the next stage of the journey. If not, there would be many bones left to whiten in the desert sun, vultures circling overhead marking the spot. And while the male citizens of the upper classes went about their business in the senate and the market place, their wives and daughters also conducted themselves as only highborn women can. Slaves were employed in abundance with the clear distinction between freeborn and slaves underlined by the varied use of the veil – as important in pre-Islamic society as now. Highborn women, as well as women given the status of official concubines, were expected always to veil themselves while slaves were forbidden to do so. There was even a code – the Ashur Code – which laid down strict rules about the veil in which, as usual, women of lower status came out worst: "A harlot must not veil herself...he who has seen a harlot veiled must arrest her, produce witnesses and bring her to the palace tribunal; they shall not take her jewellery away but the one who arrested her may take her clothing; they shall flog her fifty times with staves and pour pitch on her head...."

But power – and its companion greed – got ahead of itself and it is at this point that the story gets both interesting and a little fanciful. Despatched by his Roman masters to deal with a threat from the west, Odeanthus met his death, as did his son and heir by a previous wife. Though suspicion points to Zenobia as the cause of both deaths there are no verifiable facts, and explanations are as numerous as the books written about Zenobia. While she had a lot to gain from her husband's death and since his firstborn still stood between her and power, it was imperative that he too should be removed. Whatever the truth – or let's say the facts – with both men gone Zenobia's son Vaballathus by Odenathus now stood next in line but since he was still a minor, his mother acted as regent, a role she filled with matchless audacity by pushing westwards to take Egypt as the final jewel in her self-made crown, claiming it as her right since she was, she said, descended from the union of Mark Anthony and Cleopatra.

All this, however, was too much for Rome. Realising that she was getting out of control, the Emperor Aurelius marched southwards in 272CE, recaptured Egypt then travelled on to Palmyra, captured Zenobia, brought her back to Rome and displayed her in his triumphal march, shackled in chains of gold.

The images of Zenobia are many. One source portrayed her as a queen, another as a slave girl. Aurelius was so taken by her beauty, it was said, that he gave her a present of a villa in Tivoli where, later married to a Roman senator, she settled into a safe old age. Another version has her meeting an early and violent death from poisoning. I dug and delved in the Bodleian catalogue and decided Zenobia must surely be rated the Maggie Thatcher of her day: domineering and obstinate. Not a woman to tinker with nor one to be proud to share one's gender with. Not unsurprisingly, an Arab News website portrays Zenobia as a queen of valour and chastity, blessed with pearly teeth and with eyes that sparkle with fire. "Her manly understanding," the site continues, "was strengthened and adorned by study." In Syria, she is tremendously popular. All over the country there are cafés, restaurants and bars named after her. In Tadmor, there is a camel named for her, one which takes tourists on rides through the remains of the city that she made famous. There is even a Zenobia supermarket in my adopted city of Oxford.

My efforts to walk around the ruins have led to nothing. I just don't have the energy and in any case, it seems easier to sit in the square and watch life go by. The best time to do this is in the evening when the day has cooled. The shop next door to the hotel has a row of dates hanging up like clothes on a coat hanger. The palm trees themselves are a brilliant green, the branches exploding from their centre like frenzied fireworks. In the fading light, the boys play wheelies with a porter's trolley but break off to chase a dusty bus as it arrives in from the desert while at the same time, two taxis move in slowly for the kill. The first couple of backpackers are already being targeted and I smile: I've been there.

This evening, I watch as a man in a baseball cap gets off the Damascus bus to be immediately hijacked by a teenage hustler. The hustler, from the hotel opposite, grabs his bags and the man tries to hold on to them, smiling at the same time to show he's not annoyed though he is clearly embarrassed. That is how I found myself in my own hotel – hijacked by a boy who today, incidentally, is wearing a fez, perhaps because he feels it lends him some street cred with the tourists.

Earlier, I found him fiddling with the gears on my bike – something that annoys me terribly – but though I tried to show him how they worked it was a fruitless exercise. He flicked the tiny lever back and forth and eventually jammed the chain. I've done a basic course in bike maintenance – how to remove a link in a chain and that sort of thing – but bikes are so well made nowadays, especially the ones I ride which tend to be urban bikes with sturdy tyres, that I haven't bothered to bring any tools. No pump, no Allen keys, no bike oil. And so to release the chain I have to borrow a small hammer for the job, getting my hands covered in oil in the process. I know, of course that, more than anything else, the boy wants to have a ride on the bike and I dither between generosity (I don't really feel generous) and being realistic: if he screws the bike up, I'm up shit creek without a paddle. So I say no, firmly, though tomorrow he will again start pleading for a ride.

He's 15, he tells me, and stopped going to school a year ago and there is no doubt he works extremely hard. With no one else around the hotel and though I seem to be the sole occupant, he dusts, sweeps, rearranges the furniture, moves my bike from one wall to the other and shouts across the street to his counterpart in the hotel opposite. At night, he becomes a watchman, sleeping in the lobby, on an old sofa. Most mornings, he scrubs the outside steps supervised by a wily old man in a keffiyeh who drives a people carrier and who I think may be the owner of the hotel. If the boy gets a quiet moment, he rests his head on his arms and sleeps. He calls me babu which means grandmother and though he never seems to go there, says his home is three kilometres away.

When I'm not watching people in the square, I read Colin Thubron on Arab culture. He seems sedate and uses strangely archaic words like descry for discover and has an elderly way of looking at things even though I suspect he is about the same age as myself. Nevertheless, although he knows his Arabic history, he has the usual white, western European Christian outlook so that I find it easy to put him to one side, ignoring the fact that I too am white, western European and of Christian stock.

When I eventually walk out among the ruins, I try to analyse the feeling of desolation that overcomes me. Somehow, this place evokes a sense of imprisonment, of being back in the classroom of my Irish boarding school when the soft resounding plop of a tennis ball hitting a racquet beckoned and the seductive, toffee-scented smell of new-mown hay waited to entice the scholar away from the dry flat pages of a history book. Here, the tall, straight pillars give off a smell of conformity, correctness and predictability – the very structures which sustained the often stifling society of the convent school. Power and domination are celebrated in the straight lines of the avenues, the enormity of the pillars, the visible wealth expended to create this awesome city. The long lines of the colonnaded avenue look like a drawing designed to illustrate the theory of infinity. An early exercise in crowd control, the pillars were used to funnel people and camel trains in one gate and out the other as they passed on their way through Palmyra and beyond: step outside the boundaries and you stepped outside the law. Zenobia did and suffered for it. In fact, the more I learned of her – a crazy, malicious, overpowering mother and focused fighter – the more interesting she seemed in comparison to these emblems of Roman greatness.

Still, I had to admire the magnitude of this former empire so that with a four-day moon shining calmly in the daytime sky, birds fluttering among the columns, a man weaving on his bike between them selling Coca-Cola, I find myself softening and walk back to sit in the square, my feet and sandals both now covered in soft white desert sand. Another bus draws up and disgorges its load of visitors: middle-aged, in regulation baseball caps and stone-coloured safari vests, festooned with cameras like a convention of retired news photographers. The elderly ones turn sideways to descend from the bus. They are led towards rows of tables at the Palmyra Hotel, guided across the road to the museum, fed back on to the bus again to go to their hotel.

I got talking to a guide at the museum myself yesterday. "Tomorrow," he said, "the guy fucks."

"I beg your pardon?"

He fucks? Who fucks? Fucks who? What on earth can he mean?

"Tomorrow is the day, is it not? November 5th?"

Of course, tomorrow is Guy Fawkes Day. He is interested in the fact that I cycled along the Furat. "You not afraid of ships?" he asks.

"No, not really. Well, there weren't any on the road between Deir ez Zour and Raqqa."

"No ships?"

"Wait. You mean sheep? Oh, yes, lots of sheep."

"You afraid?"

"Of ships? Sheep, I mean no, not really."

"Sheep. Ba-baa."

"Yes, I know what you mean." But he shakes his head, shows his teeth, snarls horribly at me then starts to gnaw viciously on his hand.

"Ah, dogs? Yes, I am afraid of dogs, wild dogs," and he nods, satisfied.

The museum director is helpful, his eyes kindly behind his spectacles, his voice soft as he offers me cinnamon-flavoured coffee and fresh Palmyrene figs. Sunlight filters through the yellow-paned window glass and palm fronds sway in the morning breeze. How could I possibly have found Tadmor unsettling?

The director tells me there were once seven sources of water here with the Agfa the most important. Now, the springs are all dry. Too many wells were drilled though the government does plan to pipe water to here. Eventually. Piping water to an oasis? It seems the ultimate obscenity of the 21st century though I don't think the director shares my view. The scheme will cost money and this is where problems may arise for the waters of the Agfa belong to the farmers. In the old days, there were 21 families and they had access to the water for ten hours rotated over a period of 21 days. People with small gardens like the ones I cycled around, could buy water from one of the 21 farmers. Long before that, he said, the share-out of water was decreed by the God Bel and you couldn't argue with a God.

"In Roman times?" I ask but the director shakes his head. "Before the Romans. When there were many Gods." At once, I feel better. With Gods you know, more or less, where you stand. Whim is the order of the day which gives you as good a chance as the next poor devil. With the Romans, however, it was codified, drawn up, laid down. No room for chaos, a system too neat and tidy for me.

The museum director passes me on to a couple of his friends who run a Bedouin camp for tourists. One of them, Azim, is a poet.

"I think I saw a mirage as I was coming here on the bus," I tell him. "It was a large shimmering lake of blue which might have been water."

He nods as he pours me some mango juice: "What you saw is the relationship between the sun and the sand."

"So, was it a real mirage?"

The question hangs in the air like a metaphysical conundrum to which there are many answers. Maybe it was salt pans I had seen. When the US writer Robert Casey saw them near here, in 1929, he said they smelled of sulphur. I look to the poet but he's on a roll, not to be distracted by reality: "At the moment of supreme love," he suddenly starts to intone, "the man longs for his eyes to be big enough to take in his beloved. Then he will close his eyelids and keep her from the gaze of others."

The poet wears a blue and white striped shirt that looks freshly ironed. His smile is sweet, his eyes dark, his voice low and gentle as the words of his love poem. I pull myself together and, reaching for my glass of juice, turn to the safety of the poet's brother who is down to earth and checks to see if I know of the Balfour Agreement, Said's theory of orientalism and enquires if the problems in Northern Ireland are based on religion or economics.

Then he explains the problems they face in Syria: "Before, we were all friends. We exchanged ideas about our different religions. But colonialism divided us and the propaganda about Arabs was not good. Maybe now we will start to exchange ideas again – your technology and our oriental soul."

The poet interrupts: "Did you know that the blind Sufi philosopher, al Ma'arri, passed through Tadmor on his way to Baghdad? He knocked his head on the branch of a tree and coming back the same way, some years later, ducked his head at exactly the same spot."

"To avoid the branch!" I exclaim, shaking my head in wonder but the poet's brother interrupts: "In fact, the tree had been cut down. There was only the stump left." And we sit, the poet and I, deflated by this factual contribution. His brother, though, wants us to continue talking about Syria's ongoing situation or at least to zoom in on events of the last hundred years.

"What France and Britain did was unforgivable," I say in a craven attempt to distance myself from European colonialism. "The way they carved up Syria to suit their own purposes."

But the brother interrupts me: "There is no need to tell us. We know all about betrayal. It is written on every page of our history."

The poet moves back in to philosophical mode: "We must all love each other. We breathe the same air, drink the same water, weep the same tears. Syrian, American, Irish person. Even Jew." As a farewell gift, they give me a beautiful picture which I have since had framed. The poet explains that it is about good and evil and depicts the killing of a Minotaur. When I get back to the hotel I have a good look at it and clearly it shows two men out hunting a tiger. No more, no less. And I wonder why many Syrians so frequently need to exaggerate, to dress up, to bestow more importance on something than is really needed. The picture, blazing in gold, turquoise and crimson, is fine as it is and has no need for embellishment. And then I chide myself for not seeing things with the eyes of a poet.

Leaving the brothers, I find a café that has been mentioned in the Lonely Planet and decide to avoid it. These cafés display the Lonely Planet notices in their windows and the backpackers crowd into their safety zone while other cafés remain empty. The café I choose offers a mediocre meal: a plate of rice continuously buzzed by flies. I put a separate plate of rice to one side as a decoy and cover the rest with a paper napkin but the flies merely commute from one plate to the other. When I get back to the hotel, the boy is asleep in his clothes, lying on the sofa in the lobby. Only his shoes have been removed. He is covered by a blanket which he stows away each morning under the sofa. Last night, he and another boy crouched over an electric fire watching a murky TV screen.

In the middle of the night, I wake and the reason for my sense of unease comes to me: it is here, in Tadmor, that political prisoners were brought to be tortured and killed. And in the dark middle of the night, I remember a bus journey I had made to Hama. A man sat on the seat in front of me, the skin on his shaven head wrinkled and folded in on itself, three deep crevices running parallel from his neck to the crown. I had to shift in my seat to try to remove this unsettling sight from my line of vision. In the course of my readings, I had come across a publication by Amnesty International, documenting some of the treatment given to political prisoners here in Tadmor: "The 'barbers' are military prisoners and they shave off all the hair of every inmate so quickly and recklessly that very few inmates manage to emerge without injury. The hair cutting tools are blunt and they 'plough' the heads, making deep furrows in much the same way as the blade of the plough cuts into a plot of fallow land."

In 1980, following the assassination attempt on the life of President Hafez Assad, the 138th Security Brigade, under the command of the president's brother, had been helicoptered in to Tadmor and political prisoners had been brought out in batches of ten to be executed. The prison is now closed and no one speaks of it but lying awake at 3am, I hear the groans of men in pain, their screams of fear. I smell blood and faeces. I sense the tightening of tendons, feel the thud of a stick against a skull, hear the snap of finger bones breaking. There is a lot more I want to see in Tadmor – the Temple of Bel is one – but when the first light comes, I get up, stuff everything into my rucksack, collect my bike and catch the first bus back to Damascus. Maybe when I return, I will be better able to deal with the dark secrets of Syria's recent past.

Chapter 14

Late love in Damascus

The house is now a ramshackle gathering of rooms, stairs and arched openings, bits of it taken apart and put together again to make a home for four or five families. They keep a low profile in case the government decides to oust them in order to exploit its romantic history, for this is where the three-times married English woman and utterly enthralling Jane Digby used to live. The house, near King Faisal Street, is difficult to find but Faitti Darwish, my friend and guide, has brought me here as she has done countless others who want to make the Digby pilgrimage. I'm taken with Faitti. She's a bit of a mystery and when I ask her about herself she says she'll tell me later – but she never does. She could be 60, 70, 80 and I'm certainly not asking. Once a week, she tells me, she goes to visit and bring food to a group of people who have leprosy and who live just outside Sham. Faitti speaks English with a Leeds accent, is married to a doctor here, worked in radio in Beirut and wears such fashionable clothes that she might well be a Parisian.

We walk down some unstable stairs, up another set equally precarious, then down again to where the living arrangements become clearer. The original house had an octagonal roof the lines of which have long-since disappeared, just as the once-grand courtyard has been divided between three or four families with, built in to a corner of it, a very small room partitioned off with plywood and topped by a flat roof. The courtyard itself, what's left of it, is for eating and talking in with a small curtained-off part assigned to cooking. The partitioned room is a tiny throbbing bit of the 21st century and belongs to Fadi, the son of one of the families though which family I can't be sure.

He unlocks the new plywood door and invites me into his secret
room which is about three by two-and-a-half-metres, the floor
covered by mats and with halogen lamps lighting a desk on
which is a computer flanked by a sound system. Stacked on
the desk are piles of popular music CDs – Kylie and the rest
of them – as well as a lot of B-movie DVDs. On another desk,
which runs at right angles to the first one, is a TV and beside that
a spray of dried flowers. Above all this is a built-in bunk-bed
that could, just possibly, sleep two – though there isn't much
room between the bed and the ceiling. It's an amazing and clever
use of a very small space, a private place which you don't often
see in Arab households. Fadi works in a gym, advising people
how to lose weight though I suspect this may be a relative
concept for he himself is a chubby little guy. When I look up
at the ceiling of his small cell, I notice, stuck on to it, a poster
showing a blonde woman striking a sexy pose in a bikini and
studded hip belt. I imagine Fadi lying on his bunk, feasting his
eyes on this image of western sex, then falling asleep beneath
her pendulous breasts the way his ancestors must have fallen
asleep beneath the stars.

Faitti and I go next door into what had originally been part
of Jane Digby's very elegant Damascene house and here we
meet another family: a man, his wife and their very beautiful
daughter-in-law whose two tiny, curly-haired children hide
behind her skirts but who come out, from time to time, to stare
at the foreigner. Their mother has her long, thick dark hair tied
up casually in a purple scarf which falls to her waist over an
ankle-length fuscia dress, creating for me, an image of gorgeous
wantoness. When I ask if I might take a picture of her she bundles
all her hair away, puts on her hijab and the moment is lost. The
father of the house indicates to his wife that she should wipe
down the white plastic chair that he invites me to sit on, which
leaves me feeling uncomfortable, for though his wife looks ill and
worried she nevertheless complies with her husband's instructions. We sit and drink chai zurat (herbal tea) on the liwan which

is hung with graceful layers of creamy lace fabric behind which is stacked the family's bedding. In another room – and this one shows traces of what it once was with fretwork cupboard doors, arches leading to another room and walls decorated with faded murals now darkened with age – we meet the only occupant, a man lying on a bed who, though old and weary, tries to rise to offer us some stale biscuits he keeps in a tin high on a shelf. Faitti pats his shoulder and scolds him for getting up, fusses round him until he sinks back onto his grubby pillow again.

Climbing back up the squeaking stairs, we pass two cages hanging on the handrail, each of them occupied by a canary. Because Faitti's husband is a doctor, when people were short of cash she tells me, they came to the door to pay him in canaries. "I had so many," she says, "there was nowhere to put them all."

I have to smile at her kind-heartedness: "The din must have been terrible though."

"No, not really. Canaries only sing when they are separated."

And right enough, in the two cages on the stairs where the birds are within sight of each other, they are silent and content. But by the door, out of sight of everyone, a tiny yellow bird sings its heart out.

We leave, then turn out of the alley into the deafening noise of present-day Damascus, searching for a taxi: "It's a short ride," says Faitti, "but not easy to find on foot."

The taxi drops us at the gates of the English cemetery and we walk along the path until we come to the caretaker who is carefully brushing away the golden leaves that have fallen on a gravestone which is flat and depressingly grey in colour. Then he stands back to allow me look at the inscription on it: "Madam Digby El Mesrab."

This corner of Damascus is a well-kept secret and only those who know of Jane Digby, and her tumultuous love life, will succeed in finding it. For me, it is a closing of the circle. A few years ago, I published a book about women travellers and explorers in which Jane had had a star part. My research then, however, had been done mainly in the Bodleian Library, long before I had ever set foot in Syria. Now, having visited what was once her dream house – what remains of it – I'm standing at her grave, where the last act of this marvellous love-story was played out, the narrative coming alive here in the city that gave her romance and adventure at a time when she had least expected it. Damascus was, of course, a seductive city, full of magic. And still is.

Jane was born in Dorset, England, in 1797, wayward daughter of a family whose riches came from plundering Spanish treasure ships. She was something of a beauty – tall, with long fair hair, blue eyes shadowed by dark lashes – but at the age of 17, she was married off to a man nearly twice her age. Within a couple of years they were divorced. The very public court case rocked an English moneyed and titled class whose affairs, infidelities and marital upsets were tolerated as long as they were conducted in private. By the age of 23 therefore, Jane Digby's reputation was already tarnished.

To make matters worse, she continued as she had begun – starting an affair with a cousin, having children by various men, some of whom she married and divorced, becoming the mistress of Ludwig I of Bavaria and then of his son – before finally choosing to dispense with men altogether. To strengthen this resolve, she took to travelling until finally, arriving in Syria, she met her fate in the unexpected form of Abdul Medjuel El Misrab.

Medjuel was Sheikh of the Misrab part of the Sbaa tribe – an offshoot of the larger Anizah tribe of Syria – and the two met when Jane, planning a journey across the desert to Palmyra, employed him as her armed escort. Inevitably, her camel train was attacked and, equally inevitably, Medjuel shielded the English woman with his own body. Jane was 46 and he was some 17 years her junior – a short, dark-skinned alpha-male in flowing robes, fluent in Arabic, French and English, an expert camel rider and, as it turned out, an experienced lover. What more could this tempestuous woman want? Medjuel spent half the year in the desert which was his real home and half the year with Jane in the town house she had had built which, its garden full of roses, was as close to an English garden as she could get. Not that she pined for England with its grey climate and class-ridden society in which women like her were sinning outcasts.

"I would gladly be as you are," she wrote to her mother, "but I cannot change my nature. I am different. How different I hardly realised."

Indeed, what would her mother have thought of a woman, her own daughter at that, who entered into a marriage of dubious legality with a sheikh, a woman who delighted in washing the desert dust from the feet of this man many years her junior. And it got worse. From time to time, Medjuel retreated to his black, goatskin tent in the desert to spend time with his tribe and where his nomad wife tended to his needs. These absences were terrible for Jane who, eaten with jealousy, feared she might never see her lover again. When she finally got to see her rival, she was annoyed to find her quite attractive for Medjuel, clearly to allay her fears, had told her his desert wife was fat and ugly. Jane returned to England and paid a rare visit of filial duty to her ageing mother noting in her diary, with amazement, that, despite having just celebrated her 50th birthday, life was so very good: "Here I am still with a beating and burning heart."

As soon as she had paid her daughterly dues she hurried back to her desert love, stopping off in Paris to buy a piano and have it shipped to her house in Damascus. Back in Syria, however, love and the fear of loss awaited her in equal measure for Medjuel's absences were increasingly hard to bear. Once, when he had failed to return from the desert and the waiting had become intolerable, she decided to leave her Damascene home forever and was, in fact, making preparations to do just that when a horseman rode up with a message: "A letter from Medjuel," she recorded in her diary. "Oh, what a moment! And that he was coming in a few hours. I nearly fainted."

She mounted her swiftest Arab mare and rode out to meet him, only too eager to believe the diplomatic reasons he offered for his absence: "Oh what sweet explanations and doing away with all doubts and jealous fears," she wrote. Now all would be well. Until the next time he stayed away from her bed when she would again fret and worry about her rival, still not able to cope with the doubts and demands that formed part of her daily diet: "It is now nine months and 20 days since Medjuel last slept with me," she mourned. "What can be the matter?" A possible reason – though it wasn't one that had suggested itself to her – was that Medjuel was ageing and could perhaps be forgiven for not coming to her bed as often as required, especially if he had his desert wife to attend to as well.

Jane died of pneumonia in 1881. The Christian community rallied, offering Medjuel a place in the lead funeral coach. This was too confined a space for a desert sheikh, however, so that he jumped out of it before the cortege reached the cemetery. The burial service continued without him but just as it was ending, the sound of horse's hooves was heard on the street. Medjuel galloped up to the grave, reined in his horse, gazed down upon the coffin for one terrible moment then turned and left, to ride out into the desert that was his real home. There, he killed a camel and sacrificed a lamb in memory of the English woman who had loved him so well. In her will, Jane left him a bridle encrusted with coral and jewels.

Faitti looks down at the gravestone. "They spelled her name wrong," she says sadly. "Madam Digby El Mesrab. It means the black sheep."

"It does?"

"Yes. But the stonemasons in London made a mistake. It should be Misrab."

I look at the stonemason's name: J Houghton, 212 Great Portland Street, it says.

"And what does Misrab mean?"

"It means a little stream, like the ones that water the gardens in Palmyra." A slight breeze moves the leaves of the syringa tree which throw some shade over the grave. Around us, the cemetery is alive with filaments of light filtering through the lovely green, peppercorn trees.

It is this that I want to remember – the company of Faitti, the sunlight on the filfil leaves and Jane's poem about affirming love:

> *And she will ever thee adore*
> *From day to day with ardour new*
> *Both now and to life's latest hour*
> *With passion felt alas by few.*

I could have wept for this brave, exuberant woman who had grasped the nettle of life, disregarding its stings. She had broken all the rules while herself remaining unbroken. And, if I am truly honest, I envy her her desert lover.

Village woman, al Raqqa

Street food vendor, Deir ez Zour

Noria (water wheel), Hama

until sundown. "But what if you're cooking," I ask her. "Are you allowed to taste the food to see if you've enough salt and spice". Laylah is a marvellous cook. She nods: "Oh, yes. I can taste it but I mustn't swallow anything."

This reminds me of when, as a child, I would queue up at the altar rails to receive the small, round, white wafer, the ceremony known as Holy Communion. The form was that you held it on your tongue until you had gone back to your seat and only then could you swallow it. And you had to swallow it. No chewing or letting your teeth touch it. What we were required to believe was that we were taking not a small piece of what felt like thin card but the flesh of Christ, and to chew on the body of the Divine was unthinkable. You also had to fast from the previous evening so that the sacred flesh was not milling about with the other ingredients in your stomach. Chips or fried egg do not make good companions for the Divine. The most difficult and nerve-wracking part, however, was trying not to bite on the sacred wafer.

All that has changed, of course. Latin has given way to English, Limbo has been abolished and you can go to Sunday Mass now on a Saturday. With the loss of Latin has also gone the loss of mysticism, the theory of transubstantiation. I quite liked the very pagan idea of eating the flesh and drinking the blood of your hero so that you might, just possibly, take on board some of his very desirable attributes.

The weather has become changeable. Marwan has put plastic sheeting over the date palms in the courtyard to protect people sitting below. This keeps the rain from dripping down on us and means I can enjoy the light, if not the heat, of the sun. When it shines, a luminous yellow-ochre glow spills across the tiled floor. The current group of people who are staying here now don't know what it was like during those earlier, slow autumn days.

We are a mixed bunch. There's an Iraqi man who seems to have acquired a girlfriend since his arrival last week, a New Zealand journalist just returned, starry-eyed, from looking at war damage in Beirut, a German cyclist en route to meet his brother in Yemen who, I suspect, is marking his 40th birthday with this journey. Liz, an English woman here to learn Arabic, is attending a course and tells me, while we share an arghilah one evening, about a student in her class, an American woman, aged 32, married to a Syrian who is six years younger than she is. He has his first wife, also older than he is, in the US. His second wife would like to teach English but the husband says no because it would mean her socialising with strange men. She accepts this explaining to Liz that, before she met her husband, she was bad but that Islam has made her good. The subplot is that she was abused as a child and has had five abortions. It seems a pretty grim plot, sub or otherwise, and then to end up with a controlling husband.

Today, while I am in my room, the cannon goes off. Once, twice, three times. I try to keep count and it seems as if 23 rounds are fired but that can't be right. Anyway, after waiting all day it's a relief to know the moon has been sighted. I go up the uncertain stairs that lead to the roof where you can bed down on a mattress for a few coins. It's been chilly lately and the only sign of life here are the cats that have foregathered on one of the mattresses, rolling themselves up into one single unit for warmth. From the roof, I can see, just a street away, the minaret of my neighbourhood mosque, the al Ward al Jabeera, the large flower mosque. The minaret, a Mameluk one is squat and square. Far beyond and across the rooftops, the Jabal al Sheikh rises upwards towards a sky shading to deep blue. I can just make out the tiny sliver of moon and find myself staring at it long and hard. The Christian calendar has only one date which is governed by the cycle of the moon and that is Easter. I feel sorry for those people, bureaucrats in Brussels, who are so disengaged from their natural surroundings that they should want to make Easter a fixed date.

Next morning, it's even more cloudy and for the first time, I have to put on my sweater. Downstairs, there's a sombre feel to the place. No one is having breakfast and the courtyard is empty. It's worse than Lent and a whole month of it lies ahead. Unusually though, there's hot water in the boiler. That means I can make myself some tea. The hot water is because yesterday evening, Liz pointed out that there was no hot water for her coffee, which she badly needed after a hard day at college wrestling with Arabic grammar. However, being English and not wishing to make a scene, she had lodged her complaint in what she called a "jolly" way. So jolly was it, though, that Marwan had failed to register it as a complaint at all. She then had to "act out" being annoyed and stormed out of the hotel. Returning later, full of conciliatory smiles, she was met by Marwan, Tariq and Zulaykhan all polite but bemused by her inexplicable array of emotions. "You want hot water but for your shower?" Tariq asked at which point she gave up. Still, it's an ill wind. This morning, he got up early, at 7.30 am, to make sure the boiler was lit.

Out on the street, quite a few shops are shut. The ice cream shop is open but the chairs are stacked up as if to say: "Come in but only if you've absolutely got to". Business during Ramadan will be slack so a lot of people take the opportunity to close up and go away for a holiday or to Mecca on the umrah – the shortened version of the haj. There are suddenly a lot of beggars on the street – and for a reason: to give during Ramadan attracts a greater blessing to the giver and any beggar worth their salt would be foolish not to exploit that.

In one of the deep drawers of the lovely old and ornately carved dresser that once belonged to my English mother-in-law, there are a couple of white tablecloths folded and starched, each with a silvery pattern of roses woven into it. They are damask tablecloths so precious that I use them only for special occasions and am always fearful that someone will spill a glass of red wine on them. Now here I am with Laylah and her small daughter, Noor, two women and a little girl on a mission: I have to locate and buy a damask tablecloth right here in one of the souks in Damascus.

Laylah brings me from shop to shop and in each one I try to explain what I am looking for. It's a difficult task as most tablecloths nowadays, though attractive, are made of synthetic fibres, the heavy fabric dyed to the rich colours so beloved of Syrians – crimson or plum-red, trimmed with gold thread, bordered with strips of brocade and with red and gold tassels at each corner. In fact, they are so lovely I buy a small table covering and two cushions and, though they are not at all what I want, they will go well with the arghilah and the beaded lamp I inadvertently bought in Aleppo.

Meanwhile, we press on with our search. Noor, however, is getting tired which is not surprising since, although she is only two, she is expected to walk everywhere: prams and strollers are not widely used in Damascus. Then miraculously, a man directs us to a shop off the Souk Hamidiyeh and yes, there I find what I am looking for. Almost. The tablecloth is snow white and the threads run against each other to give the distinctive Damascene sheen. It is long enough to cover a banqueting table. The only thing is, it is very lightweight cotton and not the heavy, voluptuous damask linen I associate with cigars, cut glass and sparkling silver ware. The salesman goes into his patter, unnecessarily if he but knew, for I have already decided to buy. Spreading the tablecloth along the counter, he slips his hands underneath it so that it wafts up gently before settling again across his upturned palms like a supplicant prayer coming to rest.

"How much is it?" I ask and he smiles.

"You won't see tablecloths like this anywhere else. I don't sell to tourists. Only to embassies and people from the United Nations." I nod. Of course. But how much is it?

"This is the last one I have and with Christmas coming I have many people who want to buy it."

"Yes. But how much is it? I have a budget to keep to. I may not have enough money with me, you see."

He takes his hands out from underneath the cloth and places one of them on his breast:

"That is not a problem. How much have you got? Give me

all you have and you may pay me the rest tomorrow. I will have your name written in my heart."

I appeal to Laylah to help me and briskly she takes over. The tablecloth will cost £100. It is a lot but it is the real thing and in any case it is truly lovely. In no time at all, it's folded and wrapped up, a small lacy cushion cover included as a gift. Then I have the difficult task of revealing that I also want to buy a gallabiyyah. Not any old gallabiyyah: I want a man's one, beautifully tailored with the neck and cuff of a shirt. They sweep to the floor and have two side pockets cunningly concealed in the side seams. I possess no night clothes of any sort – neither pyjamas nor dressing gown – and the tailored gallabiyyah will be perfect back home for opening the door to the postman or for putting the rubbish out on the street. I might even risk going to the corner shop in it to buy the morning paper. The only thing is that I usually lie when buying such garments and say it's for my husband but with Laylah with me, I feel I have to tell the truth. She, and this I know because I have asked her, would never wear a man's garment but instead would choose something with coloured flowers on it. The problem is I am neither a flowery nor a pink sort of person and so I stick with tailored brown.

"How big is your husband?" asks the man and I have to confess it is for me. He is unabashed. "May Allah forgive you," he says, beaming.

Before I can stop him, of course, he brings out a selection of gallabiyyah and holds them up for inspection but I am adamant: I will buy one and one only.

"Look, I'm not buying anything else," I tell him firmly and then, to my surprise, hear myself asking: "Do you have it in blue as well?" and we all laugh.

"It's alright," the man says as he wraps up two of them for me, "you'll save money this month because you're fasting."

Out on the street, Noor does that thing you can only get away with if you're drunk or aged two: she allows her knees to buckle so that she sinks to the pavement like a rag doll. She has had enough and is going no further. Taking the hint, we call it a day.

Now that we are in to the second week of Ramadan, there seem to be a few more people on the streets. A new shoe shop has even opened next door. Obviously, Ramadan is like March in reverse: it starts big then peters away. At al Ward, things have got into their stride. Three tables have been pushed together and about 12 people are sitting down to break their fast: all the usual people plus a few others who drop into the hotel from time to time. The man who mends shoes is there as well as the tall Sudanese man who runs the tiny café at the top of the street. Voices are raised and there is lots of laughter. A festive air hangs over the meal and as I climb the stairs to my room, I feel left out. Alone.

Fasting is something I'm well acquainted with. As a child, I often gave up sweets for Lent. Forty sweetless days and then a sweet-out on Easter Sunday. Apparently, it's good for the body and the soul as it trains people to discipline themselves. It also brings about a heightened sense of perception which some people describe as being closer to God. High on hunger though, is what the cynics call it. Some anorexics say they actually enjoy the feeling of being hungry.

The association of fasting with Ramadan derives from the belief that the Night of Destiny – when the Qu'ran was revealed to Muhammad – was the most sacred of times, the night when even animals and flowers bow their heads in adoration of Allah. It is so sacred that fasting became one of the five pillars of Islam. However, if you ask a Muslim which night is the Night of Destiny they will tell you they don't know, that no one knows, that it is a mystery. I am quite at home with all this too having been brought up with the mystery of the virgin birth, of her assumption into heaven, of her son's ascent to the same destination – not to mention the mystery of the changing of wine into water, or was it the other way round? A mystery, I learned pretty early on in life, was a big, convenient con for, should you try to wrestle with things like the immaculate conception while trying to make sense of this apparent contradiction, a kindly nun would always reassure you by explaining that there was absolutely no need to understand these things since they were mysteries that brought with them no such obligation. All you had to do was believe, to keep the faith.

"Fay-ayth of, our fa-ah-ah-thers, hoooooly faith," we sang, lusty voices straining our navy school gymslips while the poor nun late charged with getting us to sing plain chant, would weep with frustration: "Soften your finals," she would beg as we murdered the small black squares that were the plain chant notes in the hymn book.

Nadia Khost comes to visit me at the hotel and Ahmad, recognizing her and always the professional, is out like a flash to ask what she would like to drink but she shakes her head and says no, nothing, thanks. Like many Syrian women, she is wearing western clothes and her head is uncovered.

"Are you observing Ramadan?" I ask.

"No. But out of respect to those who are, I don't eat or drink in front of them." And so I don't either. But I do sneak off to the Cham Palace Hotel for coffee and a sandwich. There are lots of Arabs there eating and drinking so I assume they are not observing Ramadan either. Or they are Christians, secular Muslims. Or possibly Ismailis.

I first learned about the Ismailis when I met Farah when she was reading for a DPhil at Oxford and was faced with the gargantuan task of teaching me Arabic. I was not the best of students. She wanted to begin at the beginning, to lay down the ground rules upon which I could build up a working knowledge of the language whereas I wanted to jump in at the middle, learn the shortcuts, the quickies, the phrases needed to buy tomatoes, ask the way, enquire about a bus or a hotel. Despite my inadequacies, we have remained good friends.

When I first met Farah's sister Alliyah, she worked for the government office which dealt with foreign media where, she told me without guile, she censored newspapers and magazines coming into the country: "If they say anything bad about Syria, we don't allow them in." This meant anything that might be construed as negative criticism. She was vague about how she actually did this and I felt the censor's office was really more for show than anything else. After all, on one occasion I had arrived at the airport with a copy of the Guardian which carried a report on the abuse of human rights in Syria and no one had confiscated my copy. That is not to say there is no censorship. You could never be sure a letter or a packet would get through to its destination and sending books through the post was decidedly dodgy. "Anything in an A4 envelope attracts interest," a friend told me. "Whatever it is, make it look like an ordinary letter."

When I visit her in her office, Alliyah looks lovely in a yellow, sleeveless top, her face cleverly made up, her hair long and burnished gold, her fingernails polished red. Beside her computer screen sits a glass vase with a single rose in it.

Ismailis, a major branch of the Shia, are light years away from the received image of the traditional Muslim. The women don't wear the hijab. They all believe passionately in education, human rights and matters of the soul. They feel free to drink wine if they so choose and do not feel bound to put in regular appearances at the mosque for theirs, Farah explains to me, is an internal religion that leans towards Sufism. Their Imam is the Aga Khan. And now Farah's family has invited me to spend the weekend in their family home in Salamiyeh, a sizeable town on the edge of the desert and the main centre for Ismaili study.

Nadia offers to take me on another tour of Saruja when I get back from Salamiyeh and when she leaves, I go up to my room with my supper – chips, falafel, bread and water. Then I look over the balcony and shake the fig tree to attract the attention of the diners below. I want to know if there is any hot water for my tea. The usual 12 or 13 are eating together along with the

New Zealand journalist and the German cyclist. Why wasn't I invited to join, I wonder. I'd thought the Ramadan meal was an exclusively Muslim thing but clearly not. My annoyance is assuaged by the sound of the rain falling continuously on the plastic sheeting over the courtyard, making me feel cosy. It's wet and cold tonight and burrowing into my sleeping bag I pull my fleece jacket in as well and wrap it around my feet. I can dispense with the tea. Instead, I'll have an early night: the bus for Salamiyeh leaves at 6am.

Farah's father meets me off the bus. He is a striking, urbane man in a grey suit and a grey scarf. He is a retired schoolteacher and administrator who explains all about the Ismailis to me. Ismaili mosques do not have a minaret, he says, as we walk through the town to see the mausoleum where Ali Khan is entombed, though I have difficulty believing that. Surely it is someone else? Still there is a picture of Prince Ali on the edifice which is draped in dusty fabric, green and garish, which Farah's mother circles, touching the fabric from time to time. The photo shows him as the man we all know and some even have loved – in full racing gear with top hat, binoculars and various Royal Enclosure badges. Salamiyeh has a population of some 70,000 people, most of them Ismaili, and I wonder how many of them realise what a playboy reputation their leader has. Wasn't the 1940s Hollywood star Rita Hayworth a girlfriend of Ali? Later, I check all this out. Though a mausoleum in Salamiyeh does contain Prince Ali's remains, the tomb I visited was that of the 8th century imam Radi ed Din, known as the Imam Ismaili who, one day, may return. In the meantime, the Ismailis keep faith and recognize their present Imam as Shah Karim al Husseini, also known as Aga Khan IV.

On the way home, we drop in on some friends who clearly were not expecting us but who rustle up a little snack of coffee together with beans to dip in cumin and salt. We, the women, sit on the floor and there is a bit of banter between us. The friend says she'll give me her husband.

"How much?" I ask.

"Free."

"No, how much would you pay me to take him off you?"

That raises a laugh and I am pleased my Arabic is up to making a joke. The friend, however, is under the impression that I cannot understand what she says.

"I have two daughters and one son," I tell her, in Arabic.

"She has two daughters and one son," she tells the others, translating Arabic into Arabic.

"I've just said that," I want to say but don't. I am, after all a guest in her house.

That night, back home, we sit on the floor to drink wine and chat. The branch of the Ismailis who recognize the Aga Khan as their leader belong to the Nizari sect, Farah's father tells me, which means he is a direct descendent of Ali. Farah's mother loves this place. It is where her home is, where her relatives are. The place where she can sit on the floor and eat, dispensing with cutlery. In Damascus, we sit on chairs and use forks. While we chat, we drink wine which I think is cool: it is, after all, the middle of Ramadan but Ismailis, I am told, do not believe in denying themselves pleasant things. This is interesting for, under Catholicism, these were the very things you did deny yourself. When I return to Damascus, I tell Tariq I have been with some Ismaili friends. He shakes his head and says, in a low voice: "They are not true Muslims."

For a month now, since before Ramadan began, my bedsprings have been chirping like a bird in distress and growing increasingly loud. I've raised it with Tariq again hoping to link it to an agreement over how much rent I should be paying, which varies according to which room I am occupying. Because I prefer a room all to myself, and if there is no single room available, I am sometimes allowed to occupy a double room and only charged for one bed. Until the room I'm in is needed for a couple. It means I am constantly in transit but it helps me keep my expenses in check. Right now, though, the bed is giving me grief and I would like this to be taken into account.

"So," I say, "About the bedsprings, Tariq, and so on. How much?"

"I give you a good price because I like you."

"Shukran. But listen, I've been here for two months now. There's no water in the upstairs shower and the downstairs one was cold at 9am. And the bedsprings sing all through the night. Marwan says he can hear them down here in reception. It's not natural."

"It's a nice room. You have the toilet beside the door. And the bed. You like the bed?"

"It's awful. I've got serious backache."

"Does it go this way or that way?" And he makes like an airplane banking with his arms.

But we've been through all this before and now I am adamant: "Neither. It's got a sort of scoop in the middle. Tonight, I'm going to put the mattress on the floor and sleep there."

Tariq is horrified: "No, no. I bring you another mattress."

"300 SYP."

"350. It's a good price. Because you're a nice lady."

"It's Ramadan, remember."

"Let me think – OK?"

"OK…Oh and by the way, my name in the register. What does it say?"

"It says," and he scrutinises the register, "it says British Mary."

"But I'm not."

"No?"

"No."

"It's different?"

"Look, are you Israeli Tariq?"

"It's how Marwan wrote it."

"Maybe, but it's wrong."

He smiles: "Look, I write Irish Mary. So now I'm Syrian Tariq. OK?"

"OK."

Then we have one of our sporadic Arabic lessons. When you say cheerio to someone, you can add my soul, my love, my heart.

My Mary. You can throw in habibi whenever. It's like mate or love. But if you're talking to your girlfriend, you say habibti.

In my grandmother's days in Dublin people called each other jewel and when my grandmother was put, as they say, into a home for old people, the woman in the next bed called me over to her, pressed a penny coin into my hand and said: "There you are, jewel." It's a phrase that I still treasure, more than the penny.

I spend a lot of time during Ramadan walking around. The only other thing to do is to watch films about the glory days of the desert when sheikhs were sheikhs, old women wept and young women looked wistful. Or I walk the streets. One day, I wander into Ruqqaya's mosque. Ruqqaya bint Hussein was the daughter of Ali and of his wife Fatimah and therefore a granddaughter of Muhammad. Her shrine in Damascus is a major place of pilgrimage for Shia visitors, especially women. They come from all over but especially from Iran which is predominantly Shia and this is a major Shia shrine. Old women come, veiled from head to toe in black, humpbacked, with gnarled fingers and walnut faces. Younger women, sitting cross-legged, feed their babies. Girls, rocking to and fro, studiously read the Qu'ran. Small boys play hide-and-seek among the women's black skirts. Inside, the eight magnificent chandeliers are outshone by the thousands of mirror mosaics which reflect the light, shimmering, moving and never ending. The women are three-deep around the silvered shrine, touching it, kissing it or simply clinging to it.

On a small table at the entrance is a tray of what looks like brown biscuits but which turn out to be baked discs of clay. When Muslims bow down in submission, their foreheads should touch the earth, an action not possible within such a splendid place so the earthen discs are used as stand-ins. You place the disc on the ground and then lower your forehead on to it. I pick one up and momentarily consider pocketing it but decide not. Not because it would be ill-mannered or unseemly but because I might be caught. When I get back, I tell Ahmad where I've been. I've noticed him looking downhearted lately. He's probably as tired as everyone else since we are three weeks into Ramadan. His exams start as soon as it is over and I suspect that's why he's worried.

"Did you speak to Ruqayya about me," he asks.

"Yes," I lie. "She said she'd help you with your exams."

"She can't help me."

"Oh?"

"Only Allah can do that."

"But can't she talk to Allah about you?"

"No. She's not one of the prophets. She hasn't been chosen. Look," he sighs, "why did Allah give us the sky?"

"I don't know. Why did he give us the sky?"

"So that we can look up to him and pray."

Now it's my turn to sigh, remembering my own exam worries. When everything seemed utterly hopeless – what *was* dualism, where was Shakespeare's green world, what was the word in Irish for metempsychosis – you could always pray to Saint Jude, the patron saint of hopeless cases, though even he would be no use to poor Ahmad. I've brought some honey cakes to eat later and when Marwan sees them, he begs me to hide them away quickly. Iftar isn't for another two hours.

"I'm still fasting," he wails.

"I am too," I tell him and I am. Today. I feel a glow of righteousness spread all over me but Marwan isn't interested in my apparent goodness, only his own suffering.

Laylaht al Qadir, the Night of Destiny, falls on one of the last ten days of Ramadan and has an uneven date. This narrows it to the 23rd, the 25th and the 27th. To be on the safe side, devout Muslims mark all uneven nights with fasting.

The sky is darkening, with huge grey clouds that look like balloons full of water about to burst. We are all restless but with no energy to do anything except wait for Ramadan to end. I sit in the reception area, idly watching the desert film – more lamenting, some dastardly fighting, a bare-chested man in a turban brandishing a sword.

Then, walking along the Barada this afternoon, I hear an explosion. Then another. The sound racketing over the tall towers of the al Ala Hotel. Fireworks? But in the middle of the afternoon? Suddenly, I see a brilliant white light blossom into the blue sky, another tremendous bang, followed by a puff of dark smoke that drifts away and fades to nothing. It's the cannon firing to tell us Ramadan is over.

Chapter 16

Winter Solstice at Tadmor

As I usually do when I'm cold, I tuck my feet down into the arms of my fleece jacket, keep my sweater on and burrow under the thin, coarse blanket. Then I check the time again: 3.15am. My room is not quite up to city standards. Tadmor, after all, is in the middle of the Syrian desert. There's no door on the lavatory and the pipes cheep like ravers at a 1990s dance party. There's ice on the windows and the overhead fluorescent tube refuses to switch off. I lie shivering in its blinding light, wondering if I can ask for my money back. But how do you say that in Arabic? In any case, I'm here for the winter solstice and since that means the longest, darkest night of the year, I have no choice but to see it through.

The last time I was here, I had to leave because of the huge weight of unease that settled on me. Had it been because I was feeling slightly ill – something I'd eaten, perhaps – or because I felt oppressed by the fearful recent history of Tadmor and the killings that had taken place in its political prison? Whatever the cause of my unease I had to leave, I realised, in order to return in a different frame of mind, with any luck a more positive one. I do a second time check and find it's 3.30am: only 15 minutes have passed. I hump over in the bed. Another few hours to go and the worst will have passed. The earth will tilt slightly towards the ball of fire and we will have started the long slow climb back to spring sunlight. The desert nights will get warmer. It has to happen: 21 December is Bel's day.

Bel, God of fire, who orders the stars, guides the world and gives it fertility; Bel, whose ship is a snow-bearing cloud and whose voice is the sound of thunder. Bel – lord of the earth,

mightiest of warriors. In fact Bel has many such incarnations.
As Osiris, he filtered through to Syria from the Mediterranean,
carried there from Egypt by the seafaring Phoenicians.

By a happy coincidence, people in Oxford celebrate this
mighty God on the first day of May (known locally as May
Morning) when town and gown, young and old, gather at 6am
at the foot of Magdalen College Tower to sing the awakening
earth back into life:

Te Deum Patrem colimus
Te Laudibitur prosequimus
Qui corpus cibo reficis
Coelesti mentem gratia.

This sun-worshipping reminds me of all the May Mornings
I've celebrated in Oxford where few people know why exactly
they party until dawn. "Bealtaine," I want to whisper to them,
"The fire of Baal, the emerging heat of the spring sun, that's what
you're celebrating." And though they say the Romans never got
as far as Ireland, how is it that the Irish word for the month of
May is Bealtaine which comes from Beal (from Baal) and taine
– more properly tinne – which is the Irish word for fire. Together,
they make Bealtaine, the first of May, the day still celebrated by
some in Ireland and elsewhere.

Christianity has colonised both feasts, of course, and
Communism raided them as well by trying to make May Day
a worker's holiday. But among the hundreds who brave the chill
of an Oxford spring morning to listen to the clear voices of the
choristers singing their Latin hymn, there are always a few
subversives who know that this event is really about fertility;
about the sap rising and the darling buds of May. Basically
about getting, and having, sex. Why else do young women
sing of gathering their nuts in May, heavy-bellied Morris men
stick flowers in their hats and innocent school children dance
decorously round the greatest of English phallic icons, the
May pole?

Today, however, is the winter solstice and were I back home in Ireland on this day, I'd be with a group of other sun-worshippers, standing by the great megalithic passage grave at Bru na Boinne, one-time home of the God An Dagda known also as the Good God. From this vantage point, people look expectantly across the frost-white fields to the north-eastern horizon over which, at around 9am, the sun will rise in all its glory to dazzle us once again with its fire. And as it moves upwards, a single, brilliant beam of light will slice through the gap above the entrance of the ancient tumulus and strike like a sword at the heart of the stone which lies on the cool floor of the chamber and which is engraved with three interconnected spirals. This has been happening at Bru na Boinne for 3,000 years, in parallel with other sun-worshipping rites all over the land which today is called Syria. Have I come home, I wonder? Far from Bru na Boinne but walking along a road to the Temple of Bel, I smile for I am a regular sun-worshipper, at ease in this pagan world of the all-powerful flame.

It's 8.30am and the day is warming up. A few young boys in blue overalls collect the bits of paper and soft-drink cans that litter the side of the road. Their hearts aren't in it but they carry on, bending, picking up, bending again. This is the road to the other part of Tadmor – Roman Palmyra – and the authorities want it to look good, to show that they care about what is undoubtedly the greatest 1st century place of worship in the Middle East.

The Temple of Bel is an electrifying 200 metre square rectangle of towering pillars, altars and divine mystery. At its centre is the sublime Propylaea, the huge vestibule fronting the inner sanctum with a majestic stairway, 35 metres wide, leading up to its eight-pillared entrance. To the left of the Propylaea is the altar on which the animals were slaughtered and, to the right, the pool where the priests cleansed their death-dealing axes and washed the blood from their hands. Though much of the Temple is in ruins – it is, after all, over 2,000 years old – it is still possible to sense the presence of the huge crowd of people gathered to enjoy the spectacle of the sacrifice, to imagine the sight of the priests in their ceremonial robes and head coverings going about their sacred tasks. With blood regarded as the essence of life, the practice of sacrificing animals, camels, bulls and rams – though rarely pigs – was an important act since, during the ritual, the priests spilled the animal's blood on the altar thereby returning it to the Gods to whom all life belonged. Naturally, brought up in a religious culture which daily re-enacts the death, 2,000 years ago, of a political activist in Roman Jerusalem whose followers believe they are drinking the blood and eating the flesh of the sacrificed man, I was intrigued to learn what the people in this Roman outpost got up to at the same time.

As I make my way to the Temple entrance I notice, in the main outer wall, just by the little wooden ticket hut, a tunnel which disappears under the wall and reappears on the inside. Through this tunnel the sacrificial animals were driven, already washed and decked out in coloured ribbons, in preparation for the sacrificial ceremony. If the animal to be sacrificed was a bull, his horns were painted gold. Once through the tunnel, the animal was then driven up a ramp to the waiting priests. But to be performed in an official manner, the ceremony required more than ribbons and gilded horns. Care had to be taken that the animal displayed no fear as it was led to the slaughter. If it did, then the sacrifice was considered to be polluted and had to be repeated with a different animal. To avoid this, someone had the job of bending the beast's head downwards in a visible display of humble acceptance of its fate. If this proved to be a problem, the beasts were first stunned with a blow from a heavy stick.

Once the animals were killed, they were cut open and their entrails examined. If no abnormalities were found, the sacrifice was deemed to have been accepted by the Gods. Occasionally, the priests were given the liver of the animal to "read" for portents of good or evil. At that point, the carcass was cut up and the heart and lungs set aside as offerings to the Gods while the rest was given to the people to be consumed later at a festival banquet. The heart and lungs were then carried up the wide steps to the Propylaea and into the inner sanctum where, to the right, there are still steps leading to the roof where the actual offering to Bel was made.

I sit on a warm stone to gather my thoughts and make a few notes and within minutes, one of the ticket men approaches to stand watching me as I write. His artless curiosity is at first disconcerting and then annoying.

"I can't write while you stand there," I whinge.

"I'm sorry," he says immediately and moves away leaving me to feel, as always, regretful for my surly attitude.

I return to my notes and, book in hand, mount the steps that lead into the inner sanctum where, in recognition of the fact that Palmyra was both a major trading city and a powerful military outpost of the Roman Empire, its walls – those that are still standing – reach 18 metres high. The inner sanctum is a wide hall with what looks like a large inglenook fireplace at each end but which turn out to be altars to other, lesser deities. Though Bel was the leader of the pack, the Palmyrenes had a few local ones as well including Yarhibol, God of the sun, and Aglibol, God of the moon. There were caravan deities too: Samas was one, his symbol a camel. Leading up to the south altar is a set of shallow steps which end at a niche where a small statue of Bel was usually displayed. During ritual processions, it was taken from here and paraded round the Temple. The ceiling of this altar alcove puzzles me. The guide book speaks of a burst of acanthus and lotus leaves, of a zodiac circle with Jupiter/Bel in the guise of an eagle in a starlit sky presiding over the celestial movement of the planets and thus regulating the destiny of humans. But the ceiling is black with age and smoke for, as often happened in Syria, local people moved into these sacred places and made them their own. In his book Palmyra, Iain Browning has an aerial photo of the Temple showing it crammed with flat-roofed, mud-brick houses packed tight as commuters on a Tokyo train and crowding right up against the inner sanctum. This was because people intermittently made their homes here until, in 1929, the French occupying powers developed the neglected town of Tadmor almost a kilometre away, so the Temple area could be cleared of local Arabs.

As the Roman Empire declined, so too did Palmyra's importance until, in 634CE, it was taken by the Muslim army whose leaders overlaid a mosque upon the existing stones, steps and pillars. Allah is said to be the God of all Gods but the attempt to superimpose one religious building on another was in vain, for Islam remains dwarfed by the Temple of Bel, who still reigns supreme in his awesome building, while all that remains of Islam is a mihrab and a Sufic inscription dating back to 728CE.

I rest for a while on a fluted fragment of a fallen pillar, ornate with carved grapes and twisting vine, shielding my eyes which are blinded not only by the brightness of the midwinter sun but also by the grandeur of the Temple. The silence, thick as heat, is broken by a sudden flap of pigeons' wings and a small, white feather drifts down onto my notebook. By my foot is a rusty soft drink can and beside it a piece of wire snaking upwards from the sand. I follow the wire with my eyes but it ends a few feet away with no apparent reason for its existence. The driving heat of the sun nails the day to the buff-coloured earth and the encroaching desert smothers the ghosts of the people who once came here to worship their Gods. Solitude lies like a shroud across the sand. A flock of pigeons wheels across the sky before settling on top of the temple wall. Halfway up the wall, a homely tuft of grass grows out of a niche. Higher up, much higher up, a series of large romanesque windows, empty and blind, frame a neat section of blue sky across which, Chirico-like, a puff of white cloud floats.

Much of the temple is built of huge squares of granite brought from Egypt though the pillars that loom over me are made of local grey sandstone. I get a sudden flash of a Hollywood film I once saw in which the blind Samson – played by Victor Mature – pushing against the huge pillars of the Temple, brings it crashing around him. The Palmyran pillars, as enduring as the Great Wall of China, have stood here for 2,000 years but what if they suddenly toppled down upon me? This could be the year they fall, disturbed by a distant earthquake, a shifting of the sands. By a movement of the Gods. Nervously, I stand up. After all, who could have foreseen the toppling of the Berlin Wall?

A faint chug-chug frees me from these superstitious thoughts and when I climb the walls to look beyond the Temple towards the narrow, shady lanes that border Tadmor's fertile gardens, I can just make out a distant truck moving along a sandy road like a tiny, speeding beetle. Then, right below the wall, I see the camel boy I talked to briefly yesterday. He's riding one camel and leading another, bringing them to Palmyra's famous Colonnaded Street in search of tourists who, he hopes, will buy a ride. Yesterday, when he approached me, I was curious only about the camels and their names. The brown one, he said, was Casanova, the white one Zenobia. Husband and wife, he explained. His easy, fatuous sales patter annoyed me and I walked away. Tourist I may be but not that dumb. Today however, is Bel's day and I feel a celebration would be right and proper.

I clamber down the broken steps of the wall, walk out through the ticket office and across to the Colonnaded Street to where the boy now sits feeding grain to the camels. When he looks up, I see that he has soft olive skin and dark, knowing eyes.

"How much for an hour's ride?" I ask.

"700 SYP."

"Too much."

"Madam," he says reproachfully. "700 SYP is not much. We have to buy food for the camels, look after them, train them."

"I'll give you half that."

He shakes the red tasselled rope of the nearest camel but doesn't look at me: "600 SYP."

"Five."

"Six."

"Five."

"OK."

The camel I want to ride is making a terrible business of eating grain from a shallow, leather bucket, grunting and smacking her lips and scattering her food over the side of the dish. She looks terribly cross.

"I'd like to ride the white camel," I say. "That one there."

But the boy shakes his head: "She's eating."

"I'll wait."

"The other one is better."

"I want the white one."

Zenobia, I knew, was the one for me.

"The brown one is better. More comfortable." But I shake my head. The white one or nothing. I look at the boy and try to guess his age. His face is smooth and pure, his movements lithe and his frame slim.

"How old are you?" I ask.

"Seventeen." Perhaps he is. On the other hand, he could also be 25.

"And what are you called?"

"Rabiyeh."

"Hi, Rabiyeh. I'm Mary." And he gives me a sweet smile and the hint of a formal bow. I'm curious about the camels. They used to be big business. Up to a few years ago, there were even camel races here in Tadmor.

"What does it cost to go off camel riding for a whole day?" I ask Rabiyeh.

"About 1,300 SYP. You like to do that?"

"No."

"1,000 SYP for you because you are kind person."

"No thanks. I was just curious."

I do some calculations and work out that would be about £100 for a week. I'd love to do it but not today.

"And suppose you wanted to buy your own camel?"

"10,000 SYP. You want to buy? My family has many camels."

"No thanks. Just wondering."

"1,000 SYP to buy wild. Then you have to train it."

"How long does that take?"

"Six months maybe. And feed it. Another 10,000 SYP."

For a moment I consider disappearing into the desert for six months but the thought quickly evaporates. The camel complains about having to get up, about having to turn round, about having to kneel down again so that I can get myself up onto the big leather saddle decorated with red tassels and green ribbons. She complains again when instructed to straighten her back legs so that I tip forward and then her front legs so that I tip backwards but I've done this before and the familiar seesaw movement is really nothing for either of us to complain about. Rabiyeh leads her forward and she complains again, growling and snarling at him: "She's just singing," he says and smiles. As we start to pad off along the paved street, a man appears from behind a pillar and has a few words with Rabiyeh who hands over the money I have just paid him.

"Who was that?" I ask.

"My uncle."

I hope he won't get into trouble for not striking a harder bargain then tell myself not to worry: he's undoubtedly far better at haggling than I am.

"Have you got a camera?" he asks. "I can take a picture of you. And I have spare batteries as well." This boy has thought of everything.

Zenobia settles down to an amble, the leather saddle creaking comfortingly as I rock backwards and forwards. Rabiyeh walks ahead, tattered red lead rope in his hand. He looks back every so often to check I'm OK and I am. I can think of no better way to celebrate the winter solstice than to ride a camel called Zenobia along the main street of the ancient city of Palmyra. Rabiyeh considers himself something of a guide though much of what he tells me, I later discover, is incorrect.

"You see those brackets high up on the walls of the pillars," he says. "They were where they put statues of the Gods." But not so. They were where the statues of local Palmyrene dignatories were put. Still, he's cheerful and willing and in no time at all, we're chatting away. His family still live in the desert, he tells me, and he visits them every couple of weeks. For some reason, we get on to the subject of women who decorate their hands and face with henna patterns.

"Does your mother do that?" I ask but he shakes his head. "Muslim women don't do that," he says but they do. I have seen many Bedouin women with decorated faces.

"Are you Muslim?" I ask. He shrugs: "When I am with my family, out there, I am Muslim. Here, I am Christian." A true survivor.

We move along in companionable silence past the remains of the Temple to Nebo who was Bel's son and whose job it was to mediate between his father and the world of humans. Nebo's other responsibility, my guidebook tells me, is to care for the "scribal arts" for which I am grateful.

Rabiyeh is keen to ride right to the end of the ruins that lie far out in the desert.

"But if we go there, maybe I could ride the camel with you," he says. "It's a long way."

I've become territorial about Zenobia and don't really want anyone else up here with me but it seems churlish to refuse and after all, the desert code demands it. Interdependency is the mainstay here for no one can survive on their own in the relentless and unforgiving heat.

He tugs at Zenobia's rope and when, grudgingly, she allows him to climb up, he settles himself on the saddle in front of me and instructs me to make myself comfortable behind him.

"Put your arms around my waist," he says. Instead, I reach round him decorously and steady myself by holding on to the front of the saddle but this means grasping a large brass knob which is even more suggestive than clinging to this beautiful boy. He urges me to let go of it and put my hands round his waist. Finally I do and next I am invited to move forward on the saddle so that I am closer to him.

"Closer," he says. "Move closer. It is more comfortable."

I'm not at all happy about this arrangement. Riding a camel

in the desert with an unknown if beautiful youth could well be every woman's dream but the proximity of my crotch to his buttocks is unsettling. Surely an Arab woman would not ride like this? Then I think of the many European women who lost their hearts to the romance of the desert and wonder what on earth is wrong with me. Should I throw caution to the hot winds, I ask myself? Ride out into the desert with this olive-skinned beauty? No, is the stern reply.

Zenobia gathers up a little speed and Rabiyeh and I move up and down in a rhythmically disconcerting manner.

"Relax with me," he says. "It's comfortable, isn't it? Hmm? Like sleeping. Closer. Come closer to me."

Truly, I cannot decide if his language and behaviour is that of an innocent or sexually-knowing teenager. Come to that, I'm no longer sure what age I am.

But I pull myself together. The desert is littered with the shattered hearts of European women like me seduced by the charms of dark-skinned young men. Margaret Fountain is one, Lady Jane Digby another. Thinking of them, I bring the proceedings to a halt.

"Stop." I say. "I have a bad back." How I hate myself for such a despicably lame excuse. I really should be stern and haughty. But, somewhat to my disappointment, the lame excuse does the trick. Rabiyeh slides off the camel and shakes his head apologetically.

"It's not good, riding a camel with a bad back. We'll walk carefully." And suddenly, we are back to the slow pace which, it is clear, is what Zenobia wanted all along. At the end of the ride, I clamber down but back away from Zenobia as she snarls at me, her huge yellow teeth yawning horribly, saliva drooling in gobbets from her rubber lips.

"Zenobia is glad to be rid of me," I say but Rabiyeh shakes his head.

"This isn't Zenobia. This is Casanova. The husband of Zenobia. He's more difficult to manage. That's why I wanted you to ride the other camel. She's more comfortable."

"But yesterday, you told me the white camel was Zenobia."
"Did I?" he asks. "Sometimes I forget." And once again, I
realise that in Syria, people tend to tell you what they think you
want to hear.

I have a last walk, alone, along the paved street, thinking of
the many people who trod these stones. One was the Emperor
Hadrian, who built the wall named after him in distant England.
There was Barates, a Palmyran merchant who followed the
Roman army to Britain supplying it with military standards.
While there, he bought a young local slave, freed her and married
her. Her tombstone, found in South Shields, states mournfully
in Aramaic: "Regina, freedwoman of Barates, alas."

And there was the English traveller, Hester Stanhope, whose
arrival in Palmyra in 1813 so impressed the locals that she found
herself overcome by their adulation: "I have been crowned
Queen of the Desert," she cried, "under the Triumphal Arch of
Palmyra and, if I please, I can now go to Mecca alone. I have
nothing to fear. I shall soon have as many names as Apollo. I am
the sun, the stars, the pearl, the lion, the light from heaven and
the Queen." She had an escort of 25 horsemen and her party was
accompanied by 22 camels which carried tents, firewood, wine
and corn – the whole expedition costing £150.

Lost somewhere along this timeline that stretches back 2,000
years, I fail to respond to a small persistent sound that niggles at
the edge of my mind until it gets louder and louder: Blip wheep!
Blip wheep! Blip WHEEP! BLIP WHEEEEEP! It's my mobile
phone displaying a text message from my daughter Freya in
England: Happy Winter Solstice, the message says and for a
nano second the gap between my two worlds is closed.

In the distance, I catch a glimpse of Rabiyeh kicking up a spray
of sand as he gallops away among the pillars of the colonnaded
street, his white scarf flying out behind him. He turns and waves:
"Bshoofak badin," he calls over his shoulder. See you later.

I smile. "Bshoofak badin," I reply but the words are carried
away on the warm desert wind.

Chapter 17

Christmas 3,500 feet up a mountain

The monastery bell wakes me at 7.30am – late for a monastery – and when I come down the rickety wooden stairs I find the day is already well ahead of me, the sky filling the world with a bright and brilliant blue. I'd forgotten that sunlight and shadow are so much a part of the mountain day. There's the usual crowd of Christmas orphans gathered here in Mar Mousa and though I only arrived last night, I've got to know quite a few of them already: the very fact of being here gives one carte blanche to ask everyone their business though I'd do that anyway. There's the bubbly little American from Texas, Sally, who had visa problems back in Hama and whose cute pigtails make her look like a child though she's a divorcee, travelling to forget her troubles. The best thing about her three-year marriage, she tells me, is that it gave her her former husband's grandfather – a Baptist minister. Tommy is also from the States and used to own a string of ice cream shops. I keep away from him because he tends to complain about small things and I don't have any excess energy to expend on sympathy. Wilhem is a postgraduate law student from the Netherlands who speaks perfect English even to the extent of getting the intonations right. Then there's a curly-haired Mexican in his 20s who tells me that most governments are corrupt though none as corrupt as Lula's and Chavez's which makes me wonder about his politics. He's in banking and is coming to work in Syria next year.

"Why?" I ask. Because both countries have oil, he tells me which throws light on his political ideas.

"In Mexico," he continues, "We have oil which we sell to the US and they refine it for us."

"And then they sell your own oil back to you, I suppose?"

"Yes. That's it."

He doesn't see anything wrong in this and I'm not surprised. It's how it works. In Ireland, Shell buys offshore oil from us, refines it and sells it back to us again – at market prices – a deal formulated by the government of the day though, in the culture of the brown envelope, I can't help wondering whether a few changed hands.

"The Sandinista must be thrown out," the Mexican continues, warming to his idea.

"How?" asks Toby, a German who's travelling with his girlfriend. They are both psychology graduates working in the field of psychiatric care and are looking for somewhere in the world where the commune idea really works.

"They'll be thrown out by the army," the Mexican says.

"Not by democracy then?" asks Toby.

"No, the army. That's what it's there for. Soldiers have to be ready for everything. Look at Katrina. They brought in supplies and civil volunteers by air and then they set off in convoys with a tank at the top and a tank at the bottom."

"Why a tank?" asked Toby but it was rhetorical: the Mexican saw nothing strange in all this militarism.

I have been to Mar Mousa before and each time I approach it with a certain amount of superstitious dread. This is due to a combination of things which include Paolo, the Jesuit priest who set up this neo-Christian community 15 years ago, the forbidding aspect of the monastery building itself, its location, and finally the religious ethos.

The actual building was once a 2nd century Roman fort and still looks like one, rising up from the plain below, its blank walls, sheer and grey, cornered with sharp angles that slice across the pupils of my eyes. From its ramparts, the soldiers of the Empire had a panoramic view of the wide flat expanse of desert far below and could monitor the huge caravan trains which passed beneath, plying between Damascus and Tadmor and far beyond.

Outposts of empire are sad and lonely places and this is what I feel when I come here. Hacked out of limestone, the monastery is surrounded by mountains pockmarked with caves which became dwellings for the early Christians who moved in when the Empire fell. Desolation, the mindset of the hermit, lies everywhere.

The first time I came here, I bedded down in the dormitory wearing everything I had. My room-mate was Ann, a postgraduate student doing her doctorate on the origins of Mar Mousa. Ann seemed to carry on her shoulders more problems than she could cope with. One was that she sleepwalked and had to have a chair wedged against the door to stop her opening it in the middle of the night. Her other problem was Paolo who, though not her supervisor, seemed to control her every waking moment, deciding what work she should do and stipulating she should devote five hours a day to contemplation, not something a time-pressed doctoral candidate usually wants to do.

Paolo is certainly unnerving. In his 50s, bearded, with a bulky body that imposes itself on whatever space he enters. His voice is loud and, at mealtimes, he has a way of reaching across anyone for whatever he wants. The Buddhist precept – take only that which is given – is one I want to remind him of, finding it hard to equate all this unpolished physicality with the fact that he is a Jesuit and therefore, one assumes, an intellectual with a fairly sophisticated idea of self. He has adopted the headdress of the local men – a rolled-up-sausage of keffiyeh, set like a pancake on his head – and harangues rather than talks to people. I took an instant if irrational dislike to him the first time we met.

That first time, I slept badly, had nightmares, wrote a story in my head about waking up to find that I had gone back in time and that I was alone and trapped in this fearful place. After the second night, I lied to Paolo and said I had to return immediately to Damascus.

But Mar Mousa remained unfinished business for me and once back home in Dublin, its shadow continued to flicker at the back of my mind. I got the story down on paper, entered it in a competition for a ghost story. Now, two years later, I'm here again perhaps to lay that ghost. This time, however, it's different. It's Christmas and there's an air of heightened expectancy to things. There are tiny pastries to be made for tomorrow night's Christmas Eve party and we all sit around the communal table cutting, rolling and shaping the dough. For the first time in a long while, I am on the inside, part of a group. During Ramadan, it was the opposite. Always on the outside, I was a lone stranger peering into cafés where groups of Syrians were laughing and talking, gathered together to share the evening meal. Paolo joins us and sings Old MacDonald had a Farm, in Arabic. I do my party turn – a music hall number called That's Peggy O'Neill – because it's very short. Everyone shouts out the last line con brio: That's Piggy-oooo-neel. A French woman sings Clair de la Lune so very prettily that Paolo pinches her cheek. Then Ann sings a song from her days at primary school. She sings it girlishly as if she were still ten, and I remember that at dinner last night Paolo had admonished her for putting bread on the table rather than on a plate. He treats her like a child and she behaves like one. But as I look around me, I know that the cosy feeling of oneness is illusory. I am not part of a religion that includes in its daily practice the worship of a political leader and feel ill at ease among people who appear so isolated from this Arab land.

It reminds me of something I had previously found disturbing: the fact that the people connected with the monastery seemed safely removed from the world below, where poverty and the politics of the Middle East make the future far from secure – except for those who believe they have a place guaranteed in the never-never land of eternity.

Now, I find this was an unfair judgement. One of the monastery nuns, an Arab from Damascus, has a degree in biology and is working on a conservation project which includes a much-needed waste disposal system which will serve both the monastery and the nearby town of Nabk. Paolo is engaged in building houses for people in Nabk though here I have a problem: the houses are for the local Christians. This is hateful sectarianism. I say nothing but continue to roll and cut and shape, to laugh and sing so that everyone thinks I am the same as they are.

After a while, I slip away to have a look at the frescoes painted on the plastered walls of the church. The monastery is dedicated to Saint Moses (Mar Mousa) who, in common with many saints, is a multiple-personality saint and has at least two identifiable incarnations. Though they both originate in Ethiopia, only one was murdered (martyred in religious parlance) and his thumb preserved in the church in Nabk. The other Saint Moses travelled to Egypt and failed to leave any body parts lying around.

The best fresco is the one which depicts the Day of Judgement and is interesting because it shows a row of clergy who have strayed from the path of righteousness. They are identified by the black crosses painted on their white garments. Beneath them are more wrongdoers, pictured with the things which indicate their sinfulness – a scales, a knife, some coins – so that we know the finger is being pointed at the judiciary, the merchant class and the bankers. Below them are those who are truly damned – naked people overcome by their sensory desires who have snakes emerging horribly from between their legs which then start to coil upwards into their various orifices. I feel the old shiver of fear that used to overcome me as a child when warned that the flames of hell undoubtedly waited for children who lied, stole sweets or hit their siblings.

The church fills up for the evening service and Paolo, in a voluminous white gown and a black skullcap, delivers his sermon in different modes: shouting and roaring in Arabic or talking quietly in English. I don't follow it because I'm studying the congregation. There seems to be a certain sort of young European male who wears a Palestinian keffiyeh round the neck as a fashion item and who is attracted to Paolo's brand of Christianity. The rest of the group are men and women of different ages, though mainly in their 20s, some European and some Syrian, who light their candles, sip from the communal cup, sing along and read their bible when directed to do so by Paolo.

But it's no good. Despite the peeling paint, the ancient prayers and the murky candlelight, I simply don't get a feel for the metaphysical, for that mystical moment when the water changes into wine. Or indeed into blood. And this might be the problem. I'm not absolutely sure I like the idea of blood sacrifice. Further, I see no reason to deify Jesus. His philosophy and his political aspirations are good enough without tagging on a religious cult. Of course, if you are a political activist, young and charismatic, one of the best things that can happen to you is to be arrested, executed and finally deified. What might have happened had he merely been imprisoned for life?

But this is no time for conjecture: there's too much religion around and my feet are like ice, reminding me that we are 3,500 feet up the side of a mountain. I stand in order to get the blood circulating again and push my way through the heavy curtain at the door. Outside, the night is still and perfect, the clear sky vibrant with stars, each one a throbbing heartbeat.

Next morning, Christmas Eve, the plain below has disappeared beneath a damp, rolling mist. The kitchen is full of last night's dishes which I piously stack up but don't attempt to wash: the water is too cold. One of the nuns arrives but doesn't know how to turn on the gas stove. Nor does her pretty, dark-eyed helper who appears and starts to wash up using freezing water and won't allow me to help: "No, please. I'm used to it," she says. "I work in a home for mentally handicapped people."

The mist climbs up the side of the mountain, clawing its way over the parapet like a prehistoric swamp creature. I sit on a stone bench clutching my mug of tea to warm my hands but the cushion I'm sitting on is damp. So too are my trousers and my back is shivering. We all gather together, wrapped up in sweaters, woolly hats and scarves, following the sunlight round the courtyard before finally crowding into a corner to get the last of its faint warmth before it disappears behind the mountain: the day loses its light early at this time of year.

Meanwhile, the pastry-making, the carrot-grating, the potato-peeling and the egg-beating continue all morning while visitors arrive and are welcomed with hot drinks and cakes. We are 40 for lunch with twice that number expected later.

It starts to snow wetly, desert snow that's not the right sort. I spend the afternoon in the women's dormitory drying my socks on the oil heater. When it's dark, we make our perilous way up a mountain track to a large hall close to the nuns' quarters. The way is difficult and uneven with the billowing mist bouncing off the beams cast by our torches. We walk in single file, guided by candles set into cracks in the rocks along the way. Someone decides to guide me by holding my hand which is more dangerous than helpful and I have to pull my hand out of theirs, noting there is a parable there waiting to be dealt with later when I have time to think about it. Then we burst into the light, into a hall full of crackers and colour. There's a Christmas tree with real candles on it and a table laden with food. There's drumming and clapping and people doing the hokey kokey – in Arabic. The party takes on the feel of a bizarre film set with one of the guests, a man who is paraplegic and dressed as Santa Claus, hoisted on to the shoulders of some of the revellers and carried round the room ringing a bell. It requires one man to carry him and two to walk behind supporting his back. A reporter from the Daily Star in Beirut, takes pictures and tells me, ominously, that things in Lebanon are "simmering". Just as I am about to serve myself some carrot salad, a woman who helped prepare the food tells me that she grated the carrots until her knuckles bled into the mixture. Carefully, I replace the serving spoon.

A Spanish man plays Spanish music on his guitar in a mediocre way and a Japanese woman plays soulful English carols on her violin which no one listens to: the drummers want something lively to drum to and she isn't it. Paolo takes over on a drum and plays it without interruption, beaming at us all and failing to notice a man who whispers in his ear that there is a woman who is prepared to sing. This is Paolo's style, unaware of any action unless he is the centre of it. And yet I feel a certain kindliness towards him. He is a big, ungainly man, full of energy and ambition, who has probably never known a woman, never felt the touch of a calming hand on his face nor himself stroked the cheek of someone he loved. He is a stranger to tenderness.

Next day, clambering down the mountain with Wilhem, he tells me he doesn't like Paolo: "I asked him yesterday," he continues, "If I could get on to the monastery internet to email a friend at the Dutch Embassy in Damascus and he said no."

"Really? Why not?"

"Well, I asked him that too."

"And?"

"Well, what he said was – why don't you wash, your clothes have a bad smell."

This time I shake my head in disbelief. Wilhem does not form part of the great unwashed. In fact, he is a cut above the average backpacker and is planning to cross over into Lebanon to do a bit of skiing there. Smell he does not.

Once back in Damascus, I make for the Cham Palace Hotel. In the spacious bar, a young woman in a backless, blue sequinned evening dress is playing the grand piano, accompanying another woman in a long red evening dress who is playing show songs on the violin. The waiter brings me a bowl of nuts and I order a black coffee and a brandy. I have no trouble at all moving back into my Christmas comfort zone.

Chapter 18

Visiting the Palestinians at Yarmouk Camp

I brought a wad of US dollars with me, together with some traveller's cheques to the value of about £800 in total. The cheques are relatively safe but the hard currency is, understandably, much in demand. There is so little foreign trade that the banks tend to hang on to what hard currency they can get which is why many Syrians, travelling abroad, have great difficulty getting the currency they need. When I first arrived, I changed dollars in the hotel. Then I met up with a friend and swopped with him. On a few occasions, Ahmad has taken me down an alley, in through a door and up a flight of stairs and we did the business there but I haven't been entirely happy with all this in case I get caught. I have two body belts: one a cloth one that I wear under my clothes and the other a leather bag more easily accessible for everyday purchases. The inner bag gives me cause for worry, though, because once, cycling for a month down through France, I had carried all I needed in a cloth purse. When I pulled out my travellers cheques to use in a bank, they were so sweaty that the teller refused to handle them and I had to go from bank to bank until I found a less fastidious teller.

Today, I have decided to go to a legitimate bank even though I am accosted by two would-be money changers en route. Syrian banks are like khans and the one in the centre of Damascus that I go into is no exception. There's a sociable hum in the air as people stroll around with sheaves of paper in their hands: papers for signing, for perusing, for putting down on a desk – and forgetting. In the lobby, people shake hands with each other, embrace, talk, smoke, drink tea. Hurry is a word that has no place here.

At the money desk, everyone crowds together in easy familiarity. The idea of a queue is alien so, though people reach over the heads of those in front of them, waving bits of paper or wads of notes – US dollars mainly – no one gets ruffled since clearly there is some kind of system, if only I knew what it was. All I can do is stand, shuffle forward politely, duck when a hand comes over my head, then raise it again when it seems safe to do so. In the end, you get there. Trust is all you need: the Damascenes have been handling bits of paper for centuries and know exactly what they are doing. When it's my turn, I hand over my own bit of signed paper – I have been sent to four different people in order to get one signature – and the man behind the counter gives me my money, digging into his own pocket for the small change. I am here because I need some cash as I have two journeys to make – one to Yarmouk Camp and the other to Quneitra.

Rivers are watery conduits for delivering food, for providing opportunities for trading, for enabling people to come together for funerals and weddings. But they are also barriers to be defended or forcibly bridged. As I write this, a battle is raging in southern Lebanon around the river Litani, an infernal battle so fierce and deadly that its name will live on in history as the Boyne does in Ireland, the Tiber in Rome, the Kwai in Burma. In Syria, it's the Yarmouk, which flows south of the Golan Heights and borders Syria and Jordan.

Yarmouk was the scene of a great battle in which the Arab Muslims, in 636CE, gained the upper hand over the Byzantines. It's a name that inspires people, helps them cope with the latest disaster, the latest displacement. Helps them look down a road that seems to lead to nowhere but which some know leads back to Palestine, to the family house in Haifa or the orange grove in Jaffa to which they still have the papers and the front door keys. There's a Yarmouk Hospital in Baghdad and one in Beirut. In Jordan, there's a Yarmouk University.

In 1948, a huge number of Palestinians, fleeing their homes in Israel, crossed the border into Syria. They were offered a muddy field just outside Damascus, where the UNHCR hastily erected tents for them. The field was called Yarmouk Camp because that's what it was – a refugee camp with an inspiring name. The Palestinians were given a 100-year lease on the land but some 50 years on, though now a fully-fledged town with its own shops, tower blocks of flats, schools and mosques it is still called Yarmouk Camp.

Syria was a safe haven for Palestinians and latterly for Iraqis. And it continues to be for quite a few political groups, among them Hamas and the PFLP – the National Party for the Liberation of Palestine, a sad group of yesterday's Marxist fighters who still dream of freedom for their land. Before going to Yarmouk Camp, I want to meet up with the PFLP and so, after a few phone calls I learn that Khalil, head of the PFLP in Damascus, will meet me.

"Go to the emergency gate of the Italian Hospital, the Mashfa Tilyan," I am told and I assume the contact will be a Palestinian doctor but when I find the emergency gate, there is no one there. Wait a moment, though. Isn't the word for gate and door the same in Arabic? Maybe I am actually supposed to go into the hospital, not stand about outside.

The notice on the hospital door says *siccurro pronto* which surely means emergency help. But that door is closed in a resolute sort of way. A tiny nun – the hospital is run by the John Bosco order of nuns – arrives and I ask her about the Palestinian doctor I am supposed to be meeting. She shakes her tiny, veiled head as she pads along the corridor with me running after her. All the doctors here are Syrian, she says, except the ones who are Italian.

Outside in the street, I see two traffic policemen standing by a public phone booth but when I step in to use it and bend down to get out my notebook, one of the men reaches over my shoulder and places his phonecard in the slot. When I straighten up, he pulls his card out and gives the receiver a nonchalant whack so that it flips out of the cradle and dangles in front of me.

This loutish behaviour is unusual for a Syrian and while the culprit walks away laughing I crossly signal to his colleague that he should replace the receiver which, to his credit, he does. While all this is going on, I see a car sidle up to the kerb and decide it's for me.

"Hi," I say. "I've come to meet someone from the PFLP and sorry I'm late. I couldn't get into the hospital and then when I did, the nun didn't know of any Palestinian doctors."

The man waits for a pause in my narrative and then grabs his moment: "I no spik English."

He is merely the driver and merely is the operative word for though they deny it, the class structure in Syria is evident to anyone who can pick up the signals. He is a small, dark-skinned wizened little fellow whereas Khalil, when I meet him, is a broad-framed, pale-skinned man, confident, expansive. He speaks perfect English and I am gratified that my class antennae were tuned in, even in a culture as contradictory as this one.

In 1968, guerrillas stormed an El Al plane at Athens airport and a man was killed. One of the attackers was of Lebanese origin and Israeli intelligence suspected the assault had been planned in Lebanon with the PFLP behind the whole thing. Two days later, the Israeli Defence Force retaliated by bombing 13 planes on the tarmac at Beirut airport. That was over 40 years ago and now Khalil's large, glass-topped desk is empty with not even a paperweight or an ashtray to lend it some spurious gravity. Nothing much is happening here. The jihad is taking place elsewhere – in the West Bank and in Gaza. In New York, in Madrid, in London. In Afghanistan. But not here. Here is a forgotten corner of the struggle, as the PFLP has long been overtaken by the more brutal reality of long range ballistic missiles, of nuclear threats, of superpower standoffs.

On a shelf behind his desk, Khalil has a display of business cards, tributes to his organisation's one-time importance. I add mine to the dusty pile. On the shelf too are faded photographs of his children to whom Palestine now is a mythical country brought to life only in their father's dreams. His son is an engineer and works in Moscow. A daughter is a computer engineer in the US. Another daughter is at university. Khalil makes no mention of a wife.

The PFLP was communist-backed until the collapse of the Soviet Union which now seems a very long time ago indeed but then, with Khalil, everything seems to be in the past. He proudly shows me a tattered card with a picture of Bobby Sands on it, given to him by Sinn Fein who had brought him to Northern Ireland once, all part of that organisation's shoulder-to-shoulder policy in the days when the IRA, the MK and the PLO were buzz words in the confraternity of armed resistance. Now, only Palestine remains to be sorted.

Khalil talks as many Marxists do, droning on and on, assuming wrongly that I know nothing of his country's tribulations. He is unable to deal with a question, for that is regarded as an unwarranted interruption to his discourse. There is no exchange, no dialogue. Propaganda replaces rhetoric.

After ten minutes, I am regretting that I came but at the same time I feel remorse. He has been forced to leave his country and it is unlikely he will ever return. He sees no way in which his people can talk to the Israelis and he has no concept of mediation, no idea that he could exploit the fact that his people occupy the high moral ground. Palestinians, after all, have right on their side. They have been driven from their ancestral homes, thousands of them killed in the process. Instead, in common with many Israelis, Khalil cherishes his identity as a victim and it is from this that he gets the strength to continue to bang his head against a brick wall. I feel myself losing patience wanting, irrationally, to blame him for the wrongs done to him.

Khalil, of course, is totally unaware of my turbulent feelings which, in any case, are irrelevant to his subject. People simply have to die, he continues. There must always be sacrifice. He rejoices in the fact, as he sees it, that so many young Palestinians are still ready to die. But are they? Many that I meet in Damascus have listened to their parents and know that the dream of return has been invested in them, has been laid on their shoulders. Except that their life is now here though they can never say that.

"Would your daughter in the States want to go back to Palestine?" I ask, feeling mean because I know she probably wouldn't.

"Yes, yes," he beams. "She has promised me she will go back to our village. As soon as she has a passport." By which he means an American passport. Palestinians who have settled here have all the rights of a Syrian but they don't have Syrian passports. To take out one of those would mean giving up their right to a Palestinian one, to their claim to their own one-time homes. I feel sorry for Khalil and his comrades. On the streets, they are canonised by their reputation as former jihadists but when it comes to the negotiating table they are disempowered by their own unyielding propaganda. When I leave his office, I carry with me the weight of a great wrong done to his people and of an even greater sadness for the suffering they have endured. I wait for two days to hear from the people he said would contact me to take me to Yarmouk Camp but they never do.

I get a bus to Yarmouk Camp anyway, to have a look around but it's disappointing. Expecting to find a hotbed of Palestinian intrigue with all the men wearing keffiyehs and concealing Kalashnikovs under their long garments, I find a city going about its everyday business. The usual array of plastic bags litter the paths and the buildings look run-down as so many do to my European consumer-driven eye. Behind the main street, about 1.6 kilometres long I'd been told proudly, the linking and parallel streets, flanked by blocks of flats, are little more than red, dusty lanes full of potholes. Because the post-Ramadan celebrations are still going on, everyone is out on the streets and gathering at every corner. I am in the middle of a street party. The children ride tiny roundabouts and swings. Small girls are fluffed up in flouncy, pink dresses with matching ribbons while their small brothers are decked out as bridegroom look-alike. They scream with delight on their minuscule chair-a-planes, worked by one man turning a handle as if he were starting up an old-fashioned car. I stare at the people trying to see if they are different from their Syrian hosts but they all seem the same. Except that there are fewer women in hijabs, fewer village women in their brightly-coloured dresses, fewer keffiyehs, fewer men in cloaks. There are more girls in the cafés, though, unveiled and enjoying themselves. These are the children and grandchildren of those Palestinians forced to abandon their homes in what is now Israel. They look quite at home here and I suspect few will return to their ancestral villages.

I catch a bus back to Damascus to have tea with Zada who lives in Qudsaiyya, a large housing development set among the cool hills on the far side of Mount Qassaioun. Qudsaiyya was built some 12 years ago and will eventually have a population of 100,000 people.

"You like Qudsaiyya?" Zada asks. "We are mostly professional people here. Not TV people like some of the other developments." And I sense her disdain.

My initial feeling is that there is a desolate air to the sandy hills, a feeling of emptiness that could never make up for the bustling, noisy streets of the old city. Zada's mother likes it, however, and I join her to lean over the balcony, watching the sun flame down behind a hill.

"It's beautiful here," she says, and at that moment, I have to agree.

We spend the evening watching a film made by Hizbullah. It is a crude propaganda film showing black-clad street fighters displaying their wares and a small boy, in the West Bank, taunting an Israeli soldier. First he throws a stone at the soldier, then he gets braver and hurls another one which rings out as it pings against the soldier's helmet. The soldier takes a few steps towards the child, then hesitates.

"He is afraid," says the mother. "Watch, now. Look!" And as the child advances on the soldier, the man turns and walks away. "See," says the mother, "he is running away from a small child."

I decide not to point out that the soldier may well have suspected the child was a trap to lure him into danger and has chosen the better part of valour. That is not an acceptable point of view to hold here.

Zada's brother Messan walks with me to the bus stop. Like many Syrians, he is spending time in Saudi earning relatively good money working there as a teacher.

"When I have earned enough, I will buy a house here in Damascus and set up in business, probably in computers," he tells me. "It's pleasant in Saudi but it's not home and it's not great for women. Women there are all veiled, only their eyes showing. They are educated separately as well. They cannot have male teachers so if they go to university, all that work is done by computer. I know of one male teacher who teaches women at the university but he is only allowed to do that because he's blind. In hospital, women doctors are sometimes allowed to work partly unveiled but they can never go anywhere on their own. That is not allowed."

"Can they go alone by taxi, to work maybe?" I ask but realise it is a foolish question.

"There is no need for a taxi. Every Saudi family has its own car, two or three even as well as a driver."

"And you, where do you live?"

"In a compound." He pauses. "It's like a prison."

There is, he explains, a pecking order for foreign workers in Saudi: "A teacher in Syria might get about 5,000 SYP a month but in Saudi he can earn 25,000."

"Not too bad, even if you have to live in a prison while you're earning it," I say.

He shrugs: "Except that it varies according to what country you're from. If you're an American doctor working in Saudi, you get paid 10,000 US dollars. A Syrian doctor gets half that – 5,000 US dollars while an Egyptian doctor gets only 1,500 US dollars."

Everyone, it seems, falls into a special category. In Saudi, the Lebanese, with their long history of maritime commerce, work with money and trading. The Syrians work in teaching, the Pakistanis work with computers and the Indonesians do the manual work. As simple as that.

"But it won't go on forever," said Messan. "In a few years, there will be fewer migrants and the Saudis will have to do their own work." Do I hear a note of triumph in his voice?

There is no sign of a bus but I don't mind. I'm enjoying standing here in the calm, still, night air, looking up at the ice-white moon. Messan looks at it too and nods: "That's the three-day moon," he says.

Our bus fails to show up and as it's chilly, we share a taxi into town. Messan gets out at Jizeer al Raiees – President's Bridge – and I go on to Bab Sharaqi where I had left my bike earlier in the day. Then I have a short ride home, without lights, through the quiet, empty souks of the old city.

Chapter 19

Have I been kidnapped?

Next morning, I grab a taxi in al Thowra Street and immediately get out of it again. The driver, skinny and underfed, has a shifty look to him and the inside of the taxi smells of food. Is he a ruffian just because he looks like one? I don't have time to examine that bit of illogic. He just looks like one and for the time being that's enough. The next cab is a small neat Fiat. This driver smiles, is clean – and switches on the meter with an elaborate flourish. I sit back reassured and am immediately annoyed at what I have discovered about myself: both driver and cab fit my bourgeois expectations. Travelling with a small rucksack, a bike and on a tight budget, I'd somehow seen myself as a much freer spirit but instead have unexpectedly slipped back into the old, familiar comfort zone, the safety net of my own prejudices. That's twice already this morning and it's not yet 9am.

I exchange this unacceptable self-image for that of a Damascene commuter as, recklessly, we swing out into the morning rush hour, the air full of noisy car horns as discordant as an orchestra tuning up. We peel off to cross the Jizeer al Raiess and then on to Mezze and the military area where I have to get written permission to go to Quneitra, the administrative town in the Golan Heights captured by the Israeli Defence Forces in the final stages of the 1967 Six Day War. It is now a ghost town and I want to see it.

Obligingly, the driver takes the bit of paper on which Tariq has written where I have to go and shows it to different people. But no, each person says, the place I need is in a different building, up one floor, down another, three streets away, over the next bridge.

We drive out along the four-lane highway where there are more soldiers, more signs saying no photographs, more men leaning against railings smoking. More gates. Then I think I recognise a sign on a wall.

"That's it," I say. "This looks right. Drop me here. How much?" The driver smiles, shrugs his shoulders. I should pay him whatever I think the journey is worth are his unspoken words. But the meter, I say, what's on the meter? More mute shrugs and it slowly dawns on me: the theatrical flourish at the beginning of our journey was no more than that. Like the car I declined to travel in, the meter in this one doesn't work either.

Still, I'm getting the hang of all this and, employing one of my coping strategies, I go deaf. Please write down what I have to pay, I indicate.

"100 SYP," he says apologetically and miraculously I hear what he says. That's about £6. For a local it would probably be half that but I pay up. He has, after all, brought me to where I want to be and has acted as guide as well. Inside, I am directed upstairs and ushered into a room with the usual gallery of photographs showing the president, his father and his brother Basil, the latter, as always, wearing hitman shades which make him look like Mr Pink or even Mr Orange. Did these boys never have a mother, I wonder? If so, she has been airbrushed out of all the family photographs.

Behind an expansive desk sits a five-star military person. A friend in the US Marines explained to me once that there has only ever been one five-star *general* and that was Eisenhower. The Syrian five-star person welcomes me warmly, scribbles something on a bit of paper and says I can now go to Quneitra. Caught up in all the frustrating bureaucracy, I sometimes forget how civil and indeed friendly individual bureaucrats can be. Downstairs, however, when I show my new bit of paper, I realise that, despite the five stars, he has got it wrong. I have been misinformed and am again caught up in a web of words. True, this is indeed where you come to get permission to go

Quneitra – provided you are Syrian. Foreigners have to go Adnan Malki Street.

The uphill walk, in a morning already hotting up, gives me time to think about the character of Syrian people. One thing I know is that they all want to help, which is why, if you ask them a question, it is important to give no hint of the answer you are hoping for because that is the one you'll get: Syrians aim to please and courtesy takes precedence over accuracy. Likewise, if you ask directions, it is safe to state your required destination but never mention a possible route because that is the one they'll set you on even if it takes you in entirely the wrong direction.

"Is it up this street?" you ask and they nod delightedly, congratulating you on your cleverness. "Yes, yes. Up this street." And up and up. And when you get to the roundabout at the top, you realise they omitted to tell you where to go next in this Alice in Wonderland world of smiling, helpful people.

Right enough, at the top of Malki, there is a roundabout with a vast number of men, mostly young, standing around in black suits and dark glasses, murmuring into the collar of their jackets. So, I am in the area of the Ministry of the Interior.

Next to the Ministry is the al Salamiyeh Maternity Hospital where there are a lot of older men in casual wear talking and blowing smoke into each other's faces. Can they all be anxious, expectant fathers? No, they are part of the extended chain of employees that hang about any ministry office, not even pretending to do something useful. And why bother since they will get paid anyway: it's one way of keeping the unemployment figures down. I approach one of them and tell him what I want.

"Passport," he says and holds out his hand but this is far too informal for me. I want to do business privately, not on the street where everyone can see.

"This is your office?" I ask pointing to a ramshackle shed with a desk and chair and obligingly he nods. Once inside, I ceremoniously hand over the passport – something I absolutely hate doing – and it is then I realise the shed is just the place where the night watchman sleeps though now upgraded by me to an office.

The first man hands the passport to a second man who hands it to a third who rings a bell on a large ornamental gate behind which stands a man who opens the gate, takes the passport then locks the gate before going up the steps and disappearing into the Ministry building.

Syria is a secular state but as I watch the rigid formalities surrounding the passport a few questions arise in my mind. Why didn't man number three simply hand the passport through the bars of the gate instead of ringing the bell for man number four to open it?

Why? Because here, the military is the state religion with its top brass, its mysterious acolytes in their dark suits and shades, its rituals and its pyramid of power. While I stand waiting in the street, a young man courteously lays a sheet of newspaper on a wall for me to sit on and from this vantage point I observe four huge, heavy canvas sacks with metal handles being carried out of the Ministry and loaded into the back of a car. They look as if they might possibly have belonged to Houdini for each sack has a lock on it and requires three men to carry it. Each contains, I presume, the reams of documents this tortuous system must clearly generate. Are the sacks full of reports in triplicate, minutes of meetings held, records of people thrown into prison without trial and never heard of again? Or simply applications to go to Quneitra long since granted or refused.

Syrian bureaucrats love shuffling bits of paper about. It gives them something to do. When the Ummayyad Mosque was being built – a very costly undertaking even for the 8th century – it required 18 camels to carry away the accounting documents related to its finances. As the car drives away with its load of sacks, I wonder if one car is the equivalent of 18 camels.

My passport is handed back to me and, tucked into its pages, is my permission to go to Quneitra with the proviso that I travel the following day. Fearful I might lose this precious document,

I stop at a stall in the underpass and ask for it to be photocopied but the man shakes his head: "It is a Ministry document," he apologises. "I am not allowed." At first I am put out before remembering that back home, photocopy shops are not allowed to make copies of passports.

"Bismillah," says the radio announcer next morning on the minibus I hope is taking me to Quneitra. Then it's morning prayers. After a while, the sound of praying becomes monotonous and I stare out the window. Far off to my right, the mountains are snow-capped and the black volcanic clay of the countryside is cold and unforgiving. Then, as we get further south of Damascus, the black turns to a glowing orange with the scrub broken up, every so often, by a few blessed olive trees. Occasionally, there is a flash of brilliant green where a channel of thick, brown water reaches this thirsty land.

The bus gets hotter and the praying, though musical, sounds unmelodious to my ears and is starting to give me a headache. The other people in the bus seem oblivious to the heat. One wears a camel hair coat while another turns up the fur collar of his bomber jacket. I shift around trying to find a cool place on the hot, plastic seat and am reminded, not for the first time, that I am a north European more used to wrapping up warmly than sweating quietly in an over-heated minibus. The one-street towns we pass through all have their goods hung outside for sale, including whole carcasses gathering dust from passing vehicles and I am glad, once again, that I am vegetarian. At Karnabeh, I am told to get off the minibus and, feeling like a criminal, I am made to walk across the street behind the soldier who has been sent to accompany me. His officer smiles, welcomes me, reassures me and I have to remind myself that I am doing nothing illegal. That I have merely come to visit Quneitra.

The soldier escorts me back again across the busy street and on to another minibus.

"Do you want a guide to Quneitra?" a man at the bus stop asks.

"No thanks. I'll just walk around it on my own. But thanks."

"It's very big," he warns.

"I'll be OK."

But I'm not OK. One by one, the other passengers get off until eventually there is only myself and the driver left. At the next checkpoint, a man emerges from the nearby military office and asks me for my passport which he takes away with him. Then another man emerges and gets into the bus and we move off.

"Stop! Stop!" I am in a panic. "My passport. I don't have my passport. I can't leave without it."

"It's alright," says the new man. "Don't worry. It's being looked after."

"But who are you?"

"I work for the tourist company."

"But you came out of the military building."

He nods. "They let me use it."

His answer doesn't ring true and it quickly dawns on me that I have been kidnapped. I look around for a UN flag. They're here somewhere: the no-man's-land around the Golan Heights is patrolled by the UN.

"Where are they?" I ask.

"Who?" asks the undercover tourist man.

"The UN. Look, I have a press card. I would like to talk to someone from the UN."

The man smiles and shakes his head. "I am sorry. Their checkpoint is further on."

"But anyway I would like to talk to them. There may be some Irish soldiers among them."

The man shakes his head again: "You are not allowed talk to the UN and there are no Irish. Only Austrian."

Mentally, I go through all the safety procedures I have been trained in for my other role as an international election observer. I have even attended a kidnapping camp up in the Dublin mountains, led blindfold through the woods where the IRA were reported to have trained as well. Except that then I was with the Civil Defence and now I don't know who I am with.

In the back of the minibus, I try to recall the drill: let someone know where you are going. That'll be Tariq except he thinks I'm going to Quneitra tomorrow. Check the underside of the vehicle for suspicious things attached to it. *All* Syrian vehicles have suspicious things hanging down – bits of the exhaust system mainly. Have a spare set of clothes. I do but they're hanging on the clothesline back in Damascus. Make a note of your route, the changes in the road surface, turnings left and right, number of bridges crossed. Can't. The driver is going like the clappers. Park your vehicle so that you can make a quick getaway. But in which direction? Bring a torch with you. The battery I bought in the souk was flat even before I put it in the torch. Make a will. This last, of course, is an ironic spur of the moment addition prompted by the hopelessness of my current position.

The undercover tourist man asks would I like the driver to take me around Quneitra and the driver smiles at me encouragingly in his rear mirror. This could be a trick question and I pause before replying. If I opt to get out and walk I could be making myself even more vulnerable.

"It will cost you 200 SYP," says the undercover tourist man helpfully.

"OK." In for a penny, in for a Syrian pound. After all, I have little choice.

In a land of desert scrub water, the life force, is more precious than oil. The Golan Heights, standing 3,000 feet above the Sea of Galilee, is a place cherished by both Israelis and Syrians and coveted by Israelis. Both the Yarmouk and the Jordan rivers rise among the Golan hills and both are augmented by rainwater running off other, nearby slopes. With its fertile valleys watered by such great rivers, the Quneitra area was the breadbasket for Damascus as well being an important and historic hub for traffic. Roman trade routes and military roads crossed here, linking Damascus and Alexandria.

In the final stages of the 1967 Six Day War, the Israeli army swept into the area and bulldozed its way ahead enabling the invading tanks to begin an assault on Syria's Golan Heights. By capturing these vantage points, the Israelis would gain a significant military advantage.

At the height of this war, Quneitra, lyng in the shelter of the Golan, was the focus of attention when, on 10 June at 8.30am, Syrian radio made an astounding announcement: Quneitra had fallen. As a result, military units which had been sent to defend the town turned away and headed back for Damascus which, only an hour's drive away, was now extremely vulnerable to Israeli attack. Army units already engaged in defending Quneitra, finding themselves abandoned and with the Israeli army on their doorstep, left their positions and fled to safety, one army commander making a getaway on horseback. Two hours after the first radio broadcast, the Minister of Defence, Hafez Assad, went on air to say the bulletin had been a mistake: Quneitra had not fallen.

Commentators have offered various explanations for this disastrous episode. Either it was an appalling breakdown in military communications or the Syrians had panicked and decided to portray the situation as worse than it was in the hope that the UN might take action that would stave off further Israeli incursions. Whatever the reason, Assad's announcement came too late.

When the Israeli army arrived in Quneitra at 2pm on that same, fateful Saturday, they reported finding a ghost town only recently evacuated, its communication systems still in place and vehicle engines running. "We took Quneitra without a struggle," said one Israeli commander. The Israeli Defence Forces had gained control of the Golan Heights, having, they said, "freed the residents ...from the nightmare of Syrian military presence."

The move gave the Israeli people unencumbered access to the Sea of Galilee whose fresh waters now provide for the needs of one third of the population of Israel. And since war is about people and their homes, as the Israeli settlers moved in, the vast majority of Syrians fled the Golan. The demographic landscape had once again changed. Then, in 1973, following the Yom Kippur War, Israel agreed to withdraw from Quneitra, but not the Golan, leaving behind a war scene of flattened homes with shops, schools and hospital bludgeoned beyond recognition.

And here it is now – a stricken landscape still howling with pain. Houses originally no more than four walls of prefabricated concrete are collapsed on themselves, each wall fallen inwards with the roof, also just a large slab of concrete, lying on the top, the whole house – once someone's home – concertinaed downwards to a height of a few feet. We ride over a surprisingly good road, resurfaced, I suspect, to allow the outside world to drive along it to see for themselves and finally we arrive at what had once been the hospital. The steps up to it are smooth and shiny, polished by the tired feet of women coming to give birth, the hurrying feet of fathers come to see their new child, the slow feet of old people come to die.

There is a silence here as if someone – no more than the memory of a shadow – is waiting, holding their breath. A sudden movement catches my eye and I look up: it is a Syrian flag briefly brought to life by a delicate rush of wind. The undercover tourist man and the driver settle back in their seats. This is all familiar to them and they light up cigarettes and start to chat. On the roof of some buildings beyond the hospital, a solitary Syrian soldier squats down also to light a cigarette.

I climb the steps and enter the hospital through what was once the door but which now is a gaping hole. To the right is the stairs leading to the first floor except there is no first floor, just a sky of brightest blue and a white-hot midday sun too blinding to look at. The walls are pockmarked by mortars and a sign outside says that the hospital was used by the Israeli army for target practice. I stand in the suffocating emptiness, my own mind empty. Then I turn back to the minibus.

"The church?" suggests the undercover tourist man. "You'd like to see that?"

"All right."

I have no stomach for it but we go anyway to the Orthodox Church which escaped the bombing. Inside, it is derelict, its altar area neglected, a row of soft drink cans lined up on a window ledge as if waiting for someone to take pot shots at them. Around the desecrated town, the land is green and soft-looking. I'd like to get out and sit on it for a while and gather my thoughts in this place of lonely desolation, its bleakness floodlit by bright sunshine.

I know that Israelis too have died in this never-ending conflict; that Israeli mothers have had to cradle their dead babies, have had to gather up their pots and pans, their wailing toddlers, their ailing, ageing parents and move on. But today I have nothing left over to spare for them. Today, I think only of the shadows no longer cast in Quneitra.

In any case, the undercover tourist man seems anxious to leave and the driver starts up the engine. Ahead of us, some sheep amble across the road with their shepherd – the first sign of human life I have seen apart from soldiers at checkpoints. There are, in fact, four families who have chosen to stay on here where once there were 150,000 people. We pass one of the inhabited houses, with a washing line strung between a wall and a concrete post, the clothes on it still and lifeless in the hot air. The undercover tourist man points to a battered building. "Bank," he says briefly. I had been thinking only of homes destroyed but this was a functioning community with all the normal trappings of a main governate town. The President's father, Hafez Assad, swore to rebuild Quneitra but there are no signs of it happening. Not here.

We drive on along the road as far as we are allowed. Ahead, is no-man's-land where the UN has a checkpoint and where the old, familiar blue and the white flag hangs as useless as a withered arm. Beyond the razor wire is a green valley full of tufts of meadow grass and wild cyclamen and far in the blue distance, a high hill rises, bristling with antennae, satellite dishes and aerials. I know from the British army's presence in Ireland that everything we say can be picked up clearly by these long-distance eyes and ears.

"Hello, Israel," I shout and the undercover tourist man smiles except that, of course, it is not Israel but part of Syria. In 1981, despite previous agreements and despite the presence of the UN in the area, Israel annexed the Golan Heights having first passed a law entitled the "Law of the Golan" giving itself permission to do so.

As we return to the first checkpoint, the undercover tourist man reminds me to pay the driver 200 SYP. I wonder should I pay him too if he is a guide but before getting out of the minibus, he takes from his pocket my passport and hands it back to me and I realise what I had suspected all along: he is not a guide but my very own minder, sent by the Mukhabarat to keep an eye on me. Had I cottoned on to that at the beginning, I might have asked many more questions for he would undoubtedly have known all the answers.

Chapter 20

No, there's no bus to that place

The three men take up their positions, arms crossed, hands resting on opposite shoulders, eyes closed, holding deep within themselves a place undefinable and so private that watching them seems like an intrusion. The oud player starts and they begin to move, slowly at first then faster as they whirl, each pivoting on his own small circle. When they finish, the tourists clap before returning to the business of eating. The whirling dervishes withdraw. The oud player packs away his instrument: the weekly display is over.

Sufism, which emerged in the 8th century, is usually described as the mystical aspect of Islam, that part of the Muslim practice about which we tend to know least but which we, as European lovers of all things oriental, would probably most easily identify with. The word itself is said to derive from the Arabic word for wool (soof) from which the long robes of the wandering Sufi mystics were usually made. The aim of the Sufi is to enter a state of non-desire but learning all this, I found myself wrestling with the complexities of Sufism: the desire to cast off desire seemed to me to be a contradiction in terms. The school of Sufism familiar to most western Europeans is the Mawlawiyyah (Mevlavi in Turkish) and known as the whirling dervishes – the word crops up in the family name of Darwish. The Mevlavi dervishes grew out of the teachings and thoughts of the man considered to be the greatest of the Sufi philosopher/poets, Jelaluddin Balkhi, better known as al Rumi. He was born on 30 September 1207 in Afghanistan, at that time part of the Persian Empire, and he had a passion for music which, incidentally, characterizes Mevlavi Sufism.

The dervish usually wears a conical, maroon coloured hat that represents the tombstone of the ego together with a black cloak which represents his shroud. This he takes off at the beginning of the ceremony to show he is discarding worldly ties. Beneath the shroud, he wears a white wool top and a wide white skirt, heavily weighted at the hem, which swings out as he whirls, his right hand reaching upwards to heaven and his left hand held downwards, connecting him to the earth. As he whirls, the dervish, eyes closed, leans his head to one side so that it seems to rest on his shoulder in a strangely childlike gesture.

The dervishes chose poverty as a way of life which meant that their robes were often patched. Some, however, simply sewed patches onto their robes to indicate their transient lifestyle. Inevitably, defining rules grew around these patches – how they should be sewn on, their size or the sort of thread to be used. There were even instances of Sufis being expelled from the presence of a sheikh because the stitch they had used was too long.

I am familiar with these sorts of rituals. Brought up within the Catholic Church I know all about the taking of Communion (the Last Supper), the priest washing his hands at Mass (Pontius Pilate, the Roman governor, washing his hands of the whole Jesus thing because he regarded it as just a local issue), the three steps up to the altar (the long climb up the hill to Calvary). Though the best part of all was the very pagan ritual of the eating of the flesh and drinking of the blood of the hero, mirrored in the partaking of bread and wine at Mass and, on Easter Sunday, the eating of the sacrificial lamb: rack of lamb is always on the menu at Easter in Ireland.

Lots of dervishes passed through Syria in the course of their wanderings, often on their way to Baghdad but with Syria now a secular state, the dervishes are a vanishing tradition. Nevertheless, their mosque in Damascus, close to the Hejaz Railway Station, is readily recognisable by the conical hat on the dome instead of the usual crescent moon, though the only time I saw any of them was when they were performing for tourists in a restaurant near the Umayyad Mosque. Damascus still has some very venerable connections to Sufism however and I stumbled on one when I made my way up the Jabal to a tightly-packed community where there is a mosque from which, I had been told, you could get the best view of Sham. More importantly, though, it is the mosque which houses the tomb of the Sufi Muhi al Din also known, more formally, as the poet and philosopher Ibn Arabi. Tariq, as usual, gives me detailed instructions on how to get a bus that will take me halfway up the Jabal. But when I arrive at the place, to say bus stop would be to over-describe what is nothing more than a vague spot on the pavement, there's no sign of a bus.

"No, there's no bus to that place," says the man who offers to help and who, it emerges, is also a taxi driver. "Believe me," and he wrings his hands in an effort to overcome my disbelief. "There has been no bus to there for four years."

"But there must be," I insist. "Tariq said there was." The taxi driver shakes his head but quickly opens the door of the taxi when he sees me weaken.

Qassioun is the name of the Jabal which forms the backdrop to the city of Damascus. On its side is a densely-packed collection of higgledy-piggledy dwellings that cling tenaciously to the rock face of the mountain itself, each small home fighting for whatever spare inch of space it can get and then, once there, grappling with its neighbour to maintain its hold on existence. This is a place to which many migrants have come – Kurds, Turks, Palestinians – fitting themselves in, each successive wave of arrivals defying gravity by building their homes just that little bit higher up the Jabal so that now, at night, the dark mountainside shimmers with tiny lights bright as pinprick stars in the midnight-blue sky.

Like taxi drivers the world over, take them outside their eight-kilometre inner city zone and they're lost, which is exactly what happens to us, for this driver, though knowledgeable about non-existent buses, has no clear idea of where I want to go. Indeed, I hardly know myself. All I have is some vague notion of the whereabouts of the Ibn Arabi Mosque and as we corkscrew up, round and into yet another cobbled laneway where we hit an impenetrable rock face, I suggest we call it a day: I will go the rest of the way on foot.

Then fate intervenes in the shape of an old man selling bread outside his shop: "Sheikh Muhi al Din?" and he nods delightedly, using Ibn Arabi's formal name: "A great man." He talks about him as if the long-dead Sufi were a slightly eccentric but much-loved neighbour, one he is proud to count as an acquaintance. "He didn't like religion," the bread-seller tells me. What, no religion in this country of three major -isms, not counting communism? The man shakes his head, smiling at my surprise: "No. He didn't want any religion, only God."

Ah, a true Sufi, then. One and only. Only one. A small boy is summoned to help me find my way. The boy is a skinny seven-year-old. As we pass a bakery, the air suddenly seductive with the smell of fresh pastries, I ask him if he would like one but he makes an eloquent gesture, rubbing his stomach then deflecting, with the palm of his hand turned away from him, any food I might offer. He accepts a few coins, deposits me in the souk and I set out to wander through the throng of people that packs the tiny space in front of Ibn Arabi's mosque, picking my way among stalls selling socks, fruit, nuts, trousers, beetroot, coffee, ginger, red roses wrapped in shiny clear plastic, toys, spices, very large knickers and bras built to accommodate beer barrels. The streets are far too narrow for even small minibuses to penetrate but, parked by the mosque, are lots of tartoura, the nifty little three- and six-seater open vehicles propelled by put-puts that serve as taxis in these cramped areas. I walk down the side of the mosque in search of a lavatory: a new government ruling says every mosque must provide such a facility. The one I use is a squatting one with a hook thoughtfully placed on the back of the door to hang a bag on.

One of the strange and exciting things about Syria is that no two experiences are ever the same. I visited this mosque briefly a long time ago to get the famous view of the city and found myself unceremoniously ushered out of the main prayer hall. "They probably weren't used to tourists," explained Anis later though I took it as a personal affront to my gender. This time it's different. For one thing, I'm different. I'm now much more in tune with the way things are done here and, more importantly, I know something about the great and famous man who lies entombed in the small shrine room below the prayer hall.

Ibn Arabi was born in al Andalus in 1165 and died in Damascus 75 years later. In between, he studied law in Spain which, at that time, was under Arab rule, travelled across to Tunis where he learned something of Sufism from a number of teachers one of whom – Fatima bin Waliyyah – was a well-known female Sufi. When he was 30, he set off on his travels, went on the Haj to Mecca, met al Rumi in Baghdad and settled in Anatolia where he married and raised a family. For someone given to making metaphysical statements about the oneness of being (his favourite preoccupation), he seemed to be quite a down-to-earth sort of person. For instance, when he decided to move on to Damascus, he employed a most practical means of choosing where in the city might be the healthiest place to pitch his tent. What he did was to get four big hooks, skewer a piece of meat on each one, then hang them in four different places about the city. The place where the meat remained edible, or at least took longest to rot, was here, up the side of the Jabal. It was an excellent choice for the air is indeed cool and fresh and marvellously free of traffic noise and smells.

Ibn Arabi held that, while walking the path to oneness, we learn that the mirror and the reflection are all one. He taught that Allah is in everything: in the beggar at the gate, in the idol of the pagan, even in the man drunk with wine. He further taught that, when all desire has gone, there is nothing left except Love, the Love of the Divine. Not surprisingly, his ideas were challenged by the more conservative followers of Islam. How, they argued, could a lowly beggar be the same as Allah?

The modest little mosque which serves stallholders, traders and housewives, old men and children, beggars and gentlefolk, seems to somehow attest to the humanity and compassion of the revered philosopher known to many as the Great Sheikh. At the steps leading down to the main entrance, a small girl runs up to me and says hello and when I reply she skips away to return a few seconds later leading by the hand a very old beggar woman. Feeling slightly annoyed – I'd thought she'd wanted to say hello for its own sake – I simply nod to the child: "Badin," I tell her, dismissively. "Later." Pimping for her grandmother, I note that evening in my notebook, wondering how such an ungracious idea managed to get past my ever-vigilant filter of improper thoughts and attitudes.

I leave my shoes in a pigeonhole just inside the archway that leads through to the inner courtyard before edging past a group of men sitting cross-legged in a circle, chatting. Then I make my way down the steps, pulling my scarf up over my head, before entering the small mausoleum where the guardian – an old man in a gallabiyyah and white taqiyyah – nods and accepts some coins. The room is like many I have seen in Syria – a bizarre mixture of reverence and tat. Ibn Arabi's shrine is remarkably small though this doesn't surprise me. It's how I had imagined him – a short, benign old fellah who, for all his capacity to conceptualise and flit between metaphysical states, could probably enjoy a laugh or two with the locals.

The tomb is made of white marble – though marble that is old and worn – and stands on a plinth covered in black velveteen with gold lettering on it, all this encased within an ornamental brass cage. To give money, you post your offering through a wooden letterbox set into the brass bars and the cash passes down a homemade cardboard chute straight onto the ground within. The cage, I notice, is padlocked: even the guardians of Sufi saints have to be careful, I suppose. There are lots of people who have come to have a look at the old man's shrine, many of them Turkish. I know this because when I try to speak to them in

Arabic they look nonplussed until a man whispers where they are from. The men and women divide, the men disappearing behind a shabby green curtain while the women sit on the ground on the other side of the tomb. The Turkish group have brought their own Imam, the way some package tour groups accompany their favourite radio presenter or DJ, and he emerges from behind the green curtain muttering prayers, followed by the men who all click away with their digital cameras like Japanese tourists. Ibn Arabi's shrine is important to these visitors: Konya, in Turkey, is home to the Mevlavi dervishes. The room is full of plastic: dusty, plastic flowers, plastic lampshades, plastic chairs. Two large, orange plastic water containers stand at the side of the wall with an invitation to visitors to drink: Arab courtesy and kindliness is an ever-present quality. In contrast to the plastic, the ceiling is lit by a chandelier hanging from a green and gold cupola but, when I raise my camera to take a picture of it, I find myself focusing on an ugly pair of over-bright fluorescent tubes within it. Like hospitality, fluorescent tubes, preferably green, are never far away in any Syrian mosque.

I settle down on the floor with my back to the wall and watch a beautiful young woman lift the delicate, diaphanous black veil from in front of her mouth in order to drink some water. How do I know she is beautiful when only her eyes are visible? Perhaps it is the fact that she is tall, her back upright. That her eyes are clear and bright. That her cloak is long and trails behind her so that she walks as if the earth and all its bounty were hers by right. She has a wedding ring on her finger and both her feet and her hands are newly decorated with henna. Maybe she is recently married. Before leaving the shrine room, she stands in front of the guardian who reads aloud from the Qu'ran as the woman with her, possibly her mother, gently pats her back in a companionable way. Between them, the three make a tableau of shared warmth that I can only envy. Suddenly and sharply, this quiet scene is shattered by a small boy who throws the sort of tantrum only possible from a two-year-old. He is incandescent with anger as his mother drags him down the steps to this green-lit room. The guardian, face impassive, digs deep into the pocket of his gallabiyyah, and with fingers made clumsy with age, laboriously fumbles about until he finds what he is looking for – a handful of sweets – which he holds out to the little boy. But the child gives the old man's hand a sharp whack that sends the sweets scattering across the worn carpet. I am horrified and embarrassed for the mother but the guardian raises his hands to heaven, then clasps them together in resignation, looks apologetic as if the outburst were all his fault. The mother fails to be embarrassed, ignores the child and continues talking to her woman friend. The child's angry howling fills the room and no one pays any attention to him nor appears to be annoyed or distracted by him – except me. Later, up in the courtyard, I see him happily playing hide-and-seek among the pillars while his mother chats on her mobile phone.

I pay a quick visit to the main prayer hall from which I had been evicted on my earlier visit and try finally to peer through the barred windows at the back. But the glass is grimed with dirt and the city below is barely visible through the murky cloud of dust and exhaust fumes that lie over it. Instead, I examine the smudged, green photo of a turban-shaped hat, a stick and a padded green cloak said to have belonged to Muhammad, may peace be to him, the caption on the photograph adds. Can these really be his things? Muhammad died 1,300 years ago but then, anything is possible in a country whose history stretches back to a time the rest of us can only dream about.

Outside in the brilliant sunshine, the men sitting round the gate are now scooping up food from a large, communal tray. One of them, a man of about 45 – short, overweight, and who looks as if he has some sort of mental disability – sits among them waiting patiently to be fed. Every so often, the man beside him, breaking off from the laughter and conversation with the rest of the men, unconcernedly feeds some food into the waiting mouth which is open and hungry like a bird. I try not to look but of course I do. Where I come from, middle-aged men like that are often tucked away out of sight, excluded from a society that would prefer everyone to be perfect in mind and body.

In the noisy souk, the little girl is back again and yes, now it *is* later and so I pull some coins out of my purse. I have exactly three which is lucky because I am suddenly assailed by three sets of dirty, clawlike hands. I distribute the money to the three beggars and clearly the first one doesn't think much of it but I am unmoved, determined not to respond to my conditioning which requires me to be embarrassed into giving more.

Beggars are people we have difficulty dealing with because, in a capitalist society, to be poor is a cardinal sin. Don't give to beggars, a sign at the railway station back home admonishes would-be givers. Instead, we should make our charitable donations to an organised body like Oxfam. Here, people simply give without wasting time agonising over it. Nearby, I notice a veiled woman, standing close to the steps of the mosque, who is distributing bread to anyone who might like some. She has lots of takers. Another woman is handing out plastic bags filled with bits of bread and as she gives one to an old man, a small boy tries to grab it from him. I am confused. Do you give or do you take? Can one beggar pinch from another beggar? I don't know the answers to these questions since I am not from here. What I need is a beggar disguised as a do-gooder with a collection box telling me what he's collecting for and the number of the bank account in case I want to give even more. I want a little sticker I can wear to show I have already given so that people can see how good I am and, more importantly, so that other beggars with their collecting boxes don't bother me.

The souk now has the feel of a film adaptation of a Charles Dickens' novel. All the stereotypes are here: people on crutches, beggars, stallholders, hens, kindly women, pretty little girls, skinny dogs, naughty boys. A middle-aged man, not unlike the one being fed in the courtyard, short of stature and fat, not overly clean, clasps his arms round a much taller man, rubbing his head delightedly against the other man's chest. The tall man is delighted as well, guffawing, allowing himself to be hugged by his diminutive fan. The tall man holds a piece of bread in one hand and a cigarette in the other but somehow manages to repeatedly kiss the hand of the smaller man, both of them laughing uproariously while all I can do, in my mean-spirited way, is wonder how he can bear to bring his mouth in contact with such a dirty hand.

There is something comforting about the sense of community that seems to surround Ibn Arabi's mosque, as if his presence is still felt by the local people. Like many thinkers, he has the capacity to speak of great ideas in a simple, understandable manner. But the Great Sheikh is long dead and I would really like to meet someone who can give me some first-hand information about contemporary Sufism. For this, I'm told, I must go to Aleppo and so, when I get back down to the city, I check the buses and yes, there is one leaving from Harasta Garage early tomorrow morning.

"I'm off to Aleppo tomorrow," I tell Saleh as I pour out some water for my chai furaat. "Lots of Kurdish people there," he says wistfully and returns to his doleful task of scraping a squashed grape from the tiled floor of the courtyard, using the edge of a metal ashtray for the job.

Chapter 21

The swaying woman of Aleppo

I never saw her face, only her tall, slight frame clad in a black hooded cloak that fell from her head to her feet in perfect grace, belying nothing of the form that it concealed. Despite the hood and aware that I was transgressing, I nevertheless tried to imagine her face – skin soft as olives, eyes closed – as she pressed it against the grille, her pale fingers gripping the mesh, her body swaying slightly back and forth, back and forth, her whole being yearning towards something only she knew about. Or did she?

> *I have lived on the lip of insanity,*
> *wanting to know reasons,*
> *knocking on a door. It opens.*
> *I've been knocking from the inside!*
>
> *al Rumi*

Tariq has put me in touch with Hanno, who has agreed to help me get in touch with Sheikh Jamal al Din Hilali whose grandfather initiated the Hilali Tariqa and we meet at Aleppo's Bab Qinnesrin, the main gate which leads into the old city. Hanno is a marvellous guide – this is, after all, his own city and together we walk round it.

Anyone unwise enough to attack Aleppo had to work their way through a series of gates, the first of which was a siege gate with an iron grid that dropped down to protect those within. After that, the intruders had to fight their way through three other gates, one after the other, while running the very real risk of having boiling oil poured down on them from a hole set in the roof of the supporting arches. But that was long ago. The day is sunny and, as we walk through the gates into the narrow cobbled streets closed off by high walls, I wonder if this was what Baghdad was like in the time of Haroun al Rashid. Robed figures hurry along before disappearing round a corner. A door in the wall opens and closes quietly. A child's voice calls out and then is still. I can sense mystery and intrigue everywhere but have to remind myself that this is the 21st century and that if intrigue is simmering it is most likely happening in faraway London or Paris or wherever dissidents and the discontented gather to plot the future.

Aleppo is in the process of being restored – with the help of foreign money – though this is a mixed blessing for local people who have to leave their traditional homes and move to modern flats while their former homes are turned into upmarket restaurants and art galleries. We walk through a tangle of cobbled lanes, quiet and clean but devoid of people, passing the Karimiya mosque where a mark in a stone is said to be the footprint of the Prophet. Hanno peers in through doorways and gates and eventually spots a gate marked 10. We have arrived at the Mosque al Zawia where I am to meet the Sheikh. There are about 12 tombstones in the small courtyard, family ones mostly, and all strewn with green sprays of sweet basil. Hanno goes into the prayer hall but returns with bad news. Although it had earlier been agreed I should be allowed into the mosque during Friday prayers, the Sheikh has now decided otherwise. Hanno, however, may go in for although he is a Christian and not a Muslim, he is a man. I, however, am found wanting being neither Muslim nor male. Then the Sheikh relents and sends out an emissary: I may go into the prayer hall but will have to enter one of the small rooms off it. That way, the men will be heard but not seen and they will be unable to see me. I will not be a distraction. Amazingly, it seems as if I might be some sort of sex object. The wrangling continues. Inside, I will be warmer and will be able to hear the men chanting but, to all intents and purposes, I will be veiled. Outside, I will be chilly but I will be able to hear and, by peering through the mesh on the windows, will be able to get a view, albeit a slanted one, of what is going on inside. I opt to stay outside and that is how I am able also to observe the Muslim woman who, like me, is an outsider yet not an outsider. I sit on the concrete steps and peer through the mesh window. The prayer hall is small, wood-panelled and though it has the regulatory chandelier, it is lit only with natural light coming in through the windows opposite which are set high in the wall. The Sheikh stands in front of the men, wearing a black robe and a cream turban with a tassel in its top. He looks about 60 and has dark skin, a greying beard and sharp, bright eyes. As more men enter, they approach him to make their greeting. The more devout ones try to take his hand in both theirs and kiss it but this he discourages, flicking away their hands in an almost irritable fashion so that I feel sorry for them in their apparent rejection.

The men form a semicircle in rows two and three deep. Some wear suits with open-necked shirts. Some are in jeans and T-shirts and some are in the leatherette jerkins that are so popular here. A few wear black or brown robes, white headscarves flowing from their white taqiyyahs. One man wears a woolly cap over his white cap. Shoes pile up at the door as everyone settles down and the chanting can begin. It starts as a low murmur, growing to a growl, then gaining strength as it becomes louder and faster. And as it does, the men standing shoulder to shoulder begin to sway in one movement, rhythmically, gracefully and in perfect harmony. A late arrival sweeps in wearing a black cloak and under it a white gown. On his head is a white turban from which wafts a long piece of white muslin. He looks like an extra from a bad movie set in Morocco and tremendously sexy in a stereotypical sort of way but I sternly adjust my thoughts in keeping with the spiritual occasion I am witnessing. He goes to stand on one side of the Sheikh. Standing on the Sheikh's other side is a man of about 30 dressed in a single-breasted, oddly old-fashioned, grey suit. Incongruously, he reminds me of the English artists Gilbert and George. Who on earth can he be? A visiting tourist allowed a privileged position? A member of some other Tariqah,

perhaps? Whichever it is, he looks strangely ill at ease and I
have to wonder why he's there. As other men arrive, the Sheikh
greets them without interrupting the flow of the chanting and,
now that I am getting the hang of it, I realise they are chanting
the word Allah! Allah! Allah! Sometimes, the men drone the
word while a solo singer takes up the chant, his voice rising and
falling until, at some given moment, he sounds a single note on
a higher pitch and the men, picking this up, move into a chant
on the same note. It is mesmerising and I find myself trying
to discern the individual notes and syllables, focusing on one
sound as the men hone the edges of the vowels – al-ham-dhu,
al-ham-dhu – faster and faster so that three syllables elide into
two and finally one: ham-dhu, ham-dhu, ham-dhu, ham, ham,
ham, ham, ham, ham. Then, at a sign from the solo singer the
men switch to il-law, il-law, law, law, law, law and all the time
moving, twice to the right and twice to the left, right and left
and sometimes to and fro, to and fro, all to a 1, 2, 3, 4 beat, the
Sheikh, like a conductor, using his hands to control the speed
and then slowing down the chanting with a calming movement.

An old man breaks away from the group and pads out into
the courtyard for a smoke. Two small boys sitting barefoot on
the step below me beat out the rhythm with their shoes. Then
the solo singer, hitting a high note, holds it before intoning
an Amin, the soft sound slow as a dying breath. The woman
clasping the window mesh moves her yearning body closer to the
window. Another woman enters from the street and walks from
one tombstone to the next, laying her forehead on each one. An
hour has passed and I am growing cold. Inside, the light of the
sun catches the crystals in the chandelier and they shine bright
red, green, yellow. The singing starts again, softly but relentlessly,
Illahu, Illahu, Illahu. The Sheikh increases the tempo by slicing
downwards with his hands. The chanting is louder, faster and
through the window mesh I can feel heat coming off the bodies
of the men. There is a slight pause, a fragment of silence before
the solo singer hits a C then soars upwards to a G taking the men

with him, up and away. The solitary woman coughs, reminding me of how chilly the late afternoon air has become. Inside, the Sheikh rocks backwards and forwards and I dearly wish to be inside, to be part of what is going on.

The chanting rises to another crescendo – each one as unbearable in its anticipation as the last one – and the men chant al-law, al-law, al-law, the final syllable shortening to one sharp, staccato sound: al! al! al! Then suddenly the men are swaying silently, powering onwards like a great ship whose engine has been turned off. The Sheikh's hand maintains the beat and I realise they are whispering the word al-law, al-law, al-law. Suddenly, a single voice rises above the men's like a blues singer picking up the lament and the men join in this time singing in unison, their voices sweet and melodic.

I have been advised not to take any photographs but surreptitiously I take one of the woman, my finger pressing the shutter button stiff with cold so I can only imagine what hers must be like. Inside, the light is fading, the men no more than shadowy shapes; the crystals in the chandelier darkening to nocturnal blue and finally to nothing. As the Sheikh leaves the prayer hall and sweeps through the courtyard followed by his entourage, Hanno intercedes on my behalf, requesting a meeting.

The Sheikh pauses briefly: "How long?" he asks. "Three hours?"

I panic. Three hours is more than enough for me to reveal my ignorance of all things Sufi.

"And at what time?" he asks, "Early?"

"Would it be convenient if I came at nine in the morning?" I ask.

"Perhaps nine thirty is better," murmurs Hanno. Is it relief I see on the Sheikh's face? In Syria, nine in the morning is an ungodly hour even to the Godly.

Next morning, we visit the prayer hall and I discover that the wall-panels are doors that open onto tiny, windowless cells with just enough room for one person to sit or stand. Here, in the days of the Sheikh's grandfather, Sufis would spend their time of retreat in contemplation, sometimes up to 40 days and always during Ramadan, avoiding meat and trying not to sleep too much.

"This building is over four hundred years old," the Sheikh tells me. "It was much smaller originally but two hundred years ago my grandfather extended it and then my father did as well." I am puzzled. Surly the Sheikh's grandfather did the extension less than 200 years ago. "I think he made a small mistake with the years," whispers Hanno when we are out of earshot. We climb the steps which I had sat on yesterday, and go into an ornate room furnished with French rococo chairs. In one corner is a glass case with fragile Georgian legs, housing a copy of the Qu'ran. In front of the Sheikh is a small marble-topped table on which rests a mobile phone and an ashtray. An air conditioner stands in one corner.

The Sheikh sits on a glorious throne-like chair upholstered in red with gold-painted arms. Hanno and I sit opposite each other on tiny Regency-style settees covered in red damask. The grandeur makes me horribly aware of my walking sandals and grubby toenails. The Sheikh speaks with a slight German accent, a leftover from the time he'd spent studying in Germany before being recalled to Aleppo on the death of his father. I ask my first question and quickly realise that this will be more a discourse on Sufism than a question and answer session and for that I am relieved. We begin at the beginning. All things, the Sheikh tells me, were created by God so that there is no conflict between Islam and other religions since Islam encompasses all of them. First, there was Judaism, then Christianity and finally Islam which is the last word. The goal of the Sufi is to keep a balance between religion, people and God. If he can achieve this, he will relieve his soul of all disease. Education is important to Sufism though not everyone needs to be conversant with the sciences such as astronomy, mathematics and the nuclear sciences. I try to slip in a question but fail. The sciences, the Sheikh continues, are mentioned in the Qu'ran. God created the sun, which represents life, and the moon, which represents enlightenment, and we have the planets for calculations. Knowledge of all these brings us closer to God. Talk of the sun and the moon makes my mind wander and I slip in a question. "Does Islam mark the solstices," I ask and press on quickly. "Because in Ireland, before Christianity, the winter solstice was an important time when the holy men – our druids – held ceremonies related to the planting of seeds. It is still celebrated in Newgrange every year on 21 December."

I consider adding that the great chamber at Newgrange is older than the pyramids but then decide not to. Something that happened 5,000 years ago is only yesterday relative to Syria's impressive timeline. In any case, he is not really interested in Newgrange and shrugs away my inconsequential question. "Islam is all-embracing," he continues without faltering, "so every season has its own time. In the Islamic world, which is very big, the arrival time of each climate is different." His own background is in medicine, which is what he was studying in Germany, and his special interest is genetics. "Islam is older than any genetic science," he tells me. Oddly, I find I have finished writing this sentence before the Sheikh has finished speaking it. This is because I have become used to hearing that Islam is the most compassionate, the greatest, the most all-embracing religion in the world and wonder if this need to talk about Islam in a manner which some would see as boastful is due to the fact that the intellectualism of the Arabs has never been universally acknowledged. They feel undervalued and under-appreciated in areas of study at which they have excelled.

The Sheikh locks his long, olive-skinned fingers together and is about to resume his discourse when a man enters the room. It's the man I saw yesterday, wearing a grey suit and standing beside the Sheikh. He is still ill at ease as if terrified he is going to commit some unspeakable solecism such as tripping over the carpet, spilling coffee on the Sheikh's turban or passing round a plate of biscuits among which nestles one he has already taken a bite from. It emerges that he is the Sheikh's only son who one day will succeed him. The son, his shoulders slightly bent in what seems an obsequious manner, moves across the room to check the coffee pot on the electric ring, then leaves as silently as he had entered while his father moves on to secular matters. In the old days, he tells me, people made donations, called wagf, to the mosques and the Zawiyah Tariqah had many generous supporters. In fact, most mosques owed their existence to the generous endowments made by benefactors.

"This allowed us to have meetings and discussions about some of the things we have been talking about this morning," the Sheikh tells me. "We had retreats when people withdrew into the prayer hall for weeks on end. Then, in 1952, the state stepped in, appointed an imam and made people donate to its own Ministry of Wagf so that everyone had to make their donations directly to the state which then dispensed the money as it thought fit. This meant we were left short with only enough to open the mosque once a week for dhikr." When I discussed this later with Hanno, he explained that Syria is now a modern country, with, he implied, little room for dervishes. It is at this point that the Sheikh pauses, reaches into his trousers pocket and pulls out a packet of cigarettes, offering one to me and to Hanno before lighting up.

I have to quickly conceal my surprise. How is it that a medical man smokes and seems unaware that he is a health risk to others. Instead, he puffs away unconcernedly and, coward-like, I fail to ask him not to. In any case, he has just mentioned the important word dhikr, the most binding message in the Qu'ran whereby the faithful are exhorted to keep Allah to the forefront of their minds at all times. It is similar, I imagine, to the Buddhist cultivation of awareness.

The Sufis developed their own system for remembering Allah by repeatedly chanting his various names and though each tariqah has its own way of doing this the most common form is to chant la'illaha illa Allah. This is the first part of the shahadah – the proclamation stating that there is no God but God and Muhammad is his Prophet: la ilaha illa'illah, Muhammadun rasulullah illa-illah. The son re-enters the room and scuttles about. He serves each of us a small cup of coffee which is so bitter I fail to hide the involuntary grimace that comes to my face. The Sheikh drinks his in one go and continues his talk: "In our dhikr, we start with the word llah – a simple statement. Then we move on to the statement that there is only one God – wahid illah. Sometimes, we address him as ya Allah. Then we move to allahuma which means all in one God and finally we simply chant Allah usually in a very low voice."

He lights up a second cigarette: "Do you know how many times our hearts beat in a minute?"

I think it's something to do with 70 but wait to be told.

"70," he says.

"What I try to do is get people to double that so that we are chanting the name of Allah close to 140 times in a minute. We say Allah on the blood going in and Allah on the blood going out," and he opens and closes his hands quickly like the beat of a heart. Trying surreptitiously to breathe at that speed, I find myself gasping for air. We have been here over an hour but there are two things I still want to ask about – violence and women. The occupation of Iraq continues as does that of Palestine with jihad seeming to be the only option open to resisters. Back in Damascus, Tariq's small son is called Jihad for the word simply means struggle, not always of a physically violent nature. But if the jihad we are talking of here is about killing can it be tolerated?

"It is if it is carried out in self-defence."

"If people have a choice – to live or die. What then?"

I think of all the Syrians who have told me that they would rather die than suffer under foreign occupation. For myself, I would always choose to live. Death seems a cul-de-sac of an option and besides, I can never think of anything for which I would die. Plenty I would live for. But die? The Sheikh seems to prevaricate. Since it is inconceivable that an Arab would choose

Sufi Sheikh Jamal al Din Hilali of Hilali Tariqa, Aleppo

not to fight and die for his freedom and for his religion, does this apply to Sufis?

"If your leader felt you were not well-prepared, it might be better to surrender."

I'm too polite to comment on the unlikelihood of an Arab man surrendering and instead move on to my last question which is about women and Sufism. He nods: "There are women Sufis. Very famous ones. Rabi'a al Adawiyya is one. She was from Basra, in Iraq. But no, we don't have women here in the Zawiya. There is no place for them in the prayer hall. It wasn't designed like that when my grandfather built it. Women can listen outside, of course. The woman who came yesterday has been coming for about one year though when I was a child there were about twenty women who came. They used to meet in my grandmother's house. But for psychological reasons it is not good to have women."

Rabi'a al Adawiyya, who was raised as a slave, is the most famous and cherished of female Sufis. Her life was one of asceticism and detachment and her driving belief was that people should do things for their own sake – giving alms, caring for others – rather than because the rule book required it, even if that book were the Qu'ran. The Sheikh drinks from his coffee cup, closes his eyes: "The basis of Islam is to build up and increase the universe by having children. The idea of not marrying is not in Islam. Though that doesn't mean people cannot withdraw from life from time to time. In any case, Islam says it is best to work, to make money, to leave your children richer rather than poorer."

His own son, he tells me, wants to work in agriculture and is completing a postgraduate degree in Switzerland in food chemistry. We have strayed so far from the spiritual path that I decide to risk asking if I might take a photo. He is delighted. Would I like him to put on his cloak, he asks. He's wearing a dark suit, white shirt and grey V-necked jumper and doesn't look a bit like a Sufi Sheikh.

"That would be great. Thank you."

"And my turban. Would you like that as well?"

"Please."

He puts on the black cloak, draping it round himself carefully then, settling the red and cream turban on his head, turns to face the lens. I'm glad to have been able to talk to Sheikh Hilali but somehow the cigarettes, the certainty of his rightness and the posing for the photographs seem to diminish the spiritual aspect of the whole thing. As we go back down the steps again, I wonder if I shouldn't have stuck with dear old Ibn Arabi and his 12th century tariqah.

Chapter 22

*"The stars are setting and the Caravan starts
for the Dawn of Nothing – oh, make haste."*

Omar Khayyam

"I want to get to Baghdad," I tell Ahmad. "As soon as possible." Shortly after the attack on New York's Trade Centre and, in retaliation, the US government was threatening to bomb either Iraq or Afghanistan. Or both. A gut feeling told me it would be Afghanistan first, followed by Iraq, but that the latter would take a bit longer to organise – and to justify. Ahead lay all the rubbish about dictatorship, democracy and weapons of mass destruction. I decided to make a run for it and be in and out of the country before anyone knew I'd been there.

"It's not a problem," says Ahmad. "Just tell me when you want to go and I'll fix up a taxi for you."

I pack my rucksack, putting in a change of clothes, my camera, palmtop computer, notebook and a few biros. Secreted among all this I tuck away a roll of US dollars, mainly $50s with a few $10s – a decision I was later to regret. On top of this I fit in the Rory Bremner DVD requested by my host at the Indian Embassy in Baghdad and given to me by Bremner himself, an outspoken opponent of the UN sanctions against Iraq. Most importantly, I check I have the right passport. No self-respecting Arab country will admit someone with an Israeli stamp in their passport. Because I travel to Israel and Palestine from time to time – I have friends on both sides of the divide – I have to have two passports which can lead to the recurrent nightmare that I'm carrying the wrong one. Each passport tells its own story. I treasure the one with the graceful cedar of Lebanon stamped on it, from the time when Israel occupied Lebanon; the large stamp of the Republic of Georgia with a hologram that spreads across two pages; the shamrock used by the Carribean island of Montserrat. The passport I have now, however, has an Iraqi visa bought in a small, nondescript mews building in London, a flamboyant stamp with an image of the temple of Ishtar at Babylon and emblazoned with Saddam's three-starred flag of the Republic of Iraq. Lastly, I put in the notes I made in the Bodleian Library about Baghdad's most well-known Caliph – Haroun al Rashid. I am on a mission to discover something of the Baghdad of Alf Laylah wa Laylah.

There is a brisk trade in taxis between the two cities and, two evenings later, I walk with Ahmad to al Thowra Street where a spacious General Motors taxi, bearing the distinctive band of orange paint indicating an Iraqi registration, is waiting for me, its engine drumming.

I unroll five US$10 bills which will take me the 700 kilometres to Baghdad. Ahmad, I assume, will get a small cut. There is one other passenger, a woman, who pulls her scarf around her face and shrinks back into the darkness of the back seat when I open the car door. Her husband – a tall, strongly-built man in an open-necked shirt – is there to say goodbye to her. His wife is Baghdadi, he says, but he is from northern Iraq and can't go back, from which I guess that he's a Kurd and therefore a threatened species in Iraq. Saddam's terrible crimes against the Kurds are well-known. The constant shuttle of taxis between Damascus and Baghdad is no accident. The two countries have had a long on-off political love affair. In the 1930s and 1940s many young Syrians arrived in Baghdad to study, their minds filled with despair at the takeover of Palestine by the fledging state of Israel, a move sanctioned by the UN and by Europe and thus perceived by the Arabs as yet one more humiliating defeat.

Tapping into this unrest were two young Syrian teachers, Michel Aflaq and Salah al Bitar who, in 1943, formed the Ba'ath Party – the name means renaissance. The aim of the Ba'athists was to promote unity among Arab peoples under the

twin banners of secularism and socialism. Alliances were forged
and broken many times over. Relations between Iraq and Syria
finally soured when the former invaded Kuwait, a move which
led to Syria closing most of its border with Iraq with the sections
that remained open heavily patrolled.

Despite this public falling-out, there is a continuing swell
of social intercourse between the two countries with Iraqi taxi
drivers, basing themselves in a suburb of Damascus, rarely short
of a fare. Ahmad hands my dollars to the driver who, leaning on
the bonnet of his car, counts them out one by one and then we're
off, trundling through the night-time traffic of Damascus, heading
north then east for the desert road to Palmyra but branching off to
the right to make the border crossing. In the midnight dark, the
car speeds across the desert, along a straight road unhindered by
roundabouts or traffic lights. The Baghdadi woman sleeps but I
clutch the seat in front of me, aware that the driver has probably
come along the route, in the opposite direction, only 24 hours
previously and is unlikely to have had much sleep. I know enough
about the macho image, which is not one confined to Arabs, to
remember that such men wear their long hours of wakefulness
as a badge of manliness. And so my fingers tighten on the back
of his seat as I will him to stay awake through the long night. I
get some dubious consolation from the fact that I have recently
renewed my travel insurance, which included a paragraph on Iraq
in which I undertook to enter the country by road and not by air.
If the actuaries think it's safer by car then it must be.

Suddenly, through a windscreen spidered with cracks, I see a
huge truck hurtling straight for us, its headlights whipping the
darkness like avenging swords. Crying out, I close my eyes and
lower my head for the inevitable crash. Curiously, the truck, in
some disembodied state, passes over us and I find I am still alive.
My cry of fear makes both the driver and the woman turn to
look at me and in my embarrassment, I pretend to be scrabbling
about on the floor of the car for my purse. I try to work out what
has happened and decide that, in a half-awake state, I had seen

the truck approaching along a right-hand bend which meant its headlights were trained on the taxi until the resolving moment when both vehicles passed each other on parallel courses. The Baghdadi woman, unsmiling, continues to stare at me, making me feel foolish.

Somewhere along the route, we stop at a large roadside café, blindingly lit by fluorescent tubes, the vast, noisy canteen full of truck drivers and coachloads of people travelling to and from Baghdad. Courteously, my driver buys me a cup of tea and directs me to a corner of the café set aside for women, before joining a few other taxi drivers on the other side of the room. The tea is bitter but I drink it because it is scaldingly hot and the desert night is freezing.

At 3am we reach the Syrian/Iraqi border. The customs sheds at the crossing are lit with huge brute lights that leach the blackness out of the night, turning everything a sickly grey. Before getting out of the taxi, I check again that I have all my papers in order – passport with visa stamped in it, letter of invitation from my friend at the Indian Embassy, letter from the Iraqi Embassy in London acknowledging and accepting as valid the letter of invitation. Cash, some of it obvious, some stacked away but all of it in US dollars. The driver points me across the road and down some steps to a room in a huge, high-roofed building. The room is crowded with men, some in robes and keffiyehs, others in cheap European-style clothes, with more than a hint of 1980s about them. Everyone is pushing and shoving and waving their papers in the air as if somehow the very energy they are expending will work a miracle and get them up to the window where they will be dealt with. The high proportion of women veiled and in black makes me think they are returning from a visit to Ruqqayah's Mosque in Damascus.

I join the small queue of people who don't have Iraqi passports and work my way to the top of the line. The official glances up at me, doesn't smile but nods: "Ahlan. Welcome," he says and I am through to the next round. In the big, draughty customs hall,

I join everyone else and put my belongings on a wooden counter for inspection. Beside me, a woman in a hijab places her worn brown cardboard case on the counter and waits for it to be opened. This task is performed by a short little man with a moustache and a leatherette jerkin whom I had met outside in the chilly windswept car park.

"You speak English?" he had asked smilingly and I had been relieved to find someone I could talk to. His English was good and his manner helpful and in the spirit of camaraderie, he had introduced me to four of his friends who were standing about doing nothing much. Border officials, I decided. There to welcome foreign visitors. They were the first Iraqis I met at the crossing and when I commiserated with them in their time of trial they nodded and smiled sadly.

Now here's my new friend in an unexpected role: that of obsequious acolyte to the customs inspector who wears a peaked hat, a military uniform and a chilly expression on his face.

"Name?"

"Mary Russell."

"From where?"

"Ireland."

"Ireland?"

"Yes."

To give himself time to think about this, he turns back to the woman beside me who waits patiently for attention. Deftly, the obsequious acolyte flips up the top of her case, presents its contents to the inspector with a flourish as if it were all his own work and then stands back modestly, his job done. I glance at the case: on top are scarves, a blue top, flip-flops, a folded hijab, a bra. The two men stare down into the privacy of the woman's possessions so cruelly laid bare. At a sign from the inspector, the obsequious acolyte rummages through the woman's underwear while she looks straight ahead, expressionless. At the end of the examination, the inspector waves an impatient hand and the woman and case are dismissed.

And then it's my turn to expose myself. Silently, we all stare at the incriminating contents of my rucksack – computer, camera, pen – all weapons that can be used to promote both truth and untruth. Why on earth had I brought them I ask myself. The answer is that they are the tools of my trade. To leave them behind in Damascus was too risky. Someone might find them, fiddle about with them, lose them, drop them. The thought is unbearable. The men confer and decide I must be referred to a higher authority. The obsequious acolyte directs me to another room, informing me – his smile becoming even more servile – that I must pay for his services. I know, of course, that with the sanctions and the regime, the ordinary Iraqi has very little money and what they have cannot buy much and that payment of this sort – let's call it tipping – is another if irregular source of income. And so I open my purse, remembering too late that I have forgotten to stock up in small denomination dollar bills. I give him a US$10 bill which I know is probably too much but this is Iraq and I am a visitor here. He bows and puts his hand to his breast in a gesture of gratitude then directs me into the next interrogation room where the technical experts await. I lay my electronic wares on the table hoping that no one takes a liking to anything on display.

"What is this?" one of the experts asks, holding up the computer.

"A radio," I lie and the obsequious acolyte steps forward smartly to open the computer and display its non-existent radio potential. Nothing happens as of course a password is required.

"It doesn't work," I apologise. "No batteries in it. It is of no use to me here in Iraq," I continue in order to set their minds at rest. Nevertheless, the computer and the camera are put to one side and I am directed to another room, this time to be questioned by a senior military person who sits behind an empty desk. This is a man of about 50, tired of a desk job which has been assigned to him probably because his shelf-life will soon expire. He looks at the British Medical Association journals I have brought with me to give to any doctors I might meet in Baghdad.

"What are these?" I explain that they carry up-to-date research and news of medical progress which doctors here may not have been able to get – on account of the erratic postal system in the UK, I hastily add.

But when he gets up, walks to the door and closes it, I suddenly feel a slight chill. I have lost track of the time but guess it is about 4am. I have no idea where my taxi driver is, no one knows I am here and without my computer I don't have the phone number of my friend in Baghdad. My interviewer returns, sits down again, moves his military cap from one side of the desk to the other and says: "You have to pay me."

"Pay you? For what?"

He has caught me unawares. This man, of some status in this sad, dreary outpost, with brass buttons and a room all to himself, has had to grovel just like the wretched little acolyte outside. I see shame and embarrassment in his eyes and I too am embarrassed to see him brought so low. Nevertheless, I shake my head.

"No. I am not paying you. I have given a small amount of money to the man outside but I am not giving anything to you."

The fact of the matter is that I don't have any small dollar bills and can't afford to part with my last US$10. Added to this is the small, inner voice advising me not to be intimidated by my surroundings.

"No?" He looks at me, expressionless.

"No." I hate being a witness to his humiliation but he shrugs, gets up, hands me the medical journals then adds to my misery by shaking my hand.

The air outside is chill, the noise of engines unrelenting and there is no sign of my taxi. Close by, I notice a man of about 30 also waiting. By his clothes – thin T-shirt, unkempt jeans, rucksack – I guess he is British and I am right: he's Scottish. Thankful to be able to speak English, we chat for quite a while about where we're going, what we'll do in Baghdad, where we'll stay. It seems he's come to visit his sister who has been living there with her Baghdadi husband, a doctor, for the last 20 years.

He has just turned up out of the blue. She doesn't know he's coming and he has no idea where he will stay in Baghdad. People have given him a few hotel addresses. He doesn't speak Arabic but he's sure he'll manage. Compared to my own carefully laid plans, his insouciance is impressive. Then my taxi turns up and we say goodbye never, I assume, to meet again. Except that, a few weeks later, while meeting a friend off a plane from London at Damascus airport, I run into him. He is deep in conversation with a man in a smart suit who looks as if he is a Syrian. I wave to the Scot but though he sees me he doesn't acknowledge my wave and I get the impression he doesn't want to be seen talking to me. When the Arab man moves away, I go over to him: "Hi. How are you? On your way home?"

He looks at me blankly: "I'm sorry," he says. "I think you've made a mistake."

"No. We met at the Iraqi border," I remind him. "You were going to pay your sister a surprise visit." He shakes his head and stands up: "You've got the wrong person," he says. "I've never met you before." And then he disappears into the airport crowd.

The taxi driver says I now have to go to the medical centre for my anti-Aids injection. This is the real obstacle, the one I have been dreading. To enter Iraq, you must have either a certificate stating you are Aids free which may or may not be accepted by the border guards, or you have to submit to having an anti-Aids injection right here in this hell-like place of dilapidated buildings, diesel fumes, revving truck engines, glaring lights and men with their hands out. I could offer the excuse that I am not sexually active but how do you say that in Arabic? And in any case, this is not, as I learn, the point of the exercise. The driver takes me to a floodlit prefab building with a red cross on it which I assume is the medical centre. Here, a woman in a white coat listens to me and shakes her head.

"Did they not tell you?" she asks.

"Tell me what?"

"That you have to pay."

"Pay? For what? How much?"

"It's fifty dollars to have the injection," she pauses and I close my eyes and wait. "But sixty dollars not to have it."

I am delirious with joy. Not for the first time, those who make the rules are also those who provide you with the means to break them. The driver collects me from the medical checkpoint but, as we move away, there's a scrabbling at the window: it's the obsequious little acolyte.

"You have to pay him some money," explains the driver.

"For what? I gave him ten dollars just now."

"She gave you ten dollars just now," the driver says to the man.

"Yes," agrees the acolyte. "But I shared that with my four friends and now I have nothing for myself."

Defeated, I root about in my rucksack and hand over my last US$10 bill and we pull away.

When, at about 7am and an hour short of my destination, I get the driver to stop so that I can take a picture of the rising sun balancing on the rim of the desert horizon, I am finally ready for whatever Baghdad may have to offer.

Chapter 23

"Beyond the stars, it is always yesterday."

Robert Casey

Morning rush hour in Baghdad and the streets are gridlocked with traffic: battered Ladas, decrepit Studebakers, war-weary Chevrolets, their hingeless doors held on with wire, rope, string. Handles strapped in place with row upon row of useless Sellotape, the cracks in shattered windscreens radiating outwards in a tangled maze of spiders' legs. Cars converge on a roundabout like darts thrown at the bull's-eye on a dartboard, each one aimed at the same exit point where all movement is brought to a disconsolate halt. Disorder reigns here and, throughout Baghdad, reigns over a people whose faces are grey with tiredness: Iraq is in its 11th year of UN-imposed sanctions, its citizens are suffering and worse is on the way.

Then something lumbers in to my line of vision, a double-decker bus, and I am transported back into a London traffic jam except that this bus is worn and battle-scarred, its grubby windows filled with the faces of exhausted people. Later, I learn that these buses are part of Iraq's complex wheeler-dealer survival strategy whereby some things have their shelf-life eked out by the Oil for Food programme and by the actions of those governments who, for a variety of reasons, want to retain their trading relations with this beleaguered country. The double-deckers, then, with their bodies made in China and their engines in Germany, are a bizarre melding of one of the country's survival strategies.

My Damascus taxi inches through the traffic, past ungainly chunks of high-rise concrete that some people are forced to call home. Past broken paving stones, market stalls selling cheap cooking oil, bric-a-brac from China, plastic chairs.

Past the Rashid Hotel where there is a floor mosaic of George Bush right inside the entrance. Past delapidated Ottoman houses whose balconies hang dangerously by a single piece of timber. Past enormous hoardings carrying images of Saddam Hussein in his many guises: Saddam, the guardian of the nation's future, surrounded by smiling children; Saddam, the devoted Muslim kneeling to pray; Saddam, the Iraqi huntsman in his trademark trilby with a gun over his arm and a dog at his heel; Saddam, the saviour of his people, in full military uniform, leading Iraqis to victory over western imperialism. We pass a building site which was formerly Baghdad's old airport on which the British, during their protectorate, used to display their military aircraft. Now it has ten cranes on it because here is being built the biggest, best, most magnificent mosque in the whole world, higher than any other mosque – though not as high as the nearby presidential palace. We move into Tahrir Square with its huge, 20 foot high bronze statue of Saddam Hussein and speed across a large impressive, six-lane, two-tiered bridge with just enough time for me to read on a poster that it is called the Leader's Bridge.

"Which leader is that?" I ask the driver and he sighs wearily: "Madam, there is only one leader. Our great leader."

And then the moment I have been waiting for: my first sight of the Djila known to us westerners as the Tigris. With relief, I turn away from today's reality for it is the Baghdad that no longer exists that I want to find: the great metropolis watered by its legendary river; the Baghdad that figures in pre-Islamic texts, set in a region which had been a major focus of learning, a source of civilisations so numerous I start to make a mental list of them: the Sumerians who, in 4000BCE, gave us the plough and the wheel and, thereby the means to control water supplies. After them, the Babylonians, among whose gifts were the signs of the zodiac as well as the sexagesimal system of calculating time whereby we still, to this day, assign 60 minutes to the hour and 60 seconds to the minute. These same people gave us the first written laws codified by King Hammurabi, a lawmaker so cherished and admired that a bas relief of him is to be found on the wall of the House of Representatives in Washington.

Hammurabi's laws, published for all to see on an eight foot stela, were an early example of judicial transparency though something of a pointless gesture since few people at that time could read. The stela is now in the Louvre. His laws regulated social and commercial areas such as professional fees, the hire of slaves and the conduct of freemen – though they could be harsh at times: adulterers were to be bound hand and foot and thrown into the Tigris.

Sitting in the traffic jam, a terrible yearning enters my soul as the shadows of a past Baghdad flicker like distant lightning across the grey buildings of this suffering city, the once-glorious city that spawned Alf Laylah wa Laylah; the city of the great Abbasid Caliph Haroun al Rashid and of his compassionate wife Zubeidah; the city of the poet, Abu Nawas, whose homoerotic poetry is as humourous as it is confrontational. Baghdad is the city that survived a sacking by the Mongols in 1258, endured 300 years of occupation by the Ottomans not to mention 70 years of a British Protectorate.

"I'm getting to be rather a dab at Arab politics," wrote Gertrude Bell "but it doesn't make them seem the easier. We've shouldered a gigantic task, but I can't see what the alternative is." Under her cover as an archaeologist, Bell worked in Baghdad for British intelligence, from 1917 until her death here in 1926, supplying her superiors with lists of the names of Iraqis she felt might cause them grief.

In 1941 came an attempted intervention by pro-Nazi factions within Iraq, followed by the re-entry of Britain. Saddam Hussein, then a child of four, saw his uncle, who was also his guardian, imprisoned for his armed resistance to that particular British incursion. Now, the people of Baghdad live out their lives against a background of never-ending hardship imposed serially by their leader and by his one-time foreign supporters in the UN.

The American writer, Robert Casey, visiting Baghdad two years after Gertrude Bell's death wrote that he found it a "dust heap – odorous, unattractive and hot, its monuments (are) few, its buildings too modern to merit attention, its atmosphere that of squalor and poverty." He was probably right about the dereliction. The ruling Ottomans had shown little interest in restoring Baghdad's historic buildings or even maintaining those they themselves had built. Unlike Damascus, Baghdad was, architecturally, in a sorry state, its one and only enduring glory the mighty Tigris river with two thirds of its 1,850 kms running through Iraq. But Baghdad did have its glory days, way back, when the Abbasids shifted power from Damascus to Baghdad and Abu Jaafar al Mansur, the Abbasid Caliph, began building a new city, in 762CE.

Using the time-honoured method of finding out where was the best place to start by suspending pieces of meat from trees to discover the location at which they remained freshest – he incorporated the Tigris in his plan. The whole development was enclosed by three walled circles, the outer wall five kilometres in diameter, the Tigris making the fourth boundary. The innermost circle with its 90 metre-high sloping walls was used for the Caliph's palace and government buildings. The middle circle housed the dwellings of a few trusted citizens as well as a limited number of shops while the third and outermost wall enclosed the city's guards. The main army was billeted on the east bank in an area still known today as Rusafah – or Causeway. Finally, the Round City, as it came to be known, was divided into four, self-contained quarters. This allowed the Caliph to come and go virtually unobserved and also meant that, in the event of an invasion or a riot by the citizens themselves, whole sections of the city could be isolated. This new Round City of Baghdad took five years to build though by the time it was finished the population had swelled so much that there was already an overspill on to the east bank. Interestingly, considering how many bridges across the Tigris were destroyed by the allied bombardment during the Gulf War, the Caliphs never had a permanent bridge built, preferring to use a flotilla of yoked boats instead.

Baghdad by then was a blossoming centre of culture and learning with poetry, history, music and scientific works constantly recorded and updated. Paper had been discovered in China and its manufacture developed in Baghdad so that it is not surprising to learn that, in the time of al Mansur, there were no less than 100 stationery shops in the Round City. Al Mansur's palace was renowned for the beauty of its design and for the ingenuity of the craftsmen who worked on it and the story goes that when one such man had constructed a particularly stunning fountain he was summoned to the Caliph's presence to explain how he had designed and made it.

"And tell me," said al Mansur, "could you make another fountain like this one?"

"Yes indeed," replied the fountain-maker eagerly, "I could make many more." At which point al Mansur called his guard: "Take this man away and cut off his head." The Caliph had no wish for anyone else to have a fountain as elegant as his own.

It was al Mansur's famous nephew, Haroun, however, who put Baghdad on the map, later constructing a dwelling of such opulence that it was not only a palace but a place of aesthetic worth, built within a city that was the greatest between Iraq and China, one which prompted a correspondence between Haroun and his arch enemy, Nicephorous I of Constantinople. Haroun, as arrogant as he was powerful, wrote: "From Haroun, Prince of the Faithful, to Nicephorous, Roman dog…I have read your letter, you son of a heathen. You will see, not hear, my reply." His reply was accompanied by an army of 135,000 men and a subsequent reply by 100 lions.

The taxi driver interrupts my thoughts: "Madam, we must be close now." We have been driving for 14 hours, travelling not only in time but also along the road of history, from one great Arab city to another though the difference between the two could not have been more marked – nor more distressing for there is something of a forgotten dream here, a dream darkening into nightmare. In the old Ottoman neighbourhoods, the tall louvred doors bear memories of an elegance which has long since rotted. Overhanging balconies lean sickeningly in both directions. The pillared walkways are dirty, overrun with plastic bags. Street stalls, shaded by flapping canvas awnings which are tattered and grimy, sell taqiyyah made in China. This then is contemporary Baghdad and I have not yet seen it at its worst.

The worst is on the outskirts, in the slum area called Saddam City, a hellhole of tower blocks, deprivation and poverty occupied mainly by Shia.

"Do the people in Saddam City suffer badly from the sanctions?" I ask the driver and he shakes his head in sorrow: "Madam, the Shia suffer from everything."

Mr Pandey and his wife, Bimla – my friends at the Indian Embassy – welcome me with green tea and smiles. We first met in Dublin when something which I had written about Gandhi caught the eye of Pandey, then First Secretary at the Indian Embassy. An invitation to his home followed and we became good friends. As a diplomat, he moved round the world and was proud to tell me that his was the only embassy not to close down during the US bombing of Baghdad following Saddam's invasion of Kuwait.

His PA, Jawan, a Christian Baghdadi, tells me about the bombardment: "The bombs came night after night. At first, we tried to stay in our apartment – myself, my husband and our two small children. We put our arms around each other with the children in the middle to protect them and I told them that if we died, we would meet in heaven. The lights blew out and the glass in the windows exploded and I held the children tight. In the morning, there was no one around and we were afraid to go down the stairs because they were almost destroyed. We stayed like that for three days until someone came up and found us. We were the only people left in our block of flats."

Jawan and her family survived but two years ago her artist husband died of cancer. Now she has to face the next invasion without him.

I am to be taken on an orchestrated tour of Baghdad under the sanctions, with Mahmoud as driver. He avoided having to fight in the Kuwait war, he told me, because he was employed as a driver for the military top brass. Some of his family are already in the US and that's where he's going as well. As soon as they send him the fare.

En route, we try to visit a few mosques – Baghdad has two particularly historic ones – but Jawan says we won't be allowed enter them.

"Why?" I ask.

"Because some Christians have said that Muslims are dirt and so we are not welcome."

This is disconcerting. One of the advantages of travelling alone is that I am not constrained by other people's perceptions or indeed their prejudices – which I might not share. In any case, I have plenty of my own to keep me going. When we do eventually get into the courtyard of the great Khademain Mosque and I greet a few people who I think are probably Shia, Jawan gently reproves me. I should use the more formal religious form – Salaam alaikum – rather than the cheery secular greeting Marhaba, which I am accustomed to using in Syria. I keep my counsel but disagree. The world is changing, becoming less formal and I reserve my right to use whatever Arabic greeting I want to. Though I suspect that Jawan's self-professing Christianity has a part to play in her attitude, sustaining her identity in a country that is officially secular.

On the way home, we pass a group of people standing about on the pavement, a few of them waving banners in a half-hearted way protesting, it seems, to no one in particular.

"It's an anti-US demonstration," explains Jawan. "Organised by the Ba'ath Party. Tomorrow, there will be another one in a different neighbourhood."

"Would it not be simpler," I ask, "to organise one big one?"
But Jawan shakes her head: "They can't do that: the crowd
might get out of control."

To do the political tour of Baghdad, I first have to get accredi-
tation at the government press office. The gloomy lobby of this
municipal office is lit by a single light bulb. Male and female
officials sit at tables dealing with requests for interviews with
other officials who, the supplicants hope, may sort out their
problems.

"Watch how they hand over money," Pandey murmurs. "It's the
only way to get an interview." As he speaks, I see the cash slide
across the table and into a pocket without acknowledgement.
Low-status government officials earn the equivalent of US$10
a month.

I am assigned a Ministry of Information minder and it is
indicated that I should pay him since, apparently, he is doing
this unofficially. The sum involved should be US$10 which I
don't have with me so we agree I will pay later.

My minder climbs into our car and, with Jawan as my inter-
preter, we drive across the river to visit the bombed-out Amiriyah
air raid shelter, a must-see for any visiting westerner. En route,
Jawan asks Mahmoud to stop and explains: "Many people died
in Amiriyah and visitors are expected to bring flowers. I can get
them for you, if you like." I give her a roll of dinars, enough, in
the old days, to buy a car. Now all they will buy is a bunch of
garish, plastic flowers. Further along, we pass a crowd of men
standing on the pavement gathered round one man who looks
like an official.

"Another demonstration?" I ask.

"No," says Jawan. "That's the Libyan Embassy. They're
looking for visas so they can travel to Libya to get work there."

What I have discovered is that the embassies all cover for
each other. Once, when I was trying to get into Libya and neither
Britain nor Ireland had diplomatic relations with the Libyans
at that time, I found I could get a visa by applying through the

Italian Embassy. Here in Iraq, until the year before my visit, India covered for Egypt. With no diplomatic relations between Syria and Iraq, at the time of my visit, my re-entry visa from Iraq to Syria is dealt with through the Algerian representatives in Baghdad. Clearly, whatever the sanctions or the falling-out between leaders, it's business as usual, more or less, both for the lone traveller and the commercial entrepreneur. It's just a question of knowing who's fronting for whom.

The Amiriyah is one of 34 shelters built in 1984 by a Finnish company to be used as shelters against radiation. During the bombardment in 1991, local people poured into it. I follow Jawan down into the dark hell. Our official guide is formidable with eyes heavily outlined with kohl. A pale blue hijab flows over the power-pads adorning her shoulders. She shines her torch around the cavernous shelter which has the feel of a derelict, underground warehouse. Wires protrude from a wall on which I can just make out the blackened outline of a small hand, melted into the concrete by the inferno that followed the bombing. The beam of light swings round and down onto the ground to reveal the scorched imprint of bare feet. Then moves back up the wall to draw my attention to the shadowy outline, scarred into the wall, of people blown backwards and into it by the blast. I lay my bunch of flowers against a concrete pillar and read the messages of those already there – from the Malaysian Federation of Women, from the Syrian Consulate, from the Iraq/Australian Friendship group. The guide stands silently as I stare at this ghostly war memorial.

This is what happened. At 4am on 13 February 1991, a two-ton laser missile, fired by a US F117A Stealth bomber, burst through the reinforced concrete roof and plunged down among the people sheltering at ground level before blasting its way to the floor below. Within minutes, a second bomb neatly targeted the ventilation system, closing off the air supply so that the temperature inside rapidly soared to 400 degrees. Those women and children sleeping under the air vent took the full blast.

Most were charred beyond recognition by the intense heat, their injuries similar to people killed by napalm. The huge steel doors, which could only be opened from the inside, were welded shut. Of the 408 people – mainly the young, the old and the ill – only 14 survived. A baby, born in the shelter at midnight, was dead four hours later and, the next day, a death certificate instead of a birth certificate was issued. A mother and her six children died while her husband and son, desperately trying to reach the shelter by car in order to get to them, were killed in a collision with another vehicle.

On one wall are a number of fading photographs. One is of a group of people staring in horror at the building while, in the background, an ancient fire engine stands, useless against the might of modern war technology. In the foreground are bodies skinned, blackened, legs with feet missing, torsos without arms.

"This is the result of American terrorism," says the guide while I peer down into the black hole made by the first bomb. But why do I feel such animosity towards this cold, unsmiling woman? Why does she seem so unfeeling when my own emotions are in turmoil? I want her to give me an understanding smile which would ease my pain. But wait a minute – *my* pain?

There is a set of stairs leading downwards with a single bulb swinging on its makeshift cable.

"What's down there," I ask.

"It was a hospital," says the guide. "In case anyone needed a doctor."

And no, I can't go down there. It's too unsafe. Silently, she turns away, expecting me to follow which I do. Iraqis, I decide, are courteous but also bitter and above all, tired. The whispering voices of the dead drift round me: small children playing with each other, old men coughing, toddlers whimpering in their sleep, the low voices of women, all drowning the silence that surrounds us.

The US military version of the nightmare is that Saddam was using the people as a human shield and that below the shelter was a command centre, not a hospital. No one told the people of this allegation, of course, so that the place of safety, into which so many vulnerable people crowded on that fatal night, turned into an all-engulfing incinerator as the American precision bombs found their target.

Everything here in Iraq is rationed: each designated individual gets an allowance which includes 3kgs of rice, 500g of lentils, 500g of detergent, 2kg of sugar, eight cans of powdered baby milk. In all, the rations are worth 250 dinars which is one quarter of a government employee's month's salary. No one seems to think the sanctions are working. "There can be no solution when the hero and the villain are the same," I was told by an aid worker. Not everyone, of course, needs food aid. Of the 24 million people in Iraq, there are a few who are doing fine: friends of the Great Leader, senior Ba'ath party members, people who drive around in fine new cars smuggled in from Jordan and elsewhere. Their children are well-dressed and many of their opulent houses are newly built. There is a reason for this. The moneyed classes, loyal to the Great Leader, unable to spend their cash to travel abroad or on luxury goods, spend it all on their new homes. Not unexpectedly, builders turn to heaven in search of a profit. The UN allows the importation of some building materials under the Oil for Food programme and there is a system – Saddam's system – whereby if a developer builds a mosque, he is given tax concessions on other buildings. And so the rich get richer.

I've been invited to a women's party close to where I'm staying. The house is as big as a mansion, with a spacious hallway leading to a series of rooms full of heavy furniture, elegant but worn. Everything needs a coat of paint, a good brush, a proper dusting down. The wall hangings and the carpets are threadbare. There is an aura of despair and neglect to the rooms and a cloud of gloom hangs over the people in them. At one end of the main room, a number of veiled women sit on the floor intoning the Qu'ran while at the other end sit a group of women chatting and drinking coffee. The mater familias, a bent old woman, shakes my hand and welcomes me but her daughter – a large middle-aged woman dressed in a voluminous black gown, cigarette in hand – turns her back on me, even though I have explained that I am Irish – and not English nor, indeed, American.

A woman who works for the Federation of Iraqi Women comes to sit beside me to chat. Like most of the other women, she's dressed all in black, with kohl-lined eyes. Black is everywhere and I have to adjust my feelings to this sepulchral image because here it is a fashion statement. We chat about women's rights: all Iraqi women have them, she tells me, and all women are educated, many in the formerly male-dominated areas such as engineering and physics and, no, there is very little violence against women. "Islam does not allow man to hit woman," she explains.

Later, I take a stroll along the Tigris which is wide, bordered in places by high-walled houses and by once-pleasant embankments where a few residual purple and blue lamps still swing among the trees which give shade to the numerous riverside cafés now closed but which were once packed with families taking their ease. Running alongside the river is Abu Nawas Street. Abu Nawas al Hasan ibn Hani al Hakimi ranks as the foremost of the non-classical poets, the scourge of the caliphate, bad boy of Haroun's Baghdad and, as he describes himself:

> *the vanguard of depravity*
> *the spearhead of debauchery*
> *arch-enemy of chastity*
> *and all that smacks of sanctity.*

Clearly, another man I would have got on with. Seduced as a boy by his male teacher into whose care he had been entrusted, Abu Nawas settled in Baghdad during the time of Haroun al Rashid, dividing his lovemaking between women

and men before finally throwing in his ardent, amorous lot
with the latter:

> *Now, a toast to those days which have long passed away*
> *I can no longer enjoy the sweet fare*
> *Of that bold country lass with the well-rounded ass*
> *But the memory soothes my despair.*

His love of young men was exceeded only by his love of old
wine. His poetry mocks Islam with its rules and regulations and
though he retains a belief in a compassionate Allah, he manages
to take a swipe at the Christian's love of images:

> *Almost everything God, in his mercy, abhors*
> *You may see in my person and possibly more.*
> *But while I pay no heed to religious decree*
> *You can never accuse me of idolatry.*

Like many poets, Abu Nawas spent time in the desert with the
Bedouin in order to learn the purest form of spoken Arabic. For
his fellow writers, the dusty, windy Bedouin desert camps were
a metaphor for a lost past so beloved of romantics everywhere,
myself included.

Once, on my first journey through the Sahara, travelling with
a group of desert dwellers, though in a Land Rover and not by
camel, I was puzzled by the way in which the driver, navigating
this great void, would suddenly veer to the left and then, two
hours later, take a turn to the right.

"How do you know where to turn?" I asked him. "There are
no signs, no rocks. Nothing."

He smiled, shrugged his shoulders but didn't answer.

"I mean," I continued, "I can see how you do it at night. You
have the stars to guide you. But by day, how do you do it?"

Then he smiled again: "There are stars in the sand as well,"
he said and thus I learned I was an city dweller and not a desert
dweller.

Celestial navigation, living in tents and all the other delights of desert dwelling, held little attraction for Abu Nawas, however, whose true calling was to live here, among hedonistic city dwellers:

> *...For this is the life,*
> *Not desert tents*
> *Not camel's milk!*

Abu Nawas is celebrated everywhere. Here in Baghdad there is a statue to him and a street named after him. In Damascus, there is a wall plaque to him, in Aleppo a restaurant. And rightly so for he was a courageous lawbreaker and exuberant anarchist:

> *For young boys, the girls I've left behind*
> *And for old wine set clear water out of mind.*
> *Far from the straight road, I took without conceit*
> *The winding way of sin, because (this horse)*
> *Has cut the reins without remorse,*
> *And carried away the bridle and the bit.*

Near Abu Nawas Street, there are some interesting new buildings – a staggered landscape of concrete with curves, arches and perpendiculars in grey stone. Close by is a lovely old Ottoman house with broad steps leading up to a fretworked balcony and double doors.

Inside, I meet Dr A K al Hashimi who is small, rotund and slightly bald, the sort of Arab male whose presence is preceded by a warm swell of self-knowing charm. Educated in the US, his conversation is peppered with deliciously irreverent references to "Bush the Father, Bush the Son", so that we both know exactly where we stand. Previously, he was ambassador to France, a glittering diplomatic post that indicated his high standing with the Great Leader.

His office is expansive, his polished desk huge, the small shrug accompanying his smile, gracious. I dress him in a peacock-blue gown, place him on a divan covered with crimson silk and surround him with dancing girls. Then I pull myself together and accept the tiny cup of black coffee he slides towards me across the shining surface of his desk. I am here, after all, to hear about the sanctions.

"My dear Mary," he says, "I will tell you the facts and you, with your clever journalistic mind, will draw your own conclusions. So," and he sips delicately from his own minute coffee cup, "what we have here are the Uniteds – States, Nations and Kingdom – who are carefully and ruthlessly manipulating one of the biggest oil-producing countries in the world. They are doing this in the name," and he pauses, "of democracy." The word hangs in the air between us, swings to and fro. Defies definition.

"What about the invasion of Kuwait?" I begin but he waves my interruption aside dismissively.

"This has nothing to do with Kuwait." He smiles, refills my coffee cup, drinks himself before starting to recite facts and figures to support his claim.

"They control our oil output and, in that way, delay production." I rack my brains for figures related to this: the US, I know, uses 21 million barrels of oil a day and half of that has to be imported. Fuel security is therefore a big issue for America, as it is for all of us. But Hashimi has the bit between his teeth and demands my attention: "Listen, the UN – and remember, Iraq was a founding member of the UN in 1945 – the UN Resolution 661 allocates us 41 billion dollars for health over ten years but only 46% actually reaches us which amounts to 150 million dinar per year and divide that by twelve, share it out among 24 million Iraqis and it's less than 50 cents per person per month." He shrugs. "Then we have the dual use restrictions. We can't have this and we can't have that because it might be used to make a bomb. A bomb? What bomb? Take, for instance, a pump. A pump is categorised as dual purpose so we can't get any replacement parts for our failing electricity system. But electricity is health. So, our sanitation schemes suffer, we get polluted sewage, our children get dysentery and they die." He shakes his head and looks hard at me, determined I get his message: "It all results in a degree of deprivation that did not exist before."

While he takes another sip of coffee I try to work out the rush of figures. Do they add up to what he says? I'll have to check later because he's returned to the dual use issue: "My dear lady, dual use? What is not dual use? Look at your pen. It can be used to write a feature for your newspaper or a love letter. Or it can be used to write an equation for a nuclear weapon," and he smiles but with his mouth only. "You know, we used to be the most important country in the region," he continues, "not like some corner of Africa or South America and we always had good business partners. But they are turning away now. The international community wants to make us one big refugee camp run by the UN. So, everyone is getting nervous because we are becoming more aggressive. Especially the Americans. So they say things about us – that we are a military dictatorship. Are we? Can you see riot police on our streets? Or checkpoints everywhere? Are there armoured personnel carriers in Baghdad? Have you seen any? Are people being killed on the streets?"

I shake my head. It's true. I haven't actually seen any of these things.

"They have ruined our economy. Before, 3,000 dinar would buy you a big car. Now, as you know, all you get is a bunch of false flowers. Do they think Saddam Hussein is a one-man show? Of course he's not. He has support, people behind him. He's leading a whole economic and educational system. No, capitalism thrives on crises not on stability and that's what it's all about." Suddenly, like a machine that has run out of fuel, he slows down and asks a question to which there is no answer: "The US is afraid. They think we have nuclear weapons, chemical weapons. Weapons of mass destruction. What can Iraq do to show that it doesn't, that it is not a threat?"

At dinner with my Indian friends, to which have been invited a number of both Iraqi and foreign guests, the conversation tends to confirm what Hashimi has been saying. Everyone wants a cut of whatever's going, it seems, and if they can get away with paying less, they will. This is Iraq the underdog, after all. No one really minds what happens to its people. During the 1991 bombardment, the Indian Embassy remained open while the European ones pulled out. Now, they are all trickling back again. Hashimi did some big deals while he was in Paris, someone says, for which the French hope to be paid at some future date. Russia "loaned" arms and they too expect to be paid eventually. Romania, which withdrew its ambassador, has sent someone back, not quite with the status of an ambassador but with powers to act as one. And he's here tonight. Around the dinner table we also have an Indian businessman who repairs oil drilling equipment. Some of the big refineries north of Baghdad are dangerous: the components are old and in need of repair so a few Iraqi workers are sent to India to be trained and they have learned to squeeze whatever money they can out of these trips.

"How?" I ask the Indian businessman.

"Oh well, they say they need taxi money to get to the airport in Jordan which costs 40 dollars. Then they go by bus which costs only 10 dollars. But, you know, they're my customers so I go along with it."

There's a man from Dubai who makes oil barrels and the man from Romania who is preoccupied with his health. He has a low, sexy voice totally unsuited to the story he tells of how, when he was back home, he had keyhole surgery to remove a gallstone. If it hadn't been removed, he explains huskily, it would have split open and become infected. I put down my fork. The curry which before had tasted sublime has now lost its attraction. He has never been to Saddam City: "It's not part of my job to go there. I am the Chargé d'affaires. In any case, I have been told it's dangerous."

And no, he hasn't learned any Arabic. "Haven't had time."

The conversation shifts to women, Iraqi women. Many of them are still unmarried at 35 because Iraqi men won't work, I'm told. I suspect this is because wages are so low and there's no incentive so the women prefer their own limited independence.

Suddenly, everyone has an anecdote to tell to illustrate this though the gallstone man interrupts to tell me how great Romania is. It is, it seems, another veritable cradle of civilisation: "We were converted to Christianity by Saint Andrew so we became Christian by choice and very early on. Before many other countries." I tighten my mouth to conceal a yawn. There's an Iraqi journalist at the table as well, political editor of a national newspaper. At first, I find him loud and bombastic until I grow to feel sorry for him, for the years he's had to spend in the wilderness.

"Before, many people disliked Saddam," he tells me as we tuck on to our spicy rice and spinach, "but now they are united behind him because they see how the UN sanctions make them suffer. Look at me: I can no longer get my supply of international newspapers. I used to read ten a week. Now…"

There seems nothing to say so I concentrate on my food. "Do you know," he continues, "that the government is not allowed buy food from the farmers? The farmers must sell their produce to the UN who then sells it to the people. It's another method of control, of breaking the connection between Saddam and the people. Divide and rule." I can only nod. It's a strategy we're familiar with in Ireland.

Pandey intervenes: "We must break this impasse," he says diplomatically. "New ways have to be found. New ways of thinking." But the journalist sighs. He is not interested in diplomacy at the moment: "I can't travel. I can't take my family on a holiday. Before, I earned a thousand US dollars a month. Now it's ten dollars. What I can't understand is why Britain hangs onto America's shirt-tails," and he pokes about in his salad searching among the tomatoes and cucumber for an answer.

"You know," he says, "I like to travel and when I go to England – when I used to go – I went to London, to Soho, Piccadilly. To the pubs."

I have to smile. "And when I come to Baghdad," I reply, "I go looking for Ali Baba and the Forty Thieves."

The man from Dubai is Haji which means no wine and no women. "Of course, I look at women," he beams, "but I don't let them in to my heart." And the stream of jokes which follow from this makes him beam even more. Bimla's last course is delicious – sweet homemade yoghurt with tiny sponge cakes in syrup. For the coffee, we move away from the large table to the armchairs scattered about the room. The journalist brings his coffee and comes to sit beside me: "You must think we complain all the time but believe me, it's very hard here." And I want to take his hand, to console him. We are often caught in a trap of misery not always of our own making.

He sighs: "My paper has cut its circulation from 250,000 to 25,000 because of paper shortage. Plus the machinery is old and we are not allowed replace it because of the dual use restrictions. Do you know my mother needs a valve for her heart but she can't have that either – because the valve could be used to make weapons." His look is resigned rather than bitter. The UN is not at all popular. No one goes to them now because of their politics. And US talk of Vietnam and human rights simply makes Iraqis laugh.

"We taught the Vietnamese how to grow rice," Pandey suddenly says, a remark that surprises me, "and now they export it to Iraq." Perhaps, diplomatically, he wants to change the subject. There's a lot of talk praising Iraq – its ancient civilisation, its culture, how gracious Iraqis are under pressure. I join in, extolling the virtues of the country and its people: their stoicism, the combination of old (the hijab) and the new (middle European tat). I don't mention Saddam Hussein's ruthlessness, the sale of Russian arms to Iraq, the gassing of the Kurds. More dinner table diplomacy again though I sense the journalist knows exactly what I'm thinking. When I walk across the room to refill my coffee cup, Pandey joins me and takes the opportunity to murmur: "When they say UN, think US or maybe even UK."

I return to my chair and mention to the journalist that the former UN Weapons Inspector, an Australian, has gone to work for the CIA.

"He always did," said the journalist smiling at my apparent ignorance. When he leaves, he invites us to have dinner with him in a restaurant by the Tigris the following Saturday. "It may happen," says Pandey later, "but nothing is certain here." And he's right: it never does happen.

"Will you take some of these sweets home to your wife, perhaps?" suggests Pandey to the departing Haji who shakes his head: "I think not. I have other things for my wife." In any case, he says, he has to watch his weight: "I am 10 kilos overweight."

"You can't be, not with the sanctions," says Pandey and we all laugh.

When everyone has gone, there is a midnight knock at the door. It's my minder from the Ministry of Information.

"I suppose he's come for his money," I say sotto voce but Pandey shakes his head: "He's come for a glass of good Scotch whisky."

I pay him the US$10, he drinks a glass of whisky and as he leaves, I see Pandey slipping him a small envelope. Another form of diplomacy. Money, as a vice-president of the World Bank said to me once, is like love: you take it wherever you can find it.

Later and privately, Pandey tells me that eastern European countries will sell anything. They are even offloading obsolete Soviet Union weapons on Iraq which means Iraq now owes them US$15 billion for out-of-date military hardware. The Chinese used a similar ploy, trying to pay for Iraqi oil with goods instead of cash but the goods were so shoddy that Iraq refused to accept them.

The temperature is 37 degrees but the walkways along Mutanabbi Street are shaded by strips of fabric slung from pillar to pillar. Mutanabbi, a poet born the son of a water carrier in Iraq educated in Damascus and died in 965CE, is lauded as one of the great classical poets. He took much of his inspiration from the Bedouin way of life, and this street, one of the most famous in Baghdad, is named after him. As with many of them, however, dereliction is everywhere. Above, on the third floor, tall louvred doors open to balconies that are long since gone. This is the street where people, desperate for money, come to sell their precious books and here they are, displayed on trestle tables or scattered like discards on the ground or on car bonnets – Doris Lessing, George Bernard Shaw, medical books, a Collins dictionary exorbitantly expensive at US$15. Language books. A memoir of Hoxha. The book I want is a collection of Iraqi short stories but I can't buy it because I have no money with me. I consider borrowing from Pandey but then decide not to.

"Don't even look," he says. "As soon as they see you're interested, they'll put the price up."

This saddens me because I don't think this is true. Or maybe I just don't want to think it's true.

The Pandeys, kind and considerate, offer to take me out for the day. Leaving Baghdad, we pass through a lot of checkpoints: contrary to what Hashimi told me yesterday, people's movements are restricted in a way similar to how they used to be in Soviet Russia. No one is allowed to go outside the boundaries of the city without permission. With Haroun, it was the other way round. He didn't like his citizens to get too close and kept most of them outside the city walls.

An Iraqi Airlines plane lumbers in from Basra. People are cautious about flying because, with the sanctions and the dual purpose restrictions, no one knows if the planes have all the required nuts and bolts. We speed along the highway, flat desert scrub on either side. Occasionally, we pass black Bedouin tents and small herds of camels. Rushes intertwined with feathery yellow fronds act as windbreaks behind which I catch the odd flash of brilliant green indicating something is growing there. After Saddam's attack on Kuwait and the retaliatory allied bombardment, people started to court self-sufficiency so that there are now far more people growing fruit and vegetables. Before, oil revenues made people so rich that few bothered to work the land, finding it easier to import food from abroad. But not any more.

Rural Iraq is pleasing. The older towns we pass through have pot-plants for sale and fountains playing outside the town halls. There are few tall buildings to interrupt the huge expanse of sky. It's Friday so people have a relaxed look to them, with men sitting chatting in the sun while the women make their way back from the maize fields, bundles of greenery on their heads, their voluminous skirts leaving a cloud of dust behind them as they disappear along sandy tracks to their homes hidden among the date palms. Date palms are gracious trees, generous with their shade and since learning that they have a gender identity – the male palm is taller than the female – I feel myself part of their family. Small boys amble along the side of the road, arms around each other's shoulders. A man on a donkey trots urgently towards the crossroads with baskets of produce to sell there.

When I see an end wall painted green with, at its centre, the Iraqi flag with its three stars, this unexpected display of nationalism makes me think of Ireland. And yes, a bit further on is a half-built house with imposing pillars already in place, marking where the gates will eventually go when the money comes through. Or when the cow calves, as we say in Ireland.

The sky is too bright to look at but I have to when a flock of homing pigeons, wheeling through it, glints like a burst of falling stardust. And just for this moment, here in this treasured land, I feel a degree of happiness that is boundless.

The road – a military route that tanks trundled along to Kuwait – is long and straight but eventually we arrive at Babylon and, horribly, I am disappointed. Babylon was the capital of no less than ten Mesopotamian dynasties with the great lawgiver King Hammurabi reigning as the sixth king of the first dynasty of Babylonia c1726BCE. But the city only really came in to its own during the rule of Nebuchadnezzar which lasted from 605 to 583BCE.

Not a great deal of the original Babylon is left. Much of its precious heritage, plundered by scholarly visitors including

Gertrude Bell, is now to be seen in museums around the world including Boston, Paris, London and Berlin.

Its most famous piece is the Ishtar Gate. Ishtar: Light of the World, Opener of the Womb, Righteous Judge, Bestower of Strength, Forgiver of Sins, Patron of Sacramental Promiscuity, "the embodiment of wanton behaviour that inspires both excitement and anxiety in all who desire her". In her many guises, Ishtar was the God of Gods but her gate here – one of eight leading into the city of Babylon – is now only a reconstruction. The real thing is in Berlin. In 1987 Saddam Hussein started a rebuilding programme, erecting tall brick walls in an effort to recreate something of the glory days of Babylon but the effect has been stultifying, resulting in huge empty spaces hedged about by high walls which do nothing to bring to life the thriving city this once was. But there are a few things that I do like. Set into some of the original walls are bas relief images of horses and dragons with each brick forming one small part of the animal, displaying a project of considerable artistic and technical skill which brings together the whole of what was originally designed as a series of parts.

Most imposing of all is Ishtar's familiar, a lion carved out of grey/black basalt with the trace of a saddle on its back indicating it was a means of transport for the Divine, though Ishtar, being the God of Gods, rode her lion standing rather than sitting on the saddle. Now, as we watch, children and adults clamber all over it. I have my photograph taken beside it to show Tariq back in Damascus for the Arabic word for lion is assad, the family name of the President of Syria. On a hill close to the old city of Babylon is a large mansion and I get Mahmoud to ask a soldier guarding the entrance what it is.

"He doesn't answer my question," says Mahmoud, "therefore we can guess what it is." In fact, everyone knows it's yet one more of the Great Leader's palatial dwellings, its roof, in a crude statement of power, taller than any building in Babylon.

Before I leave Baghdad, I have one last task to perform: I want to find the obelisk erected to the memory of Zubeidah,

Haroun's favourite wife. Haroun was a man of many parts and of as many women, though one woman who played a major role in his life was neither lover nor wife. His mother was a clever and beautiful slave girl called Khaizuran whom Haroun's father married. When she died, Haroun, barefoot, led the funeral procession through the streets of Baghdad. Zubeidah, on the other hand, was a highborn cousin of Haroun and, soon after their marriage, she became pregnant. However, a few months before the birth of what everyone hoped would be a boy, a female Persian slave died giving birth to a son also fathered by Haroun. Zubeidah took this child, al Mahmoun, into her household and raised him alongside her own son, al Amin, who was the younger of the two but had the advantage of being born within wedlock. As adults there was an inevitable falling-out between the two half-brothers. Al Amin was killed, and Zubeidah withdrew to live a life of seclusion until al Mahmoun married and his bride requested that Zubeidah go on one last pilgrimage to Mecca.

In fact, Zubeidah had already performed the Haj five times and had done much to make the route more navigable. She ordered the excavation of a series of wells along the way, making sure they were adequately guarded and maintained. In her excellent book, Women in Muslim History, Charis Waddy reminds us that it is 1,448 kilometres from southern Iraq to Mecca and that Zubeidah laid down extra wells between the older more established ones, especially for the use of those pilgrims who could only afford to walk the route. It is for this compassionate contribution to Islamic culture that she is best remembered. Now, here I am in Baghdad, in search of her memorial.

My researches in the Bodleian Library had turned up a black and white photograph of the obelisk though Mahmoud is sceptical about actually finding it. We drive around the city, he guided by his local knowledge, me by my ancient maps and drawings photocopied in the Bodleian. The obelisk is a scalloped cone on a rectangular base that should be easily identifiable and indeed, after a few hours searching, I see it in the distance, magically burnished by the setting sun. I glow too, in Mahmoud's admiration, for I have found something he had known nothing about in his own home town. It is only much later I learn that the obelisk is, in fact, dedicated not to Zubeidah but to Zummurrad Khatoun, wife of a 13th century caliph. And then I have one last job for Mahmoud – to try to find the Bab al Wastani.

When it was first built, Baghdad had many gates – the Gate of the Willow Tree, the Gate of Darkness, the Gate of the Moon. Now all are gone except one of the four main gates – the Khorasan. Mahmoud is intrigued and we drive about the city using my bit of paper covered with scribbles made on a wet winter's night in the Bodleian Library. Certain that we are in the right area, I persuade him to stop so that I can poke around the tumbledown buildings, the broken stones, the sandy, rutted tracks that seem to lead nowhere. Then I hear a shout and see him on top of a ruined archway, waving and looking mightily pleased with himself. He has located Bab al Wastani! Not much of it is left but it's there nevertheless. I am pleased that, on my last day, I have finally found a piece of the jigsaw.

I stand and stare, hearing the sound of camels plodding across the sand, the shouts of their handlers, the cries of people selling their wares, the slap of leather harnesses and creaking of leather saddles. Bab al Wastani is the gate to the east through which the caravans left on their way to golden Samarkand.

Later that night, skimming back to Damascus across the desert towards the Iraqi/Syrian border crossing, the midnight-blue sky is dotted not just with stars but with the lights of spy satellites moving steadily and quietly through the darkness. Their equipment allows them to monitor conversations taking place five kilometres below them, though I have no inclination to talk. The visit to Baghdad has sobered my thoughts. The stricken city makes me think of a beautiful butterfly pinned down by military hardware, the velvet of its brightly-coloured wings wilfully smeared across a fleeting second in its long history. The shape of Iraq may change, its borders will once again be redefined, sliced into, pared down. Men will be tortured, women raped. Its natural resources will become the spoils of war, to be plundered by self-regarding saviours operating under the guise of democracy – and with the avid participation of some Iraqis themselves. But the plain people of the country will remain faithful to their ancient and precious history which others have so carelessly disregarded, cherishing, amidst the roar of aircraft and of explosions, their language, their land and their children's heritage. It is they who will keep the spirit of Iraq alive, they and the writers and poets who give them voice.

Now that I am familiar with the routine, things move faster at the border crossing. A female customs guard takes me to a small cubicle devoid of furniture except for the broken iron frame of a chair. We smile sadly at each other. She is young and pretty and when she raises her hand to admire the necklace round my neck – an inexpensive bit of beading – I am slow to pick up the message and she, though impoverished by a system not of her making, is too well-mannered to spell it out. I still, to this day, regret that I didn't undo the flimsy clasp, take it off and give it to her.

By 4am, light is starting to seep across the sky as the taxi reaches Damascus and drops me close to al Ward Hotel. Marwan answers my knock on the door, rising sleepily from the mattress where he spends the night guarding the hotel entrance. I make my way up the stairs to the roof where I find a mattress to rest on. But though I've travelled all through the night, counting the pulsing satellites as they moved across the sky seeming to keep pace with the small taxi as it moved through the desert, sleep won't come.

In my mind's eye, I can still see the glory that I have left behind. Haroun al Rashid was known as the Peacock of the World, the Shadow of Allah on Earth, Lion of the Impassable Forests, Master of Spears, Gardener of the Vale of Islam. When he went to the mosque, he dressed all in black but rode an all-white steed which earned him the title the Rider of the

Spotless Horse. His palace, which shone white in the moonlight and pink in the sunlight, was hung with brocade from Damascus. Persian rugs covered the marble floors. In Zubediah's garden was a gilded tree on which sat golden birds which sang when a key was turned. The palace roses were nurtured with moonlight and moistened with dew. When his son, Mahmoud, married, pearls rather than confetti rained down on the bridal couple and guests were showered with balls of musk, each one containing a note entitling the guest to either a piece of land or a slave. This was Baghdad's golden age when music, poetry and the sciences were cherished, when the tables of Ptolemy were re-examined and the earth's circumference assessed at a time when, in Europe, it was still thought to be flat. Arabic words like zenith and nadir made an appearance on the world's linguistic stage as did alchemy and alcohol. The concept of nothingness as a number – cipher or zero – was developed and given a shape: 0. It was a time of mathematical magic which could encircle the emptiness, of oceans curving away below the horizon, of poets who drew words out of the air like threads of shimmering silk. It was a time when intricate patterns of Islamic design expanded ever outwards into a universe whose boundaries, to this day, still remain unexplored.

As I lie watching the night sky lighten, the muazzin from al Ward mosque begins his call to Salat al Fajr, the prayer said between dawn and sunrise. The muazzin is an old man but his voice has the sweetness of a boy's and is the aching cry of someone yearning for his beloved. I think of Baghdad where, curiously, I failed to notice even one call to prayer. And I think of Jawan lying in her husband-less bed, listening out for her father-less children, waiting for whatever the future may bring. Word has it that the US military, supported by the UK, is massing to strike Afghanistan and then Baghdad in its tireless search for terrorists and weapons of mass destruction. Does she know this, I wonder. Does Jawan know that powerful war planes, precision bombers, bunker busters, with their lethal dose of depleted uranium, will soon be aimed at her children? That heavy-booted soldiers with little education may march into her beloved city charged with the task of capturing hearts and minds? And from far away, I hear the anguished cry of a political leader, a Jewish carpenter from Galilee, first heard in Jerusalem 2,000 years ago just before he was silenced by his colonial masters: "Forgive them, Lord," he cried, "for they know not what they do." For me, it's not forgiveness I feel, but rage.

Chapter 24

Damascus, at last

I've been invited to Anis's apartment to meet his parents. "Ask the bus driver," he tells me, " to let you off at the meshfa." This is the hospital near his street. I hold the word in my mind though there's another, older word for hospital, bimaristan, which means house of patients.

There's a lovely bimaristan in Damascus which was founded by Nureddin in 1154. Or rather, it had been built with money which had come to him as ransom money paid by crusaders: war, as always, has an economic knock-on effect.

I get off the bus and cross the road, looking out for Bilal Street. If an Arabic word means something to me, I find it easier to remember it and this one is easy for Bilal had first been Muhammad's slave – perhaps servant might be a more judicious word – until upgraded by the Prophet to the job of calling the people to prayer thus making him Islam's first muazzin. He was sometimes known as the "black" muazzin since he was Ethiopian which may be why some American Muslims adopted him as a role model and symbol of dignity. Supper with Anis and Laylah is always marvellous since Laylah is such a great cook and tonight we have khubuz, white sheep's cheese, aubergines cooked with pomegranate seeds, fattoush, yoghurt, fried berak and, of course, her creamy, homemade humous.

I find myself sitting beside Anis's father-in-law, Abdul Azim. He has the sort of face I've come to associate with some Syrian men: square, no beard and similar to that of the former president Assad. Except that the Assad family is Alawite and Anis's family are Sunni. Abdul Azim has a short back and sides look to him as one might expect for, when I ask him what he does, he tells me he is a military instructor. There has been a lot of military activity in Lebanon and though everyone knows of Syria's presence in Lebanon, most people prefer not to talk about it. Syria's critics, many of whom are Lebanese Maronites, refer to it as "the occupation", although in fact, under the Ottomans, Syria and Lebanon were all one country.

I had first met Anis when he was a DPhil candidate at Oxford when, back in the days when I knew very little of Syria's complex history, he tried to explain to me something of the Maronite position. "I have many good friends who are Maronite," he told me, "although I may not always agree with their policies. I've got some reservations, for instance, about their attitude to Arab nationalism."

Now that I am slightly better informed, I think I understand his reservations. The Maronites, whose religion dates back to the 4th century, are proud of their historic and steadfast Christian resistance to Islam. Nowadays, they number France and the United States among their supporters.

"You've been to the Umayyad Mosque, of course," Abdul Azim says as, later, we sip our coffee. But I shake my head: "No, I haven't. Not yet."

He's surprised: "But that's the first place most people go to."

I know this. It is high on my list of must-sees but, although three months have passed, I still haven't been there.

"I'm saving up the best until last," I say, feeling an explanation is needed.

I had been resisting the call of Islam, knowing (but how did I?) that, like other monolithic religions, it would hold only limited attraction for me. And though reminding myself that I mustn't generalise, I grieved to see women veiling themselves, found many Muslim men kind but unreconstructed, felt unease at the sight of their physical submission to Allah, couldn't cope with the idea that Islam was held – by Muslims – to be the final word. That there is no postscript to the Qu'ran. No room in the scheme of things for a few extra Gods. For other possibilities.

271

For a bit of a laugh at Muhammad's expense whose shoulders, I imagined, were broad enough to carry the odd joke. I grieved that the concept of love was diminished by the idea that it should be limited to love between man and woman.

I enjoyed hearing the call to prayer in all its soaring forms but regretted the absence of any other music and found it distasteful to see young men in charge of street stalls selling bras and knickers. I felt irritated that so many Syrian women were invisible. All my dealings, my casual acquaintances, my on-street interactions seemed to be with men. The women were there, I knew, working behind the scenes but I wanted to meet up with them centre stage.

Once or twice, I had found myself in the vicinity of the Umayyad and had averted my eyes, not ready yet to be drawn in by its magnetism or enticed by the bright inviting lights shining through the huge entrance which, like sirens, sought to seduce me with promises of what lay within.

If you were to look at an X-ray image of the Umayyad Mosque, you would see layers of history gradually emerging into focus. This Muslim shrine is, in fact, only the most recent of a series of different shrines built on this site, a common practice throughout Syria and beyond. The cult of the God Haddad dates to 3000BCE and by 1300BCE he had become the foremost deity of the semitic Aramean peoples of Syria who had, by then, settled in the valley of the Euphrates. Haddad – lord of the skies, protector of life, who could shake mountains and blast trees – was so sacred a God that no mortal was allowed utter his name. The rulers of Damascus, however, were permitted to use the majestic title of Bar-Hadad which means son of Haddad since, by then, Damascus had become the capital city of a sizeable state whose writ ran from the Euphrates to the Yarmouk.

The temple to Haddad was the first to be laid on the site. Later, during the Roman period, it was replaced by a magnificent one dedicated to the ubiquitous Jupiter. Five arches of this temple still remain and, pleasingly, the street traders of Damascus have strung their striped awnings, white canopies, sparkling paper lanterns and electric cables from pillar to arch making a visible link between the old and the relatively new. The Christians then moved into Jupiter's temple and, later still, when the Emperor Theodosius suppressed paganism and gave legitimacy to the latest occupants, the site was elevated to the status of a cathedral and dedicated to the prophet Yahya ibn Zakariyya also known as John the Baptist, son of Zacharias. A few hundred years later, following the historic battle of Yarmouk, the arrival of Muslim Arabs in the region in 636CE (varied historic reports allow us to choose whether they invaded or were welcomed into Damascus) did not, as might have been expected, result in a struggle for use of the site. Instead, most admirably, it became a dual purpose place of worship with the Christians using the western part and the Muslims the east. Eventually, however, the east predominated for Damascus had by then become the power-base of the Umayyad Caliphate and it was thought necessary to build a place of worship that would give credence to this fact. In 709CE, work began on its construction: the Grand Mosque of the Umayyads was about to come into being. To postpone my inevitable visit to it, I engage in all sorts of displacement activities. One day, I walk the whole length of the Street called Straight and check out the places associated with Paul. Paul – Roman Saul in his first incarnation – was born in Tarsus. A tent-maker by trade, he was a Pharisee Jew who pursued with zeal the task of flushing out troublemaking Christians. Struck by the famous light on the way to Damascus which led him to go over to the other side, he went undercover and had to be spirited out of Damascus when the Jewish community there detected a pro-Christian bias in his preachings at the synagogue. My walks took me through the Christian part of the old city and into a piano bar, the walls of which were decorated with the usual sexist postcards. Not a place in which to linger.

Another day, I circumnavigate the ancient city walls following the line of gates that encircled and protected Damascus from so many dangers: Bab Sharaqi (the Eastern Gate), Bab al Salaam (the Gate of Peace), Bab Touma (named after Thomas, son-in-law of the Byzantine Emperor Heraclius), Bab al Faradees (the gate of Paradise), Bab al Sagheer (the small Gate), al Faraj Gate (Gate of Deliverance), al Jabieh Gate (leading out to the village of Jabieh), Bab al Nasr (the Gate of Victory, no longer in existence but once located at the top of the Souk Hamidiyeh). Bab Kissan, close to the place where Paul escaped capture, has been shut for 700 years. At Bab al Sagheer I pause: the muazzin Bilal is buried near here. My displacement activities continue. I wander round Marjeh Square, the old meat market in town where the French used to hang people and where the Syrians did as well. From there, I do my kamikaze dash back to the madinah qadima – the old town – and try to memorise the various souks: the souk of the saddler, the shoemaker, the spice seller, the sweet seller, the tobacco seller. At the perfume souk, I buy a small phial of sandalwood. Then I walk into the madinah qadima to visit the tomb of the great man himself.

In fact, Salahadin has two tombs. The first is a construction of well-worn walnut, plain and simple, in keeping with the legend: it is rumoured that he died owning nothing. Back in 1898, however, on a visit to Damascus, Kaiser Wilhelm II had the walnut replaced with a more ostentatious marble tomb. The bronze laurel wreath which he left there, commemorating his visit, has since disappeared and in her marvellous book about Damascus houses, Brigid Keenan suggests the wreath was given as a gift to T E Lawrence, the British officer whose military activities contributed to the infamous Sykes-Picot Agreement, formulated in 1916 whereby Syria, Lebanon, Iraq and Palestine were parcelled up and divided between Britain and France. Outside, I pause to rest in a peaceful, jasmine-scented garden to enjoy the afternoon sun and once more I catch myself out. Yes, I am loitering yet again, postponing the moment when I must visit the mosque which stands only a few feet away. I walk along the narrow alleyway between Salahadin's tomb and the wall of the mosque and come to a sign by a door which reads: "Putting on special clothes room". Inside, I buy an entrance ticket and choose a long brown hooded gown which is regulation wear for visiting women. The main entrance is on the west side of the mosque, just opposite the remains of Jupiter's temple. As I step through the small opening, a lake of brightness dazzles me: I am about to enter the Jami Bani Umayyah al Kabir. The surface of the expansive, pillared courtyard gleams as if a shower of rain has just fallen on the brilliant marble. Reflected in the marble is the blue sky, the glowing brass lamps and golden mosaics – shining in all their glory. Incorporated into the design of the Umayyad Mosque, for the first time in Syria, was the use of minarets, of which there are three. By the north entrance is the Minaret of the Bride with its distinctive, square-shaped tower. On the east side of the courtyard is the Minaret of Jesus whose position, it is said, indicates the spot where the prophet Jesus will appear on the Day of Judgement. The third is the Minaret Qait Bey.

Once inside the courtyard, I stand and stare. In front of me rises the Beit al Hal, an octagonal building which was used to hold the treasures of the citizens as well as the taxes paid by visiting merchants, although some scholars dispute this and suggest it was built for show only. Whatever its purpose, the treasury stands on eight elegant pillars and can only be accessed via a ladder. A thousand tiny explosions of light shimmer and sparkle as the sun catches the gold leaf mosaics covering the surface of the walls. To the left, a long pillared cloister runs the length of the courtyard, the shadows of the pillars, one after another, slicing across the marble floor in regular geometric patterns so beloved of Arabs. Behind the Beit al Hal, the west interior wall through which I had entered, glistens with gold and silver leaf. I walk across this shining space, past the lovely marble fountain where Muslims perform their ablutions before entering the prayer hall and which is said to mark the exact mid point between Istanbul and Mecca. Beyond the fountain, at the east end of the courtyard, is the entrance to the rooms where the head of Hussein, grandson of the Prophet, is enshrined. Hussein was murdered on the battlefield and his head brought back to Damascus and put on display here as a warning to others not to contemplate challenging the status quo.

The day I visit is the tenth day of Muharram – the fourth month after Ramadan and the one in which Hussein was killed. It has become a major time of remembrance for the Shia, the especial day known as Ashura which means, simply, the tenth day. This explains why there is a great number of Shia pilgrims here, women mostly, clad all in black, the men wearing small white taqiyyahs.

Hussein's head (if it is actually here) is kept in a small, green-lit mausoleum to which the Shia pilgrims come to touch and pray before later clustering round their imam as they are doing today, sitting in a circle on the marbled floor of the courtyard to listen to his sermon.

I walk across the courtyard, past the women bending over the water in the fountain, sleeves rolled to the elbows to cleanse themselves before praying, and enter the mosque. At the door, people have left their shoes on the ground, but having only one pair, I wonder would it be considered unmannerly, a terrible offence to local honesty, if I were to bring mine in with me for what if they're not there when I come out? Then, reading a notice telling me not to leave my shoes at the door, I realise that carrying them inside is in order.

As soon as I enter the huge, rectangular prayer room, I have to pause to get my bearings. Although it is a place of major religious significance, there is no reverential hush of the sort I usually associate with churches. Instead, it vibrates with activity and noise. The floor is covered with carpets and mats which get their loveliness from the fact that, since they are old and much trodden on, they bear the footprints of history. Small boys race across them, leapfrog over each other, skid to a halt in a perfectly executed wheelie and then start all over again.

Others turn somersaults on the railings surrounding the shrines. A young mother sits on the ground breastfeeding her tiny baby. A man dozes, leaning up against a pillar. Beside him, another man reads his copy of the Qu'ran undisturbed by the mayhem around him. Nearby two men, engaged in deep conversation, sprawl on carpets as if they were taking their ease on the sands of the desert. A group of black-clad elderly women sit side-by-side, swaying as they pray. Two small girls, pleasingly naughty, mimic the stiff walk of one old woman as she hobbles towards the exit while on the other side of the hall a boy drags his baby sister across the carpet by her feet – to her great and noisy delight. A man looks at me and touches his head: my hood has fallen back out of place.

Further along the prayer hall, beyond the mihrab which faces southwards in the direction of Mecca, a white-bearded imam is preaching, his large audience listening quietly, a row of young women, sitting apart from the men, industriously taking notes.

And in the middle of the prayer hall is what appears to be a large, somewhat incongruous, green-lit shrine to the prophet Yahya ibn Zakariyya. His end came about when, as John the Baptist, he was decapitated. The Roman Governor in Jerusalem, Herod, despatched his head to Damascus to prove to the Romans here that the deed had been done. Later, in the 4th century, the head was placed in what had by then become the Christian cathedral. And since he is revered by Muslims as a prophet, the head has been allowed to remain in what is now the Umayyad Mosque.

There are small havens of peace here but by and large, it is a place of movement, of constant murmuring, of public display of religious observances and, as often happens in Islam, of an easy coming together of the sacred and the profane. But for me, there is no quiet, no privacy, no calmness. I know these are things I should find deep within myself. But there is no space I can find into which I can withdraw, perhaps because I am so distracted by what is happening around me. Privacy is a concept foreign to people in this part of the world.

Back outside in the courtyard, the sun still shines brightly. Someone has thrown down a handful of corn and the pigeons – surely the best-fed birds in Damascus – have spread across the courtyard, beaks tapping busily against the marble, desperate in case they might miss a grain or their neighbour get an extra one. When a mosque caretaker suddenly claps his hands, they panic and take flight, whooshing upwards to wheel against the blinding light of the sun like flurries of snow. Then they start to fall through the sky like grains of pepper. Their presence calms me and I turn to look again at the mosaics of golden orchards, of flowing river waters. At the silver dwellings of paradise.

But all power eventually comes to an end and here in Damascus, the golden lantern chains in the mosque eventually blackened with age. The charismatic Caliph Walid was followed by Umar III, a conservative leader who had 600 lanterns removed because the gleam of the swaying gold was distracting. Mosaics and murals were erased with one brush of white paint when they were decreed to be as distracting as the gold lamps. Worst of all, Islamic leaders accused designers of modelling their mosques too closely along Byzantine lines.

The Umayyads were displaced by the Abbasids who subsequently moved the centre of Islamic power eastwards to Baghdad. The magnificent age of the Umayyad dynasty was closing down, leaving behind it the great city of Damascus cast now into shadow, a shadow which, 400 years later, in 1401, would darken to black and utter despair.

The shadow was cast by a child born into a nomad family of Mongol origin. It was said that his mother, a virgin, was ravished by a moonbeam and that the infant's small fists, when prised open, were found to be full of blood. That was the legend. The facts are that on 9 April 1336, the year of the mouse in the Mongol calendar, a baby boy was born in Shahrisabz, a town 129 kilometres south of Samarkand, lying in a valley between that great city and the mountains of the Hindu Kush in the country now known as Uzbekistan.

To many Asians, he is a hero, an iconic warrior of enormous stature and known to them as Amir Timur Gurigan – Lord Timur the Splendid. To Europeans, he is Timur the Lame. Unable to read or write, he surrounded himself with scholars conversant with the language and literature of the Greeks, Romans, Jews and Persians and from them he learned about the world. His tactics were as wily as they were ferocious. Horses had branches tied to their saddles and these, sweeping the sand in a wide arc gave the impression that a huge phalanx was advancing. Timur's weapons were those of the nomad: speed and surprise bringing with them the stench of fear. When his army moved, they took everything with them – women, children, silver, tents, their leader's household which included gold, jewels – and more women. Cities and empires fell before Timur. In Syria, Aleppo went under first after which he turned towards Damascus. The year was 1401 and the people of Damascus knew what was coming: refugees fleeing Aleppo had brought news of the destruction and horrors visited on their city, telling of how bodies were piled one on the other to create a tower 350 metres high and of how pyramids were built out of skulls. But so terrible were their tales and so bizarre were the details that they weren't believed. Some were even executed for spreading dismay among the citizens. But those citizens soon learned that it was all true. Their timbered houses easily burned and lead on the roof of the Umayyad melted in the heat. The mosque itself was destroyed with only its walls left standing.

After three months of terror, Timur marched out of the stricken city and headed for the cool of the Causcasus mountains. However, he was gone only seven days when he heard that the Damascenes, once they were sure he had gone, had burned everything he had touched, anything that was still left, that is, in an effort to rid themselves of the evil they had suffered at his hands. It was then that he wheeled round, rode back and set fire to even more houses before departing once again.

The loss to Damascus was enormous. Not only were the citizens tortured, the women raped, the children murdered, the houses demolished: the tyrant also took with him the best of Damascene scholars and craftsmen – the silversmiths and goldsmiths, the weavers, musicians, muralists, ceramicists, mosaicists, blade makers, the swordsmiths and the wordsmiths. Ironically, among those kidnapped was a writer who managed to escape and walk all the way back to Damascus, bringing with him tales of the magnificence of the Mongol court. However, it is not for the glory of his cities that Timur is remembered in Damascus but for his cruel inhumanity.

As for the Umayyad Mosque, much of it was destroyed by a series of events – a fire in 1069, the Mongol invasion in 1401, an earthquake in 1759 and another major fire in 1893. Nevertheless, what remains is a place vibrant with life, still stunning in all its shimmering brilliance.

Now, though I am glad I have finally seen it, I sit on my bed dispiritedly trying to repair a tear in my trousers with a bike puncture patch. Displacement activity. What I really need to do is deal with Islam and the things about it that make me feel uneasy. I'm not particularly concerned about the rules and regulations, about the dogma contained within the pages of the Qu'ran. These can always be disregarded or circumvented as indeed they are even by some Muslims.

But in common with the more liberal Muslim, I abhor the wilder aspects of Sharia law which orders the stoning of wrong-doers, the chopping-off of hands, the imposition of the death sentence on an adulterous woman. I am opposed to the whole idea of capital punishment more so when it is executed in the name of someone's God. And although I recognise that most religions rely on an unquestioning acceptance of its tenets by its own members, I refuse to be censorious of those Muslims who break some of the rules, who allow their men to eye a pretty woman or enjoy a glass of wine: they are merely human like the rest of us, no better, no worse.

Let he who throws the first stone, I think, and then recall that once, in Palestine, I had seen a woman throw stones at her own small child to stop him following her down the track to the bus stop. Try as I might to see the woman's point of view, all I could see and hear was a very small child crying for its mother. Instead, I try to concentrate on those things that interest and challenge me: the daily application of Islam, the way in which people live their lives according to their perceptions of it. And the more I think about it, the more I hark back to the Ireland of my childhood, constrained by strict rules made in Rome but which now, in the 21st century, have been partially adapted to accommodate modern times. At boarding school, I had to cover my head before going into the school chapel, wearing a blue cap on weekdays and a white veil on Sundays. But was this a religious or a social precept? No woman of a certain class – my socially-aspiring mother, for instance – would dream of stepping out from her home without first putting on a hat. In those days and in that respect, we were no better than Muslim women today. And even here I have to pull myself up: we were no *different* from Muslim women. I find myself looking at old women in the street here, clad head to toe in black, incensed on their behalf, that they have lived their lives under cover. But I have to remind myself that they are simply old women doing something they have always done, old people who want no truck with newfangled, bare-faced fashions.

But why should someone like Laylah feel the necessity to cover her lovely hair with a scarf simply because her father is coming to call. Her *father*? Arab men, I have been told by a Libyan friend, are woman-hungry. Are fathers too to be categorised in that way? Fathers, brothers, husbands, sons? Then I remind myself that most sex crimes against children are committed by male members of their own family.

Times change, of course. Here, in Damascus, it's not unusual now to see women smoking an arghilah in certain cafés. In Ireland, not so long ago, it was unusual to see a woman in a pub. The form was that the men went inside for a quick drink while their wives sat outside in the car, waiting. Even if they dared to venture into a pub, the man would be served and the woman ignored.

Now, on a Saturday night, the pavement outside Dublin pubs with their no smoking rules, are crowded with young women, glasses and cigarettes in hand, shouting, laughing and clearly enjoying themselves in a way never permitted to me.

But since, in Islam, there is such emphasis laid on a woman concealing her body, how is it that young men in a shop or working on a street stall may handle intimate female garments with impunity? I did once go into a shop in the souk to ask the man behind the counter about this and he assured me that there was a woman upstairs who could deal with female customers. But why, I had to wonder, was she hidden from view, tucked away out of sight? He smiled politely: I had once again showed myself to be an outsider, incapable of appreciating the role of women in his society.

And so I was left wrestling with the ideals to which I daily aspire – socialism, feminism and solidarity with the oppressed. Socialism is contained within Islam, a Sudanese friend had once told me but I could not agree, not while women – and men – were ruled by a male-dominated religion. Not while there were beggars on the street, while the divisions between rich and poor were so clearly delineated. While women were required to hide their faces.

All I could do was be grateful that I numbered so many Muslims among my friends and that, if I did not share all their values, I could at least celebrate some of them. It was Anis, for instance, who told me once that going to the mosque for Friday prayers wasn't merely a religious duty. "It's a social occasion as well," he explained. "You see who's there and who's not there. If someone is missing, you visit them to check they're alright." It seemed such a comforting attitude that I almost wanted to be included in it myself.

But I have met professional Syrian women in their 30s prevented from living on their own because this would bring shame to their family. One woman who runs a counselling service for abused women is not allowed to put up a sign to help clients find her office. A government department, she was told, already dealt with such matters and in any case, there is no such thing as abuse of women: the Qu'ran does not allow it.

And so once again, as so often, I have to ask myself where my place is, my home, the city where I feel at ease? Can it be Damascus, even temporarily, this intriguing city of veils and arghilahs, this city of seeming contradictions? Or is it Dublin, city of my birth, of drug dealing, cigarette smuggling and gang warfare, of brown envelopes slipped to politicians and planning officials by builders and developers; Dublin, of shabby one-time glory, of writers, actors and poets; Dublin of Leo and Mollie Bloom and Chinese bar tenders, of extraordinary wealth and extreme poverty, of garish lights and immeasurable vulgarity, where gunfire and ambulance sirens sound their hymns to the 21st century. Is this home? Or is it my adopted Oxford with its stark and beautiful quadrangles, its whispering libraries and underground bookstacks, its car factory and its hovering helicopter? Displaced as I am, for the time being, it is Damascus that offers itself as some sort of home, the voice of its imams expressing the voice of a people, also displaced in this temporal world, yearning to be in Allah's heaven. I note, though do not envy, my friends' accepting faith. Conventional Islam is too much like Catholicism – demanding, constrained, ruled by men and serviced by women, intolerant of other religions or of those with no religion.

But maybe there is a place for me here. If, as we are told, music is the brandy of the damned, I'd be drawn towards Sufism if only for its music. A failure to appreciate that aspect of Islam would be similar to forming an idea of Christianity based on Ian Paisley without any reference to the poetry of John Donne.

And so, finding solace in music deferred and despairing of ever mending the tear in my trousers I put them – and Islam – to one side and climb the rickety stairs to the flat roof to gaze out westwards across the city. The screech of street cats rises above the sound of car wheels on wet tarmac. The Jabal looks different – its rocky hillsides red, washed clean by the day's rain though I can still see purple clouds, huge and heavy like balloons of water about to burst, moving steadily towards Saruja, whose crumbling walls are still sodden from an earlier downpour, the slabs of pavement lining the narrow alleyways grey and wet. Only towards the eastern skies do things look bright and clear. Down below, a cat continues to howl, sounding disconcertingly like a woman climaxing wildly and uninhibitedly. Tomorrow must surely be better.

Next morning, it is indeed better. The TV says that there's snow in England but here it's sunny and, deep inside the tangle of houses in old Saruja, I can hear a cock crowing.

For now, this is where I want to be, in this city of conflicting and confusing messages, of inviting doors that, tantalisingly, remain curtained, this city that will never cease to challenge a stranger's values. This city of silk, of arghilahs, of secret archways where history, like romance, lies round every corner ready, inshallah, to waylay the unsuspecting foreigner.

Chapter 25

Coming home – from Zabdani

The man at the Hejaz Railway Station is uncertain if the little narrow gauge train would be running or not.

"I thought it always went up to Zabdani on a Friday," I say and he nods.

"So...?"

I don't quite know how to phrase the question. We are talking half in English and half in Arabic but none of the words seem to fit the situation. They are the wrong shape. The answer is in there somewhere, I know that, but I can't figure out how to frame the question the answer to which will contain what I need to know.

"Shall I go away and come back?" I ask, hoping for a hint. "Later this morning? Tomorrow even?"

"No, no. Stay. Please. Have some tea," and beaming, he signals to one of the women, busy behind a desk doing nothing, to bring me a glass of tea.

"Shukran. Bidun sukkar. Thanks. No sugar," I say weakly and sit down.

When I arrived in Syria, it was like seeing a vast canvas for the first time, waiting for things to come into focus, for the details to emerge, for the language to make sense. Looking for meaning, I found myself grabbing at half sentences, dissecting words, adding bits on until I learned that it needed more than an understanding of words. There were other things to be dealt with – the art of greeting someone, of accepting a gift, of acknowledging a kindness, of behaving with grace. Above all, there was the concept of time so different from the frenetic way it is measured in Dublin or London.

When was I going to get the hang of not being in a hurry?

Of not expecting things to happen that had been announced would happen? Of laughing instead of being on the edge of making a complaint? Now, here I am with a grievance but who would I take it up with – the station master? This man, without a tie, smoking a cigarette, smiling down at me, this *is* the station master, for heaven's sake. Over the glass of tea, it emerges that the train will leave at nine – if enough people buy tickets for it. As simple as that. All I had to do was sit, drink my tea and wait.

Hejaz Railway Station in Damascus had been a noisy one some hundred years ago and busier once the railway started to take passengers on the annual pilgrimage to Mecca via Madinah. I tried to imagine the din: men shouting to their wives, their mothers, their brothers. Relatives waving tearful goodbyes, giving advice about the perils of the journey, of having enough water, of hiding money, of praying for those who could not make the journey. Street sellers offering bread, coffee poured straight from the pot, tiny emblems of Khadija's hand warding off evil. I see women shrouded in black, checking their food baskets – cooked chicken, boiled eggs, water, more bread. Women fingering their money pouches hidden safely down the front of their voluminous gowns. Men fingering their masbahat or worry beads.

The annual Haj was an industry. In the old days, tent makers worked round the clock to make new tents and repair worn ones. Curtains for litters were sewn and put on sale. In the souks, there was a brisk trade in leather buckets and saddles. Camels, usually male, had to be fitted with thick felt blankets which would stay on for up to four months to protect the animals against skin sores.

Performed two months and ten days after Ramadan, the Damascus leg of the Haj was overseen by the Governor or Pasha who arrived on horseback to negotiate a price with the Bedouin who would give guidance and armed protection through the desert as well as guaranteeing access to wells.

Two hours before the start, a warning gun was fired and the

noisy procession was off. On 13 November 1876, the year the English traveller Charles Doughty joined the Haj, he recorded a caravan of 6,000 people stretching out three kilometres along the route with camels spread across it three and four abreast. Those pack animals which had been loaded with tents and awnings were sent ahead so that shade could be erected in advance.

The 1,500kms journey from Damascus to Mecca took the camel train about 35 days to complete and cost the individual Haji the equivalent of £40 though, with the arrival of the steam train in 1908, the journey as far as Madinah was shortened to an unbelievable four days. Merchants who contributed to the project were awarded the title of Bey or Pasha, depending on the size of their contribution.

Now, however, the train runs only from Damascus to Jordan or north towards Aleppo with the small branchline between Damascus and Zabdani running weekly, on Fridays, as a local attraction. But this is Friday and so yes, here it is, puffing into the station pulling behind it a tender and four carriages. We all climb on board and it's as if we're off on our holidays.

There's no glass in the window frames, though the frames in the top part of the carriage doors slide up and down as they used to on the train that carried me, each term, to my rural boarding school in the centre of Ireland. I look for the leather strap with the row of brass eyelets which click into place to hold the window frames in position. But I look in vain for there are none, reminding me that Damascus has the happy knack of moving to and fro, without warning, along the timeline.

On the carriage walls are the remains of old gaslight fittings. The seats are slatted wood and the overhead luggage compartments are small hammocks made of knotted string. I have embarked not on a journey by magic carpet as I had expected but on a rickety little train on which Hercule Poirot must surely be another passenger.

A woman with an assortment of children offers me a glass of tea which I am glad to accept. The carriage is quite cold and will get colder as we climb up out of the city. For the time being, however, we rattle like a tram along the narrow tracks through downtown Damascus, sometimes even waiting for the red traffic lights to change in our favour. At other times, we trundle alongside buses and cars as if part of the ordinary traffic, which we are. People smile, give us a perfunctory wave – they're used to a steam train pulling up at the lights – and a policeman on point duty raises his hand in greeting. When we approach a traffic intersection – chaotic at the best of times – the whistle sounds, peeping and pipping like an over-excited child. Make way, Damascus. We're coming through.

Then we're leaving the city behind and starting the steep climb up towards the mountains that divide Syria from Lebanon. In fact, this train originally shuttled all the way to Beirut and back, enabling Lebanese pilgrims to link up with the main Damascus-Madinah line. That was in the days before the French created the country of Lebanon, closed off the Bekaa Valley and established an official border between the two entities. Now, Beirut and Damascus are joined by a major highway which was bombed by the Israelis as recently as July 2006.

The train rattles on and the higher we go, the more lush the landscape becomes. We creep surreptitiously into a tunnel of greenery, leafy and secret, the carriage roof brushing against overhanging peppercorn trees through which I get a glimpse of the sun flashing on the waters of the Barada as it splashes across stones and over fallen tree trunks covered in green-moss, on its shallow way down to Damascus.

In the carriage behind me, a group of students, mostly male, are drumming and singing what sounds like an American boot camp song which morphs into something more political with lots of handclapping and far louder drumming: "Ya-ha! Hizbullah!" they shout, smiling broadly at one another. We are, after all, heading in the direction of Lebanon where Hizbullah has been active since the Israelis invaded in 1982.

Eleven kilometres beyond Damascus, we reach Ain Fijeh, and a lot of people get off. This is where the Barada forms the large reservoir which provides water for the city of Damascus and where people come to picnic and to swim.

The little engine huffs and puffs. Sometimes we go so slowly that small boys race us to the next corner while pedestrians walk beside us, chatting to each other, barely noticing our presence. There are about six people involved in driving this train. This includes the driver, the brakeman, a few men who hang on the outside of the train and shout warnings when, having stopped, the train starts slipping backwards as if someone has thrown an unlucky dice on the snakes and ladders board. There are also the four men who shadow us in a Land Rover as we run parallel with the road. These are security men and theirs must be the cushiest job in town. When they drive to the top of a rise and wait for us to catch up, I can see one of the men clapping in time to the music on the car radio. This is a busy journey with something happening all the way along the line. At one station, a canvas hosepipe is attached to a water tank and then to the tender. While the train fills up with water, the driver oils the wheels and sends his assistant to walk the length of the four carriages manually engaging the hand brake on each one. Some passengers get out for a bit of a walkabout.

Eventually, we enter the plateau of Zabdani, where Damascenes with a bit of money come to escape the summer heat. Here the land opens out. Leaves fall like rain, the earth is ploughed to a rich red and the holiday homes of the rich resemble Alpine chalets – though minus balconies overflowing with crimson geraniums. At Zabdani station, we all get out. This is the end of the line. Ahead lies the Lebanese border which is closed to us. I look around but there is nothing to see – no houses, no shops, no waiting room. We have been beguiled into enjoying this journey for its own sake and must now wait until the driver has had a rest and can take us back down the mountain again.

Syrians are resilient, of course, and do not need things to be waiting for them at the end of a journey. So, some go to sleep under a tree. Others bat a ball backwards and forwards with tennis racquets while the rest start to take out bread, cheese, falafel, plastic bottles of water.

And then I see that Zabdani station is not totally devoid of human life. At the end of the railway track there is what looks like a shop run by a small very old man and an even smaller old woman who, she tells me, has given birth to four daughters and ten sons. I buy a glass of tea, a lump of bread, some processed cheese and a wafer biscuit, which I have to spit out because it tastes of rat poison. As usual, Arab hospitality comes in to play and the pair invite me to sit on the floor of their shop while I eat. But sitting on the cold dirt floor reminds me we must be about 2,000 feet above sea level and that it is warmer outside than inside the shop.

On the way back, we stop at Ain Fijeh to pick up the swimmers, the picnickers and the drummers. This is the only train down so everyone jumps on board. Someone holds out the lid of a cardboard box full of plastic cups for a man, standing at the fountain, to fill with water and I wonder if that is his day job. Or does he just stand there out of the kindness of his heart? A few stations later, we stop for so long that a woman with children decides to get off. Perhaps she's worked it out that she'd get home more quickly by walking. It takes her a while to gather together her bags, drinking water, blanket, baby and then toddler but, finally ready, she helps the toddler off first and is about to step down herself when, with a heart-stopping lurch, the train groans and moves forward leaving her and her baby on board and the small boy alone on the platform. The mother freezes, the baby cries, the small boy wails and the train slowly gathers speed. We all look out, helpless, until a man further back along the carriage jumps out of the train, gathers up the little boy and running, hands him in through a carriage window. At this point, the train track starts to curve away from the street with trees and bushes blocking the way. The man, assessing the speed of the train, runs along the street until he comes to a break in the bushes, bursts through them, leaps towards the train, grabs a door handle, opens it and swings in. To me, he is a hero but for everyone else, he has merely done what was expected of him. The mother hauls the child back to his seat and, unleashing her anxiety, slaps him hard. The child yelps with pain and the rest of us all settle into our seats again. Family life is back to normal.

Sitting by the open window, I become icy cold and someone lends me a Palestinian keffiyeh which I wrap round me as best I can. The drumming dies away and children fall asleep, crisp packets slipping from their fingers. It's been a long day. Further along the line, a man gets off with two small children sleeping in the crook of each arm. I imagine them going home, the children being tucked up in bed, the man's wife cooking him a meal, his mother fussing about the house, his father sitting outside the door, arms folded, chatting to a neighbour.

Unusually, I've felt a bit solitary today. Surrounded by mothers and children, by families enjoying themselves, I've been reminded of my own family scattered across three continents. Is this really where I want to be – in a foreign land where the culture is so strange and the language stranger? Where the very kindnesses afforded to me confirm my otherness?

Then below us, the city materialises out of the darkening evening, the buildings lit by the yellow glow of the setting sun. The warmth in the air seems to envelop me. The minarets come into focus and as each one lights up, green and welcoming, I realise that, for the first time since being here, I too feel I am coming home.

Back at al Ward, Tariq will be there: Ahlayn, my light, my eyes, he will say. Marwan will come through with a cup of tea and ask what I have been doing all day. And I will know, though nothing is certain in this life, that for the time being at least, even though I don't belong here, Damascus is the place where I want to be.

Postscript

Friday 4th November 2011

On Friday 18 March 2011 a group of people came together after Friday prayers outside the Omari mosque in Dar'a, in southern Syria. They were concerned about the continuing detention of a group of children and young people who had been detained since the previous month after they had scrawled anti-government graffiti around the town. The gathering developed into a demonstration which went disastrously wrong when advancing government forces fired on the crowd using tear gas and live ammunition. The city was subsequently overrun and by April 29, according to a UN report, some 60 people were dead. The unrest spread throughout Syria leaving, according to the report, some 3,000 dead over the ensuing months.

At the beginning of the unrest, Bouthaina Shabaan, the government spokesperson appointed by President Bashar Assad, went on television to say that the political activity was orchestrated by outsiders who had crossed the border into Dar'a from Jordan.

I have met Shabaan in Damascus a few times. With her doctorate from the University of Warwick and my MA from the School of Peace Studies at the University of Bradford and with both of us having written books about women and different aspects of their lives, we had plenty to chat about. Some of what she has since said about Dar'a seems possible. It is close to the Jordanian border, a handy enough place in which to do a bit of smuggling. It didn't seem impossible therefore, that political activists – maybe some of them armed – had indeed been active participants in the events at Dar'a.

Wearing European-style clothes and looking stylish with it, Shabaan was a good example of a Assad follower: modern, educated, focused on seeking investment from abroad, protective of her slightly-aloof president. Later, I learned that she belongs to a small Shia-related group that is part of the Alawite and herein lies a clue to Syria's complex political system.

Of its population of some 16 million, 75% is Sunni, 13% Shia, 10% Christian and the last 2% Druze and other. But although Sunni form the main group, it is the Shia, which includes the Alawite, to which the president belongs, who hold the reins of government and who have done so since a coup brought the Ba'ath party into play in 1963. In order to maintain its power, the government banned opposition parties, kept in place a 1963 draconian Emergency Law, imprisoned dissidents and, in the case of Hama, in 1982, went into that city with tanks and guns to put down the mainly Sunni/Muslim Brotherhood uprising. To ensure continued enforcement of its law, it pays its army and police well. It has also allowed some Sunni to hold positions of power and influence.

But with many activists still detained and with the memory of Hama very much alive, dissatisfaction remained close to the surface. Then in July 2000, came President Bashar Assad's inaugural speech expected, by many, to be a reforming one.

Bashar Assad was never meant to step into his father's shoes. Working as an ophthalmologist in London, married to Asma, herself born and educated in London though of Syrian parentage, he was unexpectedly recalled to Damascus when his older brother was killed in a car crash. Thus, following his father's death, Bashar Assad was appointed president at the age of 34 in 2000.

Young, mild-mannered and with an attractive Europeanised wife, many hoped he would be an innovative president but it was not to be. Pleasant but lacking in charisma, it seemed that his father's old guard were easily able to manipulate him with Maher, his younger and military-focused brother, providing the hardline backup.

But how could the violence following Dar'a be justified? To understand the thinking of the Ba'athists on this, one has to look at Syria's geography. Bordered on the north by Turkey, to the west by the Mediterranean and Lebanon, on the east by Iraq and to the south by Jordan and Israel, Syria has always felt itself vulnerable to attack from unfriendly neighbours including those allied to the US such as Jordan and Iraq. It did, after all, lose part of the Golan Heights to Israel.

The Muslim Brotherhood uprising of 1982, in Hama, showed the length to which the Ba'ath party was prepared to go to maintain at least a semblance of stability. In the short term, the punitive actions of the government worked. Investors saw that it was OK to come in, that the government was prepared to crack down on its critics. Foreign banks set up shop, a sumptuous Four Seasons Hotel was built in Damascus while busloads of foreign tourists hurtled up and down the Syrian highway.

Nevertheless, in the long term, the iron fist has failed to maintain stability and unrest has simmered. Any apparent reforms have come too late. The Emergency Law of 1963 was revoked but the shooting of protesters continued. A bill to allow the formation of political parties other than the Ba'ath party was proposed but is still being drafted. Protestors, unable to join an opposition party or to voice their discontent without breaking the law have had little choice: take up arms, march or stay at home. Many, choosing to walk the streets, have paid the price.

The government is fast losing its friends. Turkey has turned away. The Russian president tells his Syrian opposite number to reform or quit. The Arab League has declared the government's violent response to political activism as wrong. The UN has brought out a report despite what it calls the non co-operation of the Syrian Government, in which it has found the last four decades of Ba'athist rule with its arrests, illegal detentions and torture to be unacceptable.

And as the conflict continues so the situation becomes darker with the Alawite civilian militia (Shabbiha) sniping from the rooftops, the Mukhabarat everywhere and foreign journalists banned, with the result that there is no way of verifying the reports from street activists nor reporting on the Syrian government's answers to its critics. The infamous Tadmor prison, closed in 2001, was reopened on 15th June 2011.

There is disquiet also among minority groups including Christians, about the final outcome of all this. One of its strengths is that Syria is, officially, a secular state but with many demonstrations emanating from mosques following Friday prayers and accompanied by chants of Alahu al Akbar, there is concern that the country might be declared Islamist, which would be seen by many as a move to exclude rather than include all its citizens.

At the time of writing, there is a stand-off and it remains to be seen who can survive the longest – the Syrian government or the street activists. Meanwhile, the people – like all people caught up in a war situation – get on with their lives as best they can.

Car in Damascus before 2011 unrest

A little bit of history

Religions and gods

Syrians often point out that their history predates the Roman and Greek civilisations with which western Europeans are most familiar. A look at Syria's pantheon of pagan Gods show this is clearly so. The cult of Haddad, for instance, dates back to 3000BCE.

But as usually happens, each succeeding religious group built upon the temples of the previous ones so in Damascus, the shrine to Jupiter replaced the one to Haddad. Then along came the Roman Emperor Constantine who, favouring Christianity, banned Jupiter. Paganism was out and Christianity in – with Islam following hard behind.

But old ways die hard. In her book Beyond the Veil, Fatima Mernissi quotes from Kitab al Muhabbar by Ibn Habib al Baghdadi who tells of pagan priestesses from the temples in Mecca who marked Muhammad's death by decorating their hands with henna and beating loudly on their tambourines. The cause of their relief was clear: Muhammad had first condemned and then forbidden their religious practices. In so doing, he had deprived them of their work and their status within their communities

Muhammad

Muhammad was born in Mecca, in 570 CE, into the Quraysh tribe and given the honorary tribal name of al-Amin, the faithful one. Mecca was a busy thriving city then, peopled by successful merchants some of whom had traded the traditional values of the desert dweller for the settled ones of self-interest. They worshipped a number of Gods of which Al-lah (the word simply means God) was considered the most senior.

Muhammad was a charismatic leader whose aim – one of them - was to bring Arabs back to the old values of selflessness and concern for others which the enterprising businessmen and merchants of Mecca, he felt, had abandoned.

He and his followers were convinced that the way to do this was by submitting to only one god: Allah. The religious path they would follow became known as Islam, which means submission.

However, relations worsened between Muhammad's followers and the merchants of Mecca with things coming to a head in 622CE when Muhammad, together with 70 families loyal to him, left Mecca and travelled 300 miles northwards across the Hejaz desert to the oasis town of Yathrib later renamed Medina. This exodus is known as the hejira and is the year from which the Islamic calendar is calculated.

Later, determined once and for all to unite the people of Medina and Mecca, by force if necessary, he marched back across the desert with an impressive army of 10,000 men. The people of Mecca submitted, their Gods were destroyed and Muhammad became the undisputed leader of Arabia, with Allah the only acceptable deity.

Encouraged by his success in Mecca, Muhammad sent his army off on a campaign of expansion and was soon in control of Jerusalem, Iran and Syria.

Muhammad's wives

As a boy, Muhammad travelled to Syria, working for a Meccan merchant. Later, his business acumen came to the notice of Khadija, a successful entrepreneur who took him under her wing and into her employ before eventually proposing marriage. She was 40 and he 25. Khadija was Muhammad's first wife though he went on to have 13 in all.

His third and favourite wife was Aisha who was betrothed to him when she was six and he 50. The marriage was consummated six years later which was not unusual in those days. By the age of 18, however, Aisha was a widow and would remain

Mary Russell

so for the rest of her life: none of the wives of Muhammad were permitted to remarry.

Muhammad's many marriages were entered into for various reasons: some in order to consolidate his position as leader, some because he was attracted to the women. Others he entered into with the aim of protecting widows of those of his followers who had been killed in the warring between rival tribes.

Byzantium

Syria came under the rule of the Roman Empire for seven centuries but when the empire divided along east/west lines, the Eastern Roman Empire became the Byzantine Empire with Constantinople its capital. This was a fractious time of change within the Empire which brought many repercussions. For the area between Aleppo, Ma'arrat al Numan and the coastal town of Antioch, however, it was a time of flowering. Farmers worked the land planting olive groves and vineyards which, in turn, made the region so prosperous that wealthy seaboard merchants from Antioch flocked southwards to build their summer houses there. Settlements grew and developed. In all, some 750 towns and villages sprang up in the region and with them 60 monasteries including that of San Samaan. But prosperity came at a price, a price sometimes met by those who could least afford to pay it. Divisions grew between rich and poor, between the smart, Constantinople-oriented Byzantines and their local, Aramaic-speaking neighbours. Byzantium, fractured from within, faced trouble from outside as well. In the 7th century, the Sassanid Persians invaded Antioch, destroying many of the Byzantine settlements as they advanced southwards through Syria on their way to Palestine and Jordan. The Byzantines were caught in a pincer movement and finally overrun by the Arabs advancing from the south who brought with them Islam and the words of the Prophet. The Battle of Yarmouk was a defining moment for both Arabs and Byzantines. Finally, in 1453, Constantinople, theByzantine capital, was captured by the Ottomans. Byzantium has been a powerful and cultural force in Syria for hundreds of years and its legacy rests in the marvellous ceramics found in palaces, baths and libraries and in the orthodox Christian churches still functioning in Syria today.

The Battle of Yarmouk August 636CE

Muhammad had died four years earlier and the Muslim Arabs were pushing northwards towards Damascus which was then held by the Byzantines. The fighting took place along the river Yarmouk which rises near the town of Der'aa. Leading the Muslim Arabs was Khalid ibn al Walid. His troops numbered 40,000 while the Byzantine army, at 140,000, was numerically far superior. Nevertheless, deploying a cavalry that constantly moved about the battlefield thus changing the position of the front line, the Muslim Arabs won the day. The Byzantines were defeated, their emperor, Heraclius, withdrew to Constantinople leaving Damascus to the advancing Muslim Arabs. For this victory, Khalid al Walid is celebrated as a great tactician and cavalry commander while the name Yarmouk is a proud one, found on streets and hospitals all over the Muslim world.

The Battle of Hattin July 1187

Jerusalem was in the hands of the crusaders and Salahadin was intent on getting it back again. Goaded by him, the Christian garrison left the safety of Jerusalem and marched towards the nearby city of Tiberias, with the aim of confronting the Arabs there. However, exhausted by the heat and without an adequate supply of water, the troops took all day to complete a march which should have taken four hours. By nightfall, parched and unable to go any further, they arrived at the village of Hattin where they got a dreamlike vision of the cool, blue waters of Lake Tiberias.

But their thirst was not to be quenched for, between them and the water, lined up on a plain tantalisingly filled with mouthwatering fruit trees, were the massed troops of the Arab, Turkish and Kurdish military, united under the banner of Salahadin. His army set fire to the dry grass so that the wind, carrying smoke and heat across the plain towards the Christians, blinded the already parched troops. Thus their fate was sealed and Salahadin took Jerusalem.

Salahadin, Richard the Lionheart, Eleanor of Aquitaine and Henry II of England and Ireland

The story of Salahadin's ride to triumph starts not far from a busy arterial road leading into Oxford city where there is a turning, known as Binsey Lane. Follow the lane and you come to Binsey Church. This church, St. Margaret's, is a 12th century foundation built on the site of a holy well and, to its great pride, still functions without benefit of electricity.

In 1130, a young priest, Nicholas Breakspear, was rector at Binsey Church. Not true, say the purists. But why spoil a pleasing historical link by casting doubt on the legend? Destined for stations higher than his modest country living, however, Breakspear went on to become Adrian IV England's only Pope and the one who handed down the edict known as Laudabiliter which – though this too is disputed – instructed the Anglo-Norman King, Henry II, to "enter the island of Ireland in order to subject the people to the laws and extirpate the vices that have there taken root."

Henry, the first Plantagenet on the English throne, was an ambitious young king and, keen to extend his powerbase in England while retaining his French one, he married the even more ambitious and very beautiful Eleanor of Aquitaine, 11 years his senior. Eleanor came to her 19-year-old bridegroom with something of a reputation. Married at 15 to Louis VII of France, and determined to accompany him when, in 1147, he set off on the Second Crusade, the young French queen caused scandal by having an affair on the way: "She carried herself not very holily but led a licentious life and, which is the worst kind of licentiousness, in carnal familiarity with a Turk."

But, as with Nicholas Breakspear and the Binsey Church connection, there is always more to the story than meets the eye: the love affair Eleanor had had was not with a Turk but with Raymond, Prince of Antioch, who, though he was her uncle was only a few years older than she was. The affair ended with Raymond's murder but the liaison was a clear indication that the marriage between Eleanor and Louis was over and indeed, on their return to France, Louis took to wearing a hair shirt and giving his money away to the poor while Eleanor moved across the water to exchange her French crown for an English one.

She and Henry had four sons, the second of which, Richard, was Eleanor's favourite. It was he, Richard the Lionheart, who went on to lead the Third Crusade.

Third Crusade 1189-1192

Intent on regaining Jerusalem, 30-year-old Richard, the Lionheart, sailed for Jaffa two years later. On the way, he stopped off on the island of Cyprus and there married Elizabeth of Berengaria though this was a marriage of dynastic convenience for Richard the Lionheart preferred men to women and even as he was marrying Elizabeth was eyeing her brother.

This Third Crusade was tough, expensive and debilitating and it wasn't until 1192, following Salahadin's attempt to take the strategic port of Jaffa, that Richard finally made the decision to march on Jerusalem. However, the summer heat, at its height, was wearing down his already battle-weary soldiers and, in this hot desert land, making the need for finding and transporting water vital to their survival. Richard himself was weakened by successive bouts of malaria. Added to this was the worry about his throne back in England which his brother John fancied. It seemed as if the crusaders and Arabs had reached stalemate when Richard, fearing his army might fall victim to the heat as the Jerusalem garrison had done at the battle of Hattin five years previously, unexpectedly signed a treaty with Salahadin under which Richard would get the coast between Tyre and Jaffa and Salahadin the port of Ascalon provided it wasn't used as a military base. Both Christians and Muslims were to be given free passage through Palestine. Thus the Third Crusade ended with the Arabs still in possession of Jerusalem.

The Ottomans

The Ottomans have their origins in the Turkic nomads of Turkmenistan. Around 900CE, they gravitated towards the Abassids and subsequently became a powerful force for Islam. It was the Seljuk Turk, Osman, who began the period of expansion that would define the Ottomans. Their empire existed from 1299–1923 with Ottoman rule in Syria lasting from 1515 until 1918. The Ottomans controlled the Silk Road through Syria and also the pilgrim route from Jaffa to Jerusalem.

Sykes-Picot Agreement 1915

This was an agreement signed by the French and the British at a time when the collapse of the Ottoman Empire seemed one of the most likely outcomes of the first World War. The question was what should the allies do with the countries the Ottomans had previously administered? The message was conveyed to the Arabs, via T E Lawrence (Lawrence of Arabia) that Palestine, as it then was, would be assigned to the Arabs as their homeland with Faisal of Mecca becoming king of the region, ie Syria. This was to be in recognition of the support of the desert tribes during the war against the Ottomans. However, the French and British, Francois Georges Picot and Sir Mark Sykes respectively, in consultation with Czarist Russia, drew up an agreement which sidelined the Arabs. Its main purpose was to assign Palestine and Iraq to a British Mandate and Syria and Lebanon to a French Mandate. This agreement was kept secret as it was feared that opposition politicians would object. It only came to light following the Russian Revolution when the Bolsheviks uncovered the relevant documents. The terms of the agreement were published in 1917, by the Guardian, then the

Manchester Guardian. As the poet of Tadmor said: "Betrayal is written on every page of our history books."

Kurds

The Kurds have links with the people of Iran and are therefore not Arab. Originally herders, they settled along the banks of the Euphrates and are to be found mainly in Iran, Iraq, Syria and Turkey. They speak Kurdish which is an indo-european language, related to Persian. There are about 30 million Kurds worldwide with some 1.5 million living in Syria. They are mostly Sunni Muslim.

The Treaty of Sèvres in 1920 promised the Kurds their independence but this was opposed by Turkey and has never been realised. In 1962, the Syrian government held a population census in the Kurdish area of the country only. Many Kurds failed to register, misunderstood the process or were misled as to its purpose. As a result, they were labelled as aliens, forbidden to speak their language, to set up businesses, to build houses or to wear national dress.

In the current unrest, there are those who recognise the Kurds' need for independence and those who, promoting the idea of the unity of all peoples in Syria, see Kurdish independence as a form of nationalism that could shatter this unity.

Timeline

3600BCE	Mesopotamia civilisation in existence in north/eastern Syria
1894BCE	Babylon flourishes
1750BCE	Death of Hammurabi, lawmaker, king of Babylon
1450-1200BCE	Ugarit civilisation on Syrian coast. Ugarit alphabet 1400 BC
300BCE	Dura-Europos ancient Parthian city near Abu Kamal
247BCE-228BC	Parthians rule, control Silk Road, challenge Roman Empire
64CE	Damascus comes under rule of Roman Empire
40CE	Saul of Tarsus (Paul) converts to Christianity on the road to Damascus
266CE	Zenobia, on behalf of Rome, rules in Palmyra. Extends her rule to Egypt
272CE	Zenobia's rule curtailed. Dethroned, taken prisoner, detained in Rome
570CE	Birth of Muhammad in Mecca
632CE	Death of Muhammad
636CE	Arab Muslims defeat Byzantines at Battle of Yarmuk and Byzantines flee Damascus for Constantinople
661-750CE	Damascus flourishes under Umayyad dynasty
705CE	Umayyad Mosque is built
750CE	Umayyads, displaced by Abassids, flee to North Africa and establish al Andaloos in Spain
750CE	Noria water wheels, devised in Roman times, are built in Hama
756CE	Birth of classical poet Abu Nawas
762CE	Abassids move Caliphate to Baghdad
762CE	Foundations laid for new city of Baghdad
786-809CE	Baghdad flourishes under patronage of Haroun al Rashid, Abassid Caliph and patron of the arts
800-900CE	Alawites established in western Syria
1098	Franks take Jerusalem in first crusade
1137	Birth of Salahadin

1157	Birth of Richard the Lionheart in Oxford
1187	Salahadin retakes Jerusalem
1189	Salahadin defeats third crusade, led by Richard the Lionheart
1193	Death of Salahadin
1516-1918	Ottoman rule in Syria
1581	Levant Company of London establishes its HQ in Aleppo
1883	Birth of Faisal, son of Sheikh of Mecca
1916	Sykes-Picot Agreement. Boundaries redrawn: Syria and Lebanon go under French Mandate, Palestine and Iraq go under British Mandate
1918	Ottomans defeated. End of first world war
1920	March Faisal declared king of Syria
1920	July Faisal deposed by the French
1921	Faisal moved to Baghdad by British
1930	Iraq gains independence, agreeing a British military presence until 1960
1946	French troops leave Syria
1946	Republic of Syria established
1947	Ba'ath Party formed in Damascus
1958	Republic of Iraq established
1967	Syria loses Golan Heights to Israel
1970	Hafez Assad nominated president of Syria
1979	Saddam Hussein in power till 2003
1982	Uprising in Hama suppressed. 10,000 – 20,000 killed.
1971	Death of Hafez Assad
1971	Bashar Assad succeeds his father

Glossary

abdan:	never
afwan:	you're welcome
ahlayn:	you're very welcome, literally two welcomes
ain:	well or spring
alf:	a thousand
alf laylah wa laylah:	a thousand and one nights
al-hamdulillah:	thanks be to God
arghilah:	hubble-bubble pipe, narghilah in other countries
ashura:	tenth day of the month of Muharram, marked by fasting
bab:	door or gate into a city. Gates in Damascus:
	al Faradees
	al Faraj
	al Jabieh
	Kissan
	al Nasr
	Salaam
	Sharaqi
	Touma
badin:	later
bayti baytak:	my home is your home, said when welcoming someone into your home
bey:	Turkish title for leader or honorary title similar to Mr
bidoon:	without eg bidoon sukher: without sugar
bimaristan:	17th century hospital/asylum
bshoofak badin:	see you later
burka:	female garment covering whole body including the face
chai zurat:	herbal tea
caliph:	political leader whose territory is the caliphate
djinn:	desert spirit, usually mischievous
dhikr:	devotional act made by Sufi followers by repeating the name of Allah

Franks:	name given to crusaders by Arabs
funduq:	hotel
gallabiyyah:	long gown worn by men
Haj:	pilgrimage to Mecca, made during the last month of the Islamic calendar
halal:	method of killing animals according to Islamic rites
habibi:	my beloved, my dear when addressing a male
habiti:	my beloved, darling when addressing a female
hijab:	scarf covering hair worn by women
iftar:	meal that breaks fast each day during Ramadan
Imam:	religious leader whose territory is the imamate
Islam:	religion of Muslim peoples of which:
Sunni,	orthodox Muslims and largest branch of Islam
Shia,	followers of Ali, son-in-law of the Prophet. Believed to have been his true heir
Ismaili:	Shia though diverged from main Shia line in 8th century. The Shah of Persia bestowed the title Aga Khan on their leader in 1818.
Alawite:	a minority offshoot of Shia. Assad family are Alawite
liwan:	part of room usually opening onto a courtyard, iwan in other Arab-speaking countries
jabal:	mountain
jihad:	struggle, may be either physical or spiritual. Can be used as a name
Kaba:	focal point of the Haj in Mecca
keffiyeh:	traditional black and white scarf worn by men. From the French coiffure
khubuz:	chickpea dip also called hummous
laylah:	night
madinah:	a town
madina qadeema:	old part of a town
mafish:	slang for none left, all gone.
mashfa:	hospital

Glossary

mihrab:	place in mosque marking direction of Mecca
mu'azzin:	man who calls people to prayer
Muharram:	first month of the Islamic year
Mukhabarat:	security police, often plain clothes, armed
nahr:	river
oud:	musical instrument
Pasha:	Turkish title granted to governors and generals in the Ottoman Empire
qadi:	judge
rasul:	prophet
Saracens:	name given to Arabs by crusaders
Sham:	local name for Damascus
sheikh:	elder, learned person, term of respect
shukran:	thank you
shuwayy-shuwayy:	so-so, a little bit
souk:	traditional street market
Sufism:	mystical branch of Islam
taqiyyah:	crochet cap worn by men
tell	hill
tifaddal:	invitation to eat/drink/sit to man
tifaddli:	invitation to eat/drink/sit to woman
yallah! (ya al Lah):	expression of surprise, delight, admiration. Literally Oh God!

Bibliography

Ibn Battutah *The Travels of Ibn Battuttah* translator Tim Mackintosh-Smith Picador 1958

Barks, Coleman, with John Moyne, A.J.Arberry and Reynold Nicholson . *The Essential Rumi* Harper Collins 1994

Bounni, Adnan and Al Assad, Khaled. *Palmyra, History Monuments and Museum*. Damascus 2000

Browning, Iain. Palmyra Chatto and Windus 1979

Fletcher, Richard. *The Cross and the Crescent* Penguin 2003

Rogerson, Barnaby. *The prophet Muhammad A Biography* Little, Brown 2003

Friedland,Tom. Features, various. *New York Times*

Fisk, Robert. *The Great War for Civilisation: The Conquest of the Middle* Fourth Estate 2005

Hitti, Philip K. *History of the Arabs* Macmillan 1970

Leslie, Doris. *Desert Queen*, a biog of Hester Stanhope Heinemann 1972

Blanche, Lesley. *The Wilder Shores of Love* John Murray 1954

Bell, Gertrude. *The Desert and the Sown* Heinemann 1907 Virago 198

Bell, Gertrude. *Letters* Edited by Lady Bell Penguin 1927

Madoun,M.A. *The Silk Road and Palmyra* al Namir Publishing 1996

Nicolle, David. *Acre 1291 Bloody Sunset of the Crusader states* Osprey 2005

Nicolle, David. *Hattin 1187 Saladin's greatest victory* Osprey 1993

Stark, Freya. *Beyond Euphrates* John Murray 1951

Joris, Lieve. Translator Sam Garrett *The Gates of Damascus* Lonely Planet 1996

Dalrymple, William. *From the Holy Mountain* 1997 Penguin 1998

Mernissi, Fatima. *Beyond the Veil* Saki 1985

Waddy, Charis. *Women in Muslim History* Longmans 1980

Rogan, Eugene. *The Arabs: A History* Penguin 2009

Rumi *Selected Poems* translator Coleman Banks Penguin 1995

Burns, Ross. *The Monuments of Syria* I.B. Taurus 2000

Keenan, Bridget. *Damascus: Hidden Treasures of the Old City* Thames and Hudson 2008

Bibliography

Thubron, Colin. *Mirror to Damascus* Penguin 1996

Maalouf, Amin. *The Crusades through Arabs Eyes* Random House 1989

Munqidth, Usama. *An Arab Syrian Gentleman: Memoirs of Usama ibn Munqidth (Kitab al I'tibar)* Translated by Philip K Hitti. New York 1929

Aram Journal of the Society for Syrian-Mesopotamian Studies

Russell, Alex. *A Natural History of Aleppo* London 1794

Kabbani, Nizar. *Arabian Love Poems,* translator Bassam Frangieh Lynne Rienner Publishing 1998

Doughty, Charles. *Travels in Arabia Deserta* London 1888

Mandeville, John. *Travels of Sir John Mandeville* 1371

Tergeman,Siham. Translator Andrea Rugh *Daughter of Damascus* Centre for Middle Eastern Studies Austin US 1994

Reston, James. *Warriors of God Richard the Lionheart and Saladin in the Third Crusade* Faber 2001

Huxley, Julian *From an Antique Land* London 1954

Lawrence, T.E. *Seven Pillars of Wisdom* Wordsworth Classics 1997

Neos Guide *Syria and Jordan* Michelin Travel Publications 2000

Maps Stanfords, London

Index